Deadly
Masquerade

NEW
HORIZON
PRESS

Dear Reader:

We proudly present the newest edition to our internationally acclaimed true crime editions of *Real People/Incredible Stories*. These riveting thrillers spotlight men and women who perform extraordinary deeds against tremendous odds: to fight for justice, track down elusive killers, protect the innocent or exonerate the wrongly accused. Their stories, told in their own voices, and in their own words, reveal the untold drama and anguish behind the headlines of those who face horrific realities and find the resiliency to fight back...

Deadly Masquerade: A True Story of Illicit Passion, Buried Secrets and Murder is the shocking true story of one woman's dreams slowly unraveling into a pack of lies, each one deadlier than the last, until she unearths a twenty-year-old unsolved murder..

The next time you want to read a crackling, suspenseful page-turner, which also is a true account of a real life hero illustrating the resiliency of the human spirit - look for the New Horizon Press logo.

Sincerely,

Dr. Joan S. Dunphy
Publisher & Editor in Chief

Real People/Incredible Stories

Deadly Masquerade

A True Story of Illicit Passion,
Buried Secrets and Murder

Donita Woodruff

New Horizon Press
Far Hills, New Jersey

Woodruff, Donita
    Deadly Masquerade: A True Story of Illicit Passion, Buried
    Secrets and Murder

Cover Design: Wendy Bass
Interior Design: Susan M. Sanderson

Library of Congress Control Number: 2005924250

ISBN: 0-88282-266-7
New Horizon Press

Manufactured in the U.S.A.

2009   2008   2007   2006   2005 / 5   4   3   2   1

To my son and daughter
who are the love and light of my life
to the very end

Author's Note

This book is based on the experiences of Donita Woodruff and reflects her perceptions of the past, present and future. The personalities, events, actions and conversations portrayed within the story have been taken from her memories, court documents, interviews, testimony, research, letters, personal papers, press accounts and the memories of some participants.

In an effort to safeguard the privacy of certain people, some individuals' names and identifying characteristics have been altered. Events involving the characters happened as described. Only minor details have been changed.

Table of Contents

Prologue

You can never know what the future will hold. When I was a teenager, I expected my life to play out just like my friends' lives: high school, college, true love, marriage, babies, my children's graduations, their weddings, a future like that.

Well, that wasn't the way it turned out. My too-early relationship quickly dissolved. I was a single mother with two small children when I met the real man of my dreams. My happily-ever-after finally had arrived—I thought.

But soon my existence turned into a nightmare. My trust became suspicion and suspicion made me follow a path that revealed an awful truth.

My story became a tale of lies and deception, of a woman who was not who she seemed, of a husband who was not what he appeared and of me—a person who was stronger than I had ever thought.

chapter one

The Masquerade Begins

I badly needed a fresh start. As a single mother working hard to raise two children with no support, little money to spare and few luxuries, moving from Los Angeles to a place in the heartland seemed the right thing to do. As a child I had always been part of a close family relationship and felt my children would benefit from exposure to the extended family I had there, learning the strong moral lessons and codes that taught me to be responsible for others and distinguish right from wrong. My mother, who owned several rental properties in Oklahoma, offered to let me live in one fully furnished. New furniture and no rent sounded better than the high cost of living back in Los Angeles, so I packed up our belongings and we headed to Oklahoma.

The bus ride from Los Angeles to Oklahoma wasn't the most pleasant one, especially with two young children wanting to run away at every rest stop to explore. The long hours and monotonous scenery dragged on from yellow field to yellow field, making me momentarily reconsider my decision. When the bus finally stopped in Oklahoma, my Aunt Clara was waiting for us. She scooped up Sam and Jessica in one arm each and drew them to her bosom, smothering them with kisses and bear-hugs. As their tiny faces squeezed to a purplish-blue I worried I might have to intervene and pry them free from Clara's ecstatic embrace. Luckily Uncle Ted showed up just in time. "Clara, let 'em go! You're gonna crush 'em," he said with a quiet patience, obviously having faced her enthusiastic hugs numerous times before. Just seeing my aunt and uncle standing before me brought back all the memories of my childhood.

Seeing smiles on my kids' faces and eager relatives willing to help, I really believed I had left my old life behind and a fresh start was before me. Uncle Ted and Aunt Clara let us stay with them for a few days until our furniture arrived from storage. The kids spent most of their time running around and playing outside while I tried to plan our new future. They adapted well to the laid-back lifestyle of Oklahoma; the long summer days, Aunt Clara's homemade ice cream and vegetables straight from the garden seemed to suit them fine. I, on the other hand, was having a much more difficult time adjusting; perhaps what I thought I wanted was not what I needed. I felt trapped by the slow pace of life out there. Los Angeles was always on the go, with new faces and things to do. That palpable buzz of energy had evaporated in the endless fields of farmland and while life may have been simpler it was certainly not as exciting.

Other than getting used to country life versus country living there were a whole host of new problems that Oklahoma presented. Work was hard to find in the small town in which we settled, at least enough work to support a single mother with two children. While my relatives offered to help out with my financial responsibilities where they could, I didn't want handouts and started to feel like I was becoming a burden. The townspeople seemed standoffish from the start. Most of the salt-of-the-earth people seemed to keep us at a

distance, since few remembered me as the little girl who often visited there. That attitude made it especially hard for Sam and Jessica
to get to know other kids and I felt they thought me a city slicker.

The humidity was brutal that summer. The only relief came from
the occasional downpour of rain that cooled off the night air after
thunder and lightning storms. When the rain stopped, we often sat on
the front porch, watching lightning bugs flicker in the night sky. On
one of those lonely nights I was surprised when a woman, not much
older than me, yelled a friendly hello from across the street, beckon-
ing us over. I was anxious to make a friend. Taking my children's
hands, I walked across the street to her front lawn. "I'm Gayle," she
said with a deep southern accent and a smile so warm and sympathetic you couldn't help but crack a grin in return. I soon found Gayle
to be one of the most down-to-earth people I'd ever met. Before I
knew it we became close friends.

But as August approached, the children began to miss their old
friends and school and I too found myself missing Los Angeles more
and more. Despite Gayle's camaraderie and my family's constant support, I made the decision to move back to Los Angeles. My mother
wasn't happy and felt I hadn't given Oklahoma enough time. Maybe
she was right. I was there for no more than a summer, but in my gut I
knew I didn't belong there; it didn't feel like home. My aunt agreed to
keep my youngest child, Sam, until Jessica and I got settled, which I
promised her wouldn't be very long. I knew there would be things I
would miss about Oklahoma. That close net of family love I experienced, the wonderful scenery and the slow pace—there were times
when it was nice not to be in a rush.

Arriving in California, Jessica and I stayed with a close friend,
Holly, until I could save up enough money to get our own place and
bring Sam there. It was difficult with him so far away. Not knowing
how he was doing at every moment made me neurotic beyond
description. I forced myself to limit my phone calls to one a day, or

else Sam might act out and Aunt Clara wouldn't be able to handle him. Despite my anxiety over Sam, the pace of Los Angeles suited me much better than what I experienced in Oklahoma.

My old life was suddenly new again; one day I ran into an old friend, Bob, who had started his own package delivery business. I stopped to say hello and we began to talk, catching up on all the missed times in mere minutes. Bob, knowing I'd been away, asked, "Are you dating anyone?"

I brushed off his question, "I doubt I'd ever meet a man who would really love my children *and* me, and we're a package deal."

He laughed. "Why don't you let me introduce you to someone I think you'd like? I just delivered a package to this guy; his name's David. He owns a small movie studio over there," pointing up the street. "He was up for an Academy Award for *Young Sherlock Holmes*. He's nice, handsome, single…"

Timidly, I shook my head. "Maybe some other time," I told him.

Bob shrugged, said goodbye and continued his delivery route. I stood there, intrigued. It had been years since I'd even given a man half a chance, too afraid that the children and I would get hurt again. I remembered feelings I once had of being in love and they brought a dreamy smile to my face. Maybe Bob was right; maybe it was time to give myself a second chance. I knew my biggest problem in connecting with a man wasn't my looks but overcoming my shyness; when meeting strangers I always stammered and blushed in embarrassment.

A few mid-afternoon raindrops pelted me out of my daydream and I decided, right then and there, I had nothing to lose. Taking hold of my confidence, I walked the few blocks to the movie studio Bob had told me about. Standing in the small parking lot, I suddenly felt my stomach do an anxious back-flip and I chickened out. Impulsively, I thought of another way of meeting David. I grabbed a pen and paper from my purse and, as a light rain began to fall, quickly wrote a silly

note, saying, "You shouldn't leave your car window open," followed
by my name and number. I slipped the note into the open window of
the only car in the lot and ran back down the street like a frightened
deer. Since my dating skills were so rusty, I felt my only chance was
on the phone, where I could be a little braver and less anxious without a face looking back at me.

A day passed and I became anxious that David still hadn't called.
Perhaps I was more desperate than I thought; one day and I was
already stalking the phone like a hungry leopard. I started making
excuses. Maybe the rain ruined my note, maybe he stayed in his office
so long that when he came out the ink had bled to an unreadable mess.
Or maybe he just threw my note away. Oh, I was so stupid to leave a
note! Who would leave a note in a stranger's car and expect a date?

"Will you stop pacing the floor and sit down for a minute! You're
making me nervous just watching you," Holly said with a smirk.

"Oh, I'm sorry, Holly. I just… well, I just haven't been out with a
guy for so long—I haven't even talked to a guy that I liked for so long."
I sat down next to her on the couch. I was so nervous that if I didn't
sit on my hands they would start flailing in the air like those of a mad
woman.

"Relax, Donita!" Holly told me. "It will work out. Pacing the floor
and talking to yourself isn't going to attract too many guys."

I laughed. "I guess you're right. Stay calm, stay relaxed and what
will happen will happen. Right?"

"Right—or he'll never call!"

"Holly!" I half-screamed before laughing out loud at my own neurotic behavior. "I'm going to go pick up Jessica. If anyone should
call—a guy, a realtor, the president—just take a message."

When I returned that afternoon, Holly was on the phone. "Hold
on, she just walked through the door." Immediately a puzzled look
crossed my face. I wasn't actually expecting anyone to call. She came
into the living room with a wide smile on her face and said, "A man

by the name of David is on the phone, asking to talk to you. He sounds pretty sexy!" Surprised by the call and Holly's brashness, I felt my cheeks blush a deep shade of red. I nervously picked up the phone, not really sure of what to say. I paused for a few moments, trying to hold on to my fleeing composure. When we finally began to speak David didn't seem to have those problems. He was charming and friendly, making me feel welcome and special. And as my shyness melted at the sound of his deep voice we talked and talked like old friends—he made it too easy for me. As our long conversation wound down, David asked if I'd like to see if the face matched the voice, leaving me even more intrigued. I agreed to have dinner with him the following night. As I hung up the phone, a renewed memory of love flew me into the bedroom giddy with excitement.

I stretched out on my bed, my head swimming with a spinning sensation. Soon I heard the footsteps of Jessica and Holly practically running full speed into my room and just as I thought, they wanted to hear a little gossip. I told them all about David and the plans for our dinner date the next night and I agreed with Holly, he did have a sexy voice. I was glad to see how happy Jessica was for me. I think she knew, even at her young age, how lonely being single could be and how happy the possibility of romance made me. Her support was what mattered most.

The next day inched by and that night, as I frantically searched the closet trying to find the perfect dress to wear, I felt like a teenager going on her first date. I was beyond nervous as I waited for David to pick me up, not sure what to expect. Jessica and Holly just stared at me in disbelief from the couch as I kept looking out the window for David's car.

Soon a sleek maroon Jaguar pulled up to the building. He was a few minutes late, not that I was glaring at my watch counting the time. When I finally saw David face to face, I found myself pleasantly surprised at how attractive he was. David was a handsome man with short, wavy brown hair, sky blue eyes and a wide smile that seemed to cover his face with warmth. He was a little on the short side, but so am I. He wore black business slacks and a blue button-down shirt, probably just coming from the office, and carried himself with an upright self-confidence as he marched up the stairs to the apartment. Sometime between his arrival and the restaurant he took me to, he introduced himself to me, though I honestly can't remember the exchange that took place. I think I was that taken by him.

On our way to the restaurant, David kept turning to me and smiling. "You really are very pretty," he said over and over. He was such a gentleman; all my other boyfriends only complimented me when they wanted a cold beer or a sandwich. But before I got my hopes up, I felt I should tell David up front that I had two children. It was something I didn't want to do, because it usually sent men running and I didn't want David to go anywhere. However, if tonight went well he wouldn't only be dating me; eventually he would be dating my kids as well. I knew I couldn't suspend any longer the fairy tale I had been imagining. I took a deep breath and told him, "I have two kids from a previous relationship, but it's over between us. I just thought you should know. I didn't want to surprise you." I waited silently for his answer, biting my lip and crossing my fingers.

David replied, "I'm divorced. I have a thirteen-year-old son, who lives with his mother in northern California." His sincerity relieved me greatly. Now that our kids were out in the open, I told myself I could relax and get to know David better. Without pausing, he told me all about himself: that he was forty-six, lived in Burbank and worked in the movie business. I was surprised at how much older David was than me, because he looked a lot younger, but I wasn't about to let the nearly twenty-year age gap bother me. I was already attracted to him and wanted to get to know him.

He pulled his Jaguar up to the front of a fancy French restaurant, and a valet attendant, dressed in a little red vest and bow tie, opened my door for me; soon he was off parking the car. I wasn't used to such luxurious treatment and I almost wanted to tell David not to give his keys to a complete stranger. I couldn't believe how well the evening was going. David held doors open for me and pulled out my chair. I thought he seemed very sweet and gentle and smart and sophisticated—the perfect man. With all the wonderful things happening to me on my first date back in the social scene, I felt guilty and a little uncomfortable. The restaurant's menu was in French, so I had no idea what I was ordering. All I understood were the hefty prices tacked onto the ends of the descriptions. I made out a few words and ordered the cheapest entrée there was. Even though I wasn't paying I couldn't forget that I didn't have a job yet and was living off an ever-shrinking bank account. The meal was delicious—the best since I left Aunt Clara's cooking in Oklahoma. Afterward David and I split a dessert—one plate, two forks!

After dinner, David asked if I'd like to see his movie studio and the posters of films he'd worked on. The date couldn't be going any better; I nodded my head and just waited for someone to pinch me from my dream. I have to admit, when we arrived at the studio it did seem a little scary at night with no lights and long dark hallways, but I felt more secure with David. He carried himself with a self-confidence that completely overshadowed my shyness. David gave me a private tour of the studio, showing me all the fancy, complex equipment he used to film his pictures.

David began explaining the long path of his career; how he started out doing animation and puppets for such programs as *Gumby* and *Davey and Goliath*. He also worked on commercials, helping to create characters such as Mrs. Butterworth, the Pillsbury Doughboy and the Planter's Peanut mascot. He had been working in the field for over twenty-five years and easily rattled off the names of the old Hollywood special effects masters he studied under to learn his craft.

Proud of his work, David told me his visual effects work on *Young Sherlock Holmes* garnered him an Academy Award nomination. I was impressed, but even more impressive was that David didn't act with a huge ego. We strolled down the halls of the studio looking at the posters of movies he had either been a special effects advisor on or directed. I didn't know all of the films, but some clearly jumped out at me: *When Dinosaurs Ruled the Earth; Twilight Zone: The Movie; Dolls; Ghoulies II; Batteries Not Included; Willow; Honey, I Shrunk the Kids II; Ghostbusters II* and others. It seemed that David had an interesting story or funny anecdote to tell for each film. I asked him to tell me about *Q—The Winged Serpent*, a film Jessica and I had actually just watched days before. As he told me a story about the filming I couldn't stop staring at him; the whole experience seemed to be a pleasant dream. The man I was with had created movies the whole world enjoyed.

His specialty was stop-motion animation, the technique used to film the special effects in movies like *King Kong* and *Clash of the Titans*. They made miniatures, complex puppets really, and then filmed them one frame at a time, stopping to adjust the direction of the movement ever so slightly. I was a little lost on the concept. "Almost like a picture flip-book, but instead of drawing and flipping pages to make the character move, we make models and film them one stage at a time," David explained. He said that the process was exhausting and tedious, but the results were well worth it. He did other special effects too, often supervising a whole film, but he was best known for stop-motion animation. Sadly, he told me, computerized graphics on films such as *Jurassic Park* would soon become the standard in Hollywood, making stop-motion animation a nearly dead art.

David took me to a small design room that held various puppets he was using to direct his latest movie, *Puppet Master II*. The puppets looked a little devilish, but David explained the film was a horror movie. He showed me the mechanics of each puppet: the complex system of moveable joints, hinges and rods that made the puppets come to life. Showing off, David made the puppets do a funny dance for me. Watching the intricate workings of the puppets and listening to David's explanation of how to film frame-by-frame made me realize how hard a worker he was. It took countless hours, dedication and passion to put together a movie of his. Those were the qualities that immediately drew me to David.

I had completely lost track of time at the studio and when I realized how late it was I made David drive me home so I could get up early and send Jessica off to school. I knew my children were my first priority and always would be, but I saw how easily it was to fall in love with a man like David.

As he drove me home, David reached over and gently held my hand. My heart jumped a beat and I knew, at that very moment, I was enthralled by him. He pulled up to my apartment and leaned over to kiss me on my cheek, politely asking if he could call me tomorrow to make another date.

Feeling like I was on cloud nine, I quickly said, "Yes."

After saying goodnight to David, I danced into the apartment and plopped down on the couch right next to Holly.

"I want to marry that man one day!" I said, blushing.

"But you just met him," Holly replied, laughing.

I shook my head. "I have never believed in love at first sight, but I believe it now." And as I sank deeper into the couch I realized how true it was.

With each date my feelings for David grew deeper and my day-to-day activities seemed to be less important. Jessica and I moved into a new apartment with my friends Dena and Kelly. I didn't want to leave Holly, but the rent was cheaper. And with cheaper rent I could save up some money for my own apartment and finally bring Sam home to Los Angeles. Holly still kept in touch with me, wanting to know how my relationship with David was going.

A couple of days after we moved into the new apartment, David came over to pick me up for a date. It was the first time that Dena and Kelly met David. Our dinner reservations made it necessary to keep the introductions quick and we barely had enough time to say goodnight to Jessica and leave the restaurant's phone number before David whisked me out the door for a romantic evening. I wanted my friends to get to know David and like him as much as I loved him, but that evening our time was short.

When I returned later that night, I found Dena and Kelly sitting on the couch with serious looks on both their faces. "Sit down," Dena said softly.

"Yes, do," Kelly echoed.

I grew concerned and my mind raced with the outrageous scenarios that could be behind their dour faces. "Is something wrong with Jess?" I asked in a panic.

"No, no," they both chimed in. I let out a sigh of relief, but as they began to express how happy they were that I'd met someone, I noticed the worry in their voices.

"We have a funny feeling about David, although we aren't sure what it is," Dena said. "Maybe you should go slower."

Outside of my kids no one made me happier than David, so I wrote off their premonitions. "You're being silly," I said. I had every intention of continuing to see David. "David treats me well and I think I love him."

"That's what we're talking about—you've known him four weeks!" Dena said. I could tell from their faces they both felt strongly about this conversation.

"We're not saying stop… just take a step back and slow down," Kelly added.

"That's what I'm doing. I'm taking it one step at a time," I replied. The bitterness and insincerity in my voice must have been obvious. I wasn't about to slow down with David when it felt so natural to me. All three of us left the fruitless discussion and went to our bedrooms, frustration still steaming under our breaths.

The following day my son, Sam, arrived in California. Jessica and I both were *so* excited to have him home. I couldn't wait for David to meet him. When I phoned David at the studio, he suggested we all go out to dinner that night. Although the kids felt strange sharing their mother with a new man, they wanted to try and get to know him.

Smiling, David entered the apartment, giving me a kiss on the cheek. He smiled at the kids as I introduced to him to Sam. Though Jessica had already met David, she was still shy and kind of held back.

Not so for Sam. He flew headfirst into any situation. He began asking David questions about anything that came to his mind: favorite baseball team, favorite ice cream flavor, why was the sky blue, a whole barrage of inquiry, which David answered with a smile. David patted Sam's curious head and answered all his questions, at least the ones he knew the answers to. Jessica and I shared a look, giggling because we knew how much of a talker Sam was.

That night David took all of us out to a nice dinner at a family-style restaurant. It was nice to know that David was just as comfortable eating chicken fingers and hot fudge sundaes as he was with fancy French cuisine. After David dropped us back at the apartment, I asked the kids what they thought about him. I tried my best to explain my feelings for David as well as the relationship we had. I didn't give my kids enough credit. Both of them approved of David and understood my needs to start dating again.

Jessica liked David, but I think Sam was the more enthusiastic one of the two. Every time he saw David, it was a non-stop barrage of questions about movies or science or history, fields David wasn't even an expert in. But that's just the kind of mind Sam had at that age. He needed to know everything. Sam was especially interested in the movies and David was impressed that a child Sam's age would take interest in such technical things as filming and editing.

Talking to David on the phone the next day, I asked what he thought of Sam and Jessica. He said he was already in love with them. Adding to my pleasure, David told me how well behaved they were and what a good job I'd done raising them alone. I thought that it would be nice to have a strong male figure in their lives to give some balance to my parenting, but I knew it would be a while before I let David—or any man—into my life permanently.

By October, I had saved enough money to get my own apartment and finally found the perfect place near the kids' school. When I told David he rushed over. I gave him a tour of the empty apartment, telling him all the decorating plans I had, where I would put the sofa and the dining room table, how I would arrange my bedroom. I was so excited to share my dream with David. Standing before me, he pulled out a check for five hundred dollars, made out to me. Both surprised and confused, I refused it. David explained, "You and the kids will need things for the apartment. Please take this." I had never met anyone as generous as David and, although I felt uncomfortable with his generosity, it felt so sincere. Eventually I accepted and thanked him.

Time moved our relationship in a serious direction. Just about every weekend, David took the kids and me out to dinner, museums and parks. I tried to slow him down on his gifts, but he kept insisting we needed things like new furniture and that it would take me too long to save the money to buy them on my own. Work hadn't come easily and when it did it was sporadic. David understood the hard times I was going through and knew things would eventually pick up. His generosity also came with compliments: I was beautiful, intelligent, the humble girlfriend of his dreams.

David made me feel like a princess and before I knew it, I was hopelessly in love with him. I decided to call and tell Gayle, my friend in Oklahoma, about the new love in my life. I told her how wonderful David was to the kids and me, and how giving and kind he was. "I can't wait for you to meet David someday," I said. "I've never been so happy." Gayle seemed happy for me as well. I knew I must have sounded like some love-struck teenager, but I didn't care. I didn't care who knew or what they thought—I was so happy.

Soon, David and I were seeing each other on a daily basis. He talked a lot about the movies he was working on. Eventually I started joining David on movie sets and found it most interesting. All the cameras and

sound equipment with their buttons and lights and thousands of moving parts—the buzz on the set was electric and every time the director
screamed "action" or "cut" I got shivers.

Our time together was sweet and passionate and I felt we were
gradually growing closer. But I wondered what he really thought,
since on the set David introduced me as just a friend. Maybe I was
reading too much into our relationship, but how could I when we
spent nearly every day together?

We talked a lot about the present, but he never brought up the
past. It made me wonder if he was hiding something or simply too
afraid or uninterested to open up to me completely. We talked exten-
sively about his work, but rarely about more personal subjects. At
times he would throw me dialogue to get my reaction on lines he
wanted to use in a film. Late one night, as David and I lay next to each
other talking about his work, he mumbled to me in a tired voice, "I
know someone who killed someone and got away with it."

"Was it a man or a woman?" I asked, for some reason curious as
to the perpetrator's sex.

He muttered an indecipherable reply as he drifted off to sleep.

I found it strange for a movie line, but I ignored his words,
because he was half asleep when he said them and probably wasn't
making a lot of sense. Turning over on my side, I fell asleep thinking
nothing of it.

Soon after that conversation, David started acting moody. At first
I felt he was just having some bad days at work. I did my best to comfort him about whatever was bothering him, but he wouldn't tell me
what was wrong. He began making odd comments, telling me his past
was complicated and he had no business getting into a relationship
right now and we probably shouldn't be seeing so much of each other.

I thought he was getting scared because our relationship was
becoming serious. I tried to ignore his comments, hoping whatever
turmoil David was going through would pass. Maybe, I told myself,
he just needed some time away from me to think some things over.

Not really sure of what to do, I decided to let a week pass without having any contact with him and see if it was our relationship making him nervous.

David didn't notice anything was wrong the first day, but by the second, he began calling the apartment every few hours to leave messages, asking where I was and why I wasn't returning any of his calls. When I still didn't return his calls, his messages became increasingly angry.

Conjuring up an excuse, I told David I'd been busy, but he didn't buy it and said he was on his way to my apartment. When he arrived, he was obviously concerned, telling me, "I feel you are pulling away from me," and, "I don't want to lose you."

I felt reassured, at the moment, that whatever David was going through had nothing to do with me. I adored him and was glad we were back together again and the problem was behind us. David was happy too—he hugged me lovingly and held me in his arms. He told me, "I got a phone call from an old friend named Valerie. She's invited us, along with several other people, to a brunch she is going to be having at her apartment next Saturday. I told her about the kids and you and she wants to meet you all."

I thought it was strange that David had never talked about this friend of his, but I concluded it must not be someone he kept in touch with on a regular basis, someone from his past. It was a good sign and I was glad, because it showed David was getting more comfortable with our relationship, opening up his past to me.

Saturday afternoon, David arrived to pick us up to go over to Valerie's apartment. As he parked the car in front of an expensive apartment building, it suddenly occurred to me that David's apartment was just down the street.

We walked up the marble steps to the apartment building and stood in front of a security door, waiting for the click that unlocked the entrance, which led to a beautiful garden setting. The kids and I waited behind David as he knocked on an apartment door.

A beautiful African-American woman in her mid-thirties, statuesque at about 5'10" and very curvaceous, opened the door. Shoulder-length curly black hair showcased her piercing black eyes, and her long fingernails were painted the same fiery red of her lipstick. She wore very high heels, an expensive black dress that showed off her cleavage and a bright yellow leather jacket, which was from a famed designer's current line.

Everything about Valerie seemed manicured, all the way down to her personality. As she held out her polished fingers to shake my unpolished ones, an uneasy feeling came over me and I suddenly felt uncomfortable in my simple blue dress. This gorgeous woman was David's dear, old friend. We were introduced to several other guests, some of whom had brought their children as well.

Looking around, I noticed how fancy and expensive the apartment was, from the elegant furniture to the sterling silver on the highly-polished mahogany table. When Valerie slipped off to the kitchen to get us glasses of champagne, I leaned toward David and asked in a whisper what Valerie did for a living. He told me, "She is a very successful interior designer." That explained how Valerie could afford to live such a lavish lifestyle.

Sam and Jessica went off with several other children, while I tried to mingle with the adult guests by making small talk, but I soon found myself feeling out of place.

As the afternoon wore on, I caught Valerie staring at me several times from across the room, as she took slow sips from her champagne glass. She seemed very curious about me, as I was about her. Her laugh was low and throaty and she seemed upbeat, but there was something about her that made me nervous. My appetite was lost and I wished all afternoon that David and I were alone with the kids as we usually were. Several times I ended up standing on the terrace trying to gather my thoughts and steady my nerves.

When David approached me and asked if I was ready to go home, I sighed with relief. I gathered the kids, said goodbye to everyone and thanked Valerie for inviting us. After David dropped us back home, I called my old friend Gayle, needing someone to confide in. "Valerie is a good friend of David's." I tried to be enthusiastic. "The good thing is he's finally introducing me to his old friends. I think," I said, pausing before I went on, "he's admitted to himself he's serious about me."

chapter two

False
Illusions

In April, David told me he had a two-week vacation planned for September with his mother and his son, Andy. It would be the longest time David and I had been apart since we met.

The summer came and went. September had already arrived and David had to leave, separating us for a lonely two weeks. I invited Gayle for a visit, which helped divert my attention from missing him. I showed her the sights of Los Angeles and caught up on girl talk, though neither of us seemed to want to dwell on the subject of David. Still, I missed him and was terribly glad when he came home.

Shortly after David returned from his trip, he called from work to tell me he had received a call from Valerie, inviting us out to dinner, along with her new boyfriend Brad and another couple, Rick and Carolyn.

We joined each other at a restaurant in Hollywood. Once again I found myself uncomfortable around these new people, but what mostly bothered me was that same nervous feeling I had the first time I met Valerie.

I found Carolyn the easiest to talk to, but her boyfriend Rick seemed to be sort of an oddball. Glancing across the table, I noticed that Brad, Valerie's new boyfriend, didn't seem to fit in any more than I did.

I excused myself from the table to go to the ladies room, followed by Carolyn and Valerie. The men, as men do, cracked a joke, saying it must be a "girl thing." As Valerie and Carolyn stood in front of the bathroom mirror fixing their hair and makeup, I exited the bathroom stall and stood between them at the sink.

"I hate this time of month. I have the worst menstrual cramps right now," Carolyn said, moaning and rubbing her stomach.

"I know just how you feel; I hate getting them too," Valerie replied, as she tried to console Carolyn. The three of us left the rest room and rejoined the men at our table.

A month later David told me he had a surprise for me, that he was getting plastic surgery on his face. Confused as to why, since he looked fine to me, I assumed working in the movie world, where appearance was so important, he wanted to have a more youthful look. I didn't feel I should really question his decision but did offer to take care of David during his recuperation, after surgery. Wanting David to be comfortable when he got home after the operation, I cleaned up his apartment and bought food to cook for him so I could make his recovery as pleasant as possible.

After his surgery, David first was sent to a private care facility in Beverly Hills. Two days later I arrived to pick him up. When I walked into the facility a nurse asked me to follow her down a hallway that led to his room. Slowly I entered the room, not knowing what to expect. David was sitting up in bed, his face covered in bandages as if he had been in a horrible accident.

As the nurse began explaining to David how often the bandages on his face needed to be changed, I tried to retain my composure and cautiously helped David out of bed, getting him dressed and down to the car. Wanting to get him home as fast as possible, I made the mistake of driving through the hills of Hollywood, taking Coldwater Canyon. The up and down motion of the car made David nauseous. He was shaking by the time I slowly helped him out of the car and into his apartment. Once I got David into bed, he seemed to be in a great deal of pain so I gave him his pain medication, trying to make him feel as comfortable as possible. When it came time to change his bandages, I tried to keep my expression calm, as I painstakingly peeled the bloodstained dressings away from his face. Somehow we got through those hours before I went back home to care for the kids. We talked several times a day and he reassured me he was doing fine.

A couple of days later I received a call from David, his voice distressed. "Run to the store, buy bug spray and bring it over right away," he requested urgently. David told me hundreds of termites had broken through his apartment wall and were flying towards a light shining outside his window. David sounded as if he were acting out a scene from a low-budget horror film. I desperately tried my best to keep from laughing.

Bug spray in hand, I opened the front door to David's apartment, only to find his frantic call had merit. The room was besieged by termites that had broken through a small passage between the apartments and were flocking towards the sleeper sofa David was lying on. Sitting up, David looked like a cartoon character, his white bandages sticking out from the top of his head like giant rabbit ears as he batted at the termites with a rolled newspaper, trying—and failing—to keep them away. I tried to be sympathetic to his plight, but the situation was kind of ridiculous. I went to work and sprayed the apartment before I fixed David some lunch and changed his bandages.

Just as I was going to leave and pick my kids up at school, David's phone rang. He answered it in the other room. From the living room, I could hear him arguing with someone before quickly hanging up the phone. When David returned to the living room, his posture was stiff and he told me it was Valerie who called.

"You seem angry," I said.

"Valerie thinks you're only taking care of me for my money."

Now I was the furious one.

"If that's what Valerie thinks, she can come over and take care of you herself."

David tried to calm me down, explaining, "Valerie is just being an overly protective friend. You're the one I want to care for me."

I was pacified for the moment, but still angry at Valerie.

As David recovered he started relying on me more than before. "Being able to count on you when I am down is very important to me," he said repeatedly. "You'll never know how much it means."

With Christmas quickly approaching, David took the kids and me out to buy a tree. As soon as we began decorating it, the phone rang. It was Valerie, claiming, "It's important. I have to talk to David right away." Wondering how Valerie had gotten my phone number, I looked over at David as I slowly handed him the phone. The conversation was short and David swiftly hung up the phone. The only explanation I got was that Valerie was in some kind of trouble and needed his help immediately. He grabbed his jacket and went flying out the front door.

The following day I asked David what had happened. "Valerie was in an accident after losing control of her car," he told me.

"But how did she know where to reach you?" I asked, puzzled.

"My business partner gave her your phone number."

David then admitted Valerie had been arrested for driving without a license. Seeing how upset I was, David explained, "This will be the only time I'll bail her out of trouble, but it is my duty as a friend to help her."

It seemed to be the truth. For the next few months, neither of us spoke of Valerie. David started work on a new movie, requiring him to go on location to film in the desert. He asked if the kids and I would like to join him, as he'd be there for a week. It sounded like fun for all of us. I packed a week's work of clothes for myself and the children and we headed to the desert with David, along with the film crew.

After everyone was set up in a hotel, David and the rest of the crew drove further into the desert to film some scenes. Due to the intense summer heat, the kids and I decided to stay behind, trading dry desert sightseeing for a cool wet swimming pool.

Everything seemed to be going well. David and I were happy together and the kids were having a good time. Then one afternoon at the hotel, as the kids napped, the phone rang. I quickly rushed over to answer it so it wouldn't wake them. I picked up the receiver. "Hello," I said in a low voice, but no one replied. I said, "Hello," two more times but still got no reply, only a click as the caller hung up the phone. Curious, I called the front desk, asking, "Was it a man or woman who called the room?" The clerk said it was a woman's voice. Since whoever it was never called back, I was left with the assumption the caller had been connected to the wrong room.

chapter three

Wicked Games

As Halloween crept closer, David's sister Gerri flew in to
California to pay David a short visit. When David called to say
he wanted to introduce me to Gerri, I made the suggestion of inviting
her over for dinner. I wanted to make a good impression, but my shyness made me more and more apprehensive as the evening
approached.

I spent hours meticulously preparing dinner, but as the time for
David and his sister's arrival drew near, I found myself becoming
more and more neurotic. I had the children dressed in their Sunday
best and waiting on the couch. "Please don't mess yourselves up," I
pleaded. A knock at the door made me jump; they finally were here.
After I answered it, David introduced Gerri and me to each other.
"And these are my children, Sam and Jessica," I said in an unsteady
voice, walking her over to where they were sitting.

After a few minutes of small talk, I excused myself to the kitchen
so I could check on dinner. Gerri followed me, asking if she could

help with anything. It didn't take long before she began asking me questions about where I came from, who my family was, what I did and things of that nature.

Gerri, a pretty brunette, seemed nice enough. But she asked a lot of questions, giving me the feeling I was being dissected in some grand inquisition. I felt she was trying to figure out what David could see in me and what, if anything, we had in common. My discomfort grew and to get away from Gerri I sent her out to David with a tray of hors d'oeuvres. But a few minutes later, she was back in the kitchen. She asked me to take a walk outside with her so we could talk alone. We sat side by side on the hard front steps of the apartment building.

Gerri began by telling me how pretty I was and how cute Sam and Jessica were. Wondering why she had asked me to come outside alone and away from David, I did not realize she was softening me for the blow.

Gerri soon began talking about David and his work, explaining, "He's worked so hard at his career and he is moving his way up in Hollywood." Somewhat embarrassed, she carefully tried to convince me that I did not belong with David, stating, "His type of woman is more of the glamorous type."

I sat there in disbelief. My own self-doubts and insecurities flooded over me as I listened to her explain how I would be holding David back from meeting the type of women he deserved.

I soon found it very difficult to hold back the tears welling up in my eyes. "You have no idea how much in love I am with David," I murmured, getting up. I wanted to explain that I thought she was completely wrong and though I might not be glamorous and polished, I would tenderly care for and about David forever. But in my daze I couldn't get the words out. My emotions were already spilling over too much. I quickly walked back into the building.

As I shut the door behind me, I glanced over at David and the kids, who sat together on the couch watching television; Gerri soon joined them. Not wanting the kids or David to see me upset, I walked into the kitchen, tears silently streaming down my face. When he noticed that I didn't come back, David called from the living room, "Is everything all right?"

I tried to answer "Yes," even though the tears kept coming. I didn't want to make a scene and decided to tell David what had happened later. I tried to calm down and continued preparing dinner as if nothing were wrong. When everything was ready, I brought it out on a tray and served everyone. Saying very little as we ate, I kept my attention more towards the kids, as David and Gerri talked amongst themselves.

I had begun clearing the dining room table when Gerri asked if I would like her help. My hurt feelings had now become resentment and I looked over at her, saying sharply, "Thank you, but I can do it myself."

Sensing something was wrong, David followed me into the kitchen. Quietly, he took me aside and asked, "Donita, what's wrong?" I blurted out what Gerri had said to me, tears streaming from eyes.

"I'm sorry Donita," he apologized. "I'm very disappointed in her behavior… Gerri's just being overly protective. I'll have a talk with her after we leave." He gave me a hug of reassurance and made sure I would be all right. "I love you and have no plans of leaving you. You may be certain of that," he assured me.

The visit was short, with few words exchanged between Gerri and me. The tension made all of us obviously uncomfortable.

On returning home, David assured me how much he loved me. "Gerri will love you too after she gets to know you as I have," he promised. I nodded, not trusting myself to speak, but inside I was still in pain. Not too long after this incident, David decided it was time that the kids and I met his parents.

I wasn't sure what to expect from his family and found myself with the same highly nervous feeling as the day drew near. When we arrived at David's parents' house, his mother, Dianna, was standing outside waiting for us. A petite, spunky woman, she approached me with open arms as soon as I got out of the car, cracking a joke, "You don't know how glad I am that David's finally brought a girl home. I haven't seen him with a woman in so long I was starting to wonder if he was gay."

I laughed along with her. "I know David isn't gay, he just wanted to make sure he met the right girl before introducing one to his parents." Dianna then approached Sam and Jessica, giving them hugs and welcoming them as well, as David and I made our way into the house.

In the living room, the kids and I were introduced to David's father, who, due to the slow deterioration of his memory, wasn't quite aware of the occasion, and to David's brother, Gary, a tall, strapping man who was down-to-earth and friendly. David and his mother took the kids and me into the kitchen, where we met his brother's wife, Myra. Soon I was also introduced to Tammy, David's cousin. It seemed like I was meeting David's whole family at once and I was a little overwhelmed. Tammy was very sweet and I found myself taking a liking to her right away, but David's mother was the one I really wanted to get to know.

While Sam and Jessica played in the backyard, I helped his mother, Tammy and Myra with dinner in the kitchen. The men sat in the living room watching golf on television.

As she arranged a vegetable platter, his mother talked about how proud she was of David's accomplishments, especially his Academy Award nomination. As she spoke she began raising her voice. I thought it was on purpose, in hopes that David would overhear her when she remarked that she was only invited to the luncheon, but not to the Oscar ceremony.

"And to this day, I still don't want to know who he took to the Oscars instead of me!" His mother said, in a loud voice. I could tell, even though she was trying to make light of it, deep down she was hurt he didn't take her.

As the evening went on, David's mom began to question me about my family, asking where Sam and Jessica's father was and if he was in their lives. When it became apparent that I was not comfortable discussing the kids' father, she hastily dropped the subject. At that first meeting I immediately liked David's mother a lot and she seemed to like me. We both wanted to get to know more about each other and I hoped David would take us to visit his family again soon.

With the holiday season quickly approaching David seemed happy in our relationship and asked me to go through catalogs and help pick out Christmas gifts for his family. We enjoyed decorating a tree together and participating in holiday festivities with the children, though David understandably missed his own son. However, after the holidays were over, I noticed he was withdrawing from me again.

Then one night when David came over to my apartment I saw cuts and bruises on his face and forehead. Concerned, I asked David what happened to him. David shrugged it off. "It was an accident at home," he said and abruptly changed the subject. As the weeks passed, David seemed more miserable, as if something were deeply troubling him; but the more I asked, the more he became frustrated, refusing to talk about whatever it was that was eating away at him.

I began doubting myself and thinking maybe I was the reason for David's change in behavior and his distant attitude. Deciding to confront him to find out if I was right, I waited for the right moment, when we would be alone.

Reluctant at first to discuss what was bothering him, David then cautiously mentioned my breasts as the reason behind his being less affectionate towards me. "I understand after having children, things change with a woman's figure." Confused as to why David never complained before now, I found myself feeling helpless and embarrassed that this was such an issue to him. "What can I do about it?" I asked. David's reply in return was quick and simple. "I'll pay for the surgery, if you want to get it done," he replied.

The thought of altering my body in any way, shape or form had never crossed my mind. After David left that night, I found myself standing in front of the bathroom mirror, knowing deep down if I did what he proposed it would be for the wrong reasons. I decided to wait and think about it before making a decision. At that point I was more insulted than hurt.

With spring approaching, David seemed to return to his normal self. I wondered if the dark winter season had affected him as it did some people. He started coming over on a daily basis again and spent the weekends taking the kids and me on outings and to his parents' house.

During the week David often came over to my apartment in the middle of the day. One afternoon I again noticed cuts and bruises on David's forehead and face. I knew it couldn't have been another accident, and insisted, "Tell me how you got them."

With a sigh of resignation, David replied, "Valerie caused the injuries."

"Are you kidding?" I asked, shocked and confused. David tried to calm me, saying, "It's no big deal." But I could tell something was going on that he didn't want to talk to me about.

I wasn't going to be put off. "Why did Valerie do this to you?" I asked. After I made several attempts to get the truth, David finally admitted, "Valerie called me, asking if I could take her to pick up her dry cleaning." He sighed in frustration and went on. "Valerie asked me to take her to lunch, which I did; and, as I drove her home, she threw her leftover lunch at me in an outburst of anger."

David sighed again and said, "Valerie and I were once more than friends. Our relationship ended just months before you and I met," adding that Valerie was with him the day he got in his car and found my note.

"From that day forward," David said "Valerie has been jealous of you and is having a hard time accepting that her relationship with me is over," David told me. "I told Valerie we would only remain friends."

"David," I said finally, "look at what she's done. Next time it might be worse. You need to get Valerie out of your life immediately."

Agreeing, he said he'd been trying to end their friendship slowly. But he felt badly for Valerie. Both her mother and father were dead and she had no other family. He explained that the loss of one more person close to her had driven her to an almost suicidal state.

Even though I tried to understand, I still felt there was no excuse for Valerie becoming violent with him. Nevertheless, I tried to be compassionate so as not to upset him, and to believe that he was ending his friendship with her. But I couldn't help being curious about their past relationship. I encouraged David to tell me more. He said Valerie had lived with him at one time in the house near his studio. David continued by telling me it was Valerie he took as his date to the Oscars the night he was nominated. *So that's the person David took to the Oscars that David's mother so badly wanted to know about.*

David saw my concern, "Donita, please, I don't want to lose you. I want you to try and be understanding of the situation I'm in with Valerie. Give me some time to deal with her on my own." Reluctantly I agreed to do so.

"But if she becomes violent again, you have to promise never to get back in touch with her."

He promised that he would be careful. Things quieted down and soon it was the anniversary of our first date, marking two years that David and I had been together. We had a wonderful celebratory lunch at a chic restaurant. During the meal I screwed up my courage and asked how he'd feel about us moving in together.

David cautiously explained that it might not be a good idea. He felt Valerie was finally getting over their relationship, but didn't want to endanger himself or me. He told me that if we moved in together there might be a problem with Valerie; that she was the type who would try to find out where he lived and he didn't want to risk any further problems with her.

I thought David was using this as an excuse for us not to move in together. I felt used and abused, and made it a point to avoid any contact with David for the next week. I once again let the answering machine pick up all my calls and kept quiet when I heard a knock at the door. Finally, after a week of tormenting David and myself, I decided to talk to him over the phone, making it clear I was going to break up with him and move on with my life if Valerie continued to be an issue in our relationship.

David asked to come over to talk to me. He told me, "I'll be so hurt if you and I break up; Valerie will just have to deal with the break-up of my relationship with her on her own."

The question of us moving in together did not come up again. I tried to put it out of my mind. As the months passed and winter turned to spring, our relationship grew closer. Valerie seemed to have vanished out of our relationship and David's life.

One afternoon while I was at home with Jessica and Sam, the phone rang. It was David and before I could even ask how he was doing, he blurted out, "Listen, why don't you look for a house for us to buy?"

My eyes grew large as I stood in silence for a few moments cradling the receiver in my hands. "I love you," I finally said.

"I love you, too," he replied. It seemed David was about to make my past wishes come true. Before too long we found a lovely home in a desirable neighborhood in Burbank. It was right down the street from David's studio. Never had I been so happy and he seemed to feel the same way.

Since my apartment lease was about to come up, the kids and I moved into David's apartment while we waited to close the contract on the house. The future stretched before us like a dream about to come true.

David wanted me to stay home for a while and I did too, so I could give my all to making our life together work. I started our new life together by trying to be a perfect homemaker. First thing in the morning I woke Jessica and Sam, fixed their breakfasts and packed their lunches for school. Shortly thereafter David woke up. Each morning, before he finished dressing, I put his coffee, newspaper and a hot breakfast on the table while I got the kids ready for school. As soon as I returned from dropping off the kids, David and I shared a little private time together and by 10:00 AM David headed out the door to work.

Soon there were only two weeks left before escrow closed. I became even more excited about moving into our new house. I picked out drapes and some furniture and thought about what kind of picket fence I wanted to put in front of the house.

In the mornings after David left for work, I cleaned the apartment until everything was polished and perfect. I thought things were going wonderfully, but soon I started receiving mysterious phone calls at David's apartment. I didn't think much of them at first, until I noticed they had become regular and always came at around the same time of morning, just after David left for work. Each time I picked up the phone, I said, "Hello," repeating myself two or three times before the other line went dead. I never got a reply in return. The phone calls came in sequence, three to four times, every call the same, the caller keeping silent on the other end. Though I listened closely, I couldn't hear any background noise or detect any breathing.

After a week of receiving these calls, I started to wonder if Valerie was behind them. But, I asked myself, why wouldn't Valerie just call David at the studio if she wanted to talk to him? Why would she call and hang up so systematically every morning, always after David left for work?

I started to wonder whether Valerie had found out David and I were living together. This made the most sense, so I decided to tell David about the hang-up phone calls I had been receiving. Since it was such a touchy subject, I waited for the right time to ask. I decided to bring it up with David after dinner, when the kids were settled in bed. I wanted to ask him if, in fact, Valerie knew or somehow had found out that the kids and I had moved in with him.

When David and I were alone, I told him, "You know, I've been receiving all these funny phone calls." I rushed on, "Well, I have the feeling the hang-up calls are coming from Valerie."

David looked at me, then shook his head. "No, there is no way it could be Valerie making those hang-up calls," he said firmly.

I didn't want to argue with David about it, but I needed to find out the truth. After David left for work the next morning, I called the phone company and requested *69 service, which automatically calls the last person to call a number. I was told I would have to wait twenty-four hours before the service would begin to work. That night I spent a sleepless, anxious night watching the clock.

When morning arrived, I got the kids off to school. Then I told David I had gotten the *69 service added to the phone. "Please stay home until the hang-up calls begin again," I begged. Although David felt it was a complete waste of time, he agreed to stay. As we both sat quietly at the kitchen table drinking coffee, I gazed at the clock on the kitchen wall, waiting for it to hurry past ten o'clock, the time the calls usually occurred. The first ring startled me. Making short eye contact with David across the kitchen table, I stood up from my chair and walked over to the phone. I leaned down and slowly picked up the receiver, bringing it up to my ear. "Hello, hello?" I called out, my heart skipping a beat. There was no voice, only a clicking sound as the caller hung up. Now the moment of truth was here! Immediately I dialed *69 and waited impatiently for the phone to stop ringing so someone on the other end could answer.

"Hi, this is Valerie," an answering machine tape kicked in. "I'm unable to come to the phone right now; please leave a message and I'll get back to you soon."

I told David, "Well, it's definite, now. Valerie has been making the calls." Putting the phone to David's ear, I watched as he listened to the dial tone, then I pushed *69 and handed him the phone so he could clearly hear her voice. With a surprised look on his face, he hung up.

"Now you know. It is Valerie; she has been making all those hang-up calls," I said quietly.

"Yes, yes, I believe you. I just don't understand why she would be doing this," He replied, with a confused look on his face. "I have to get to work, but when I get there I will call Valerie and ask why she's been calling and hanging up." I was glad to have gotten to the bottom of it; I wanted to know the reason behind Valerie's hang-up calls.

Later that morning, David called me from the studio, telling me he talked to Valerie and that she admitted to only making one call, that same morning, and that it was by accident. He said her excuse was that she was sleepy after taking some sleeping pills and meant to dial a friend but accidentally dialed his number by mistake. He continued to say that Valerie would be calling me soon to apologize about the accidental call. I didn't believe her excuse for one moment; I felt sure she had to be the person making all those calls, not just the one earlier in the day. I told David I wasn't happy about Valerie wanting to call to say she was sorry, that I just wanted the calls to stop.

"I told Valerie we're moving into a house together," David told me. While this made me happier, I still felt annoyed and wasn't sure I should even answer the phone the next time it rang, but since it could be Sam and Jessica's school calling if they were ill or something, I felt I had no choice.

Shortly after David and I ended our conversation, the phone rang again. It was Valerie. She began to apologize about her so-called accidental call, giving me the same excuse she had given David, claiming that she had never made any of those other calls I had received. Valerie kept insisting she knew nothing about the other calls, but I still didn't believe her. There was something very strange about this woman, something that made me distinctly uncomfortable. As she plied me with excuse after excuse, the feeling became more intense.

I wanted to hang up on her, but then she started talking about her new boyfriend Paul, wanting advice about whether she should let him move in with her or not. I told her she should, hoping it was a way to get her out of David's life completely.

I never received any more hang-up calls at David's apartment after that. But one day, looking out the window, I saw a dark car stop out front and wait in idle for a few minutes before zooming away in a cloud of dust. On the next few mornings I saw the same car lurking outside, but telling myself not to be paranoid I tried to forget it.

Soon David, the children and I moved into our new home.

The kids and I were especially excited, because the house had a huge backyard for them to play in and a big kitchen for me to prepare the gourmet meals I wanted to create for David, to show him how much I cared and how grateful I was for all he was giving me. For the first time my life was coming together. We were one big happy family. There were only two things missing from all my dreams becoming a reality: a marriage with David, and the white picket fence of which I'd dreamed for so long.

chapter four

Meetings and Confrontations

David and I had planned for Thanksgiving to be the first holiday the kids and I would spend with David's family. That day, when we arrived at his parents' house, we found it full of friendly people who warmly welcomed us. There was no shortage of laughter as we swapped stories back and forth. From the kitchen window I watched the kids playing with the dog in the backyard. I glanced over at David from across the room and smiled at him. He had made the kids and me so happy.

His mother, with a letter in one hand, grabbed me with the other, taking me away from the kitchen into the family room where she pulled out old family albums and showed me pictures of David as he was growing up. It made me feel even more connected to David, as I watched his mother laugh and smile, telling me the stories behind each picture. "I can see from the look on your face how much in love you are with David," she said. The day went by quickly, enfolded as we were in the warmth of the family gathering.

The next weeks flew by. The Christmas season was soon coming and I started decorating our home inside and out. I decided to throw a Christmas party for David's work colleagues and invited some of our neighbors as well. Everything turned out just as I had hoped. David was happy and content, seemingly relaxed and enjoying himself.

A week before Christmas, David told me he had received an invitation to a holiday party a friend of his was throwing. "It will be a lot of fun and give you a break from kids' activities," he urged. I was in such a great holiday spirit, I agreed. I figured I would already know someone there and would feel more relaxed than I usually did at such affairs.

When the night of the party came, I was rushing to get ready. As I applied eye shadow, I heard the phone ring; David yelled he'd answer it. When I finished with my makeup, I went to the kitchen for a glass of water. David was standing at the telephone. When I asked who had called, he was silent. I looked at him, waiting for an answer. He took a deep breath and said it was John, the friend who was hosting the party. "Don't get upset, but he told me Valerie, her boyfriend and his brother will also be going to the party."

John had called to ask if we could give them a ride, as Paul's car had broken down in front of Valerie's apartment. Frustrated, I asked why Rick and Carolyn couldn't pick them up. David said, "They could, but they are coming from the opposite direction and would have to go out of their way to pick Valerie up."

I felt annoyed. Thinking Rick and Carolyn had no idea of the past problems I had had with Valerie, and with us now running late, I snapped in frustration "Fine, whatever, let's just go!"

David and I drove over to Valerie's apartment. I was hoping her new boyfriend would have helped Valerie get over David. I made it clear to David as we approached Valerie's apartment that I would be polite, but I wasn't going to have any real conversation with her at the party.

As we pulled up, they were already standing outside waiting. Paul, his brother and Valerie quickly piled into the back seat, just as it began to rain.

For the twenty-minute drive, I was largely silent, while Paul, his brother, Valerie and David chatted about David's latest movie project.

As we drove along the windy, wet road, a patrol car passed us coming from the opposite direction. While he was trying to find the address of the house, David's car drifted slightly over the center line. "David," Valerie snapped, "let's not ruin the night by getting us pulled over." In the front seat I rolled my eyes, feeling Valerie was overreacting.

Pulling up the steep driveway and parking the car, we saw that Rick and Carolyn had just arrived. Greeting them, we made our way out of the sprinkling rain and inside. Rick introduced us to the owners of the house, a county sheriff and his wife. Their home was beautifully decorated for the holidays, with a Christmas tree in almost every room.

David and I quickly broke away from Valerie and her clan as we introduced ourselves to the other guests and then sat down in the living room

As David got up to get us drinks, Rick and Carolyn joined me on the couch. We were talking about what had been happening with David and his work when Valerie made her way into the room and sat down in a chair across from me. As she sat there she downed one glass of champagne after another, motioning to the waiter every time she wanted another.

Feeling very uncomfortable, I turned to Rick and Carolyn, saying, "I don't know what happened to David. I'm going to find him."

I found David immersed in conversation with two men in the movie business. Joining them, I had little to add but tried to be pleasant. As the evening wore on, David and I talked to other guests and eventually were separated. I ended up in the den with Rick and

Carolyn. Once again, Valerie found us and walked over. Rick was standing up against the fireplace with one arm on the mantle and a drink in his hand. "Well, Donita," he said with a smile, "now that you and David have moved in together, I guess the next step is getting married, huh?"

"Yes, someday down the road we probably will," I replied, smiling back.

Valerie's face became twisted with rage and she began lashing out in a hostile verbal attack against me.

"You're smothering David! You have him chained up like a dog! He has to sneak out to visit his friends because of you!" Valerie spit out angrily.

Shocked by her outburst, I was speechless and turned away so that the scene didn't escalate. Rick, seeing how upset I was, offered to join me, following me out the back door to the patio. "Are you okay?" he asked. I nodded. Nevertheless, I was shaking.

He said, "You made the right move leaving the room. Valerie can be explosive. Do you want me to stay here with you?"

"No, no," I insisted. "You go back; I just want to steady myself."

Rick returned inside but I remained outside, taking deep breaths of cold winter air for a few more minutes. Then I went to find David. I told him what had happened and asked that he take me home. David quickly moved from room to room, trying to find Rick and Carolyn to ask them to take Valerie, Paul and his brother home. But Rick and Carolyn already had slipped out and left the party. The only other people who knew Valerie well enough to drive her and the others home were the sheriff and his wife, but they couldn't leave their own party.

David walked up to me and began explaining, "We're stuck taking Valerie and her company back to her apartment."

Though frustrated and irritated at the whole situation, and wanting to get away, I felt Valerie wouldn't have the nerve to lash out again, so I nodded. "Well, let's find them as quickly as we can and take them home."

David did just that and soon we said goodbye to our hosts. Valerie, Paul and his brother slid into the back seat of David's car. Valerie sat directly behind me.

But I was wrong about Valerie's reluctance to cause another scene. As soon as David pulled out of the driveway and onto the main road, Valerie wasted no time starting in again. This time her anger was aimed at David. Between the pelting rain and my own nervousness, at first I couldn't understand what Valerie was saying; her words were slurred from the champagne she had been drinking the whole night.

But as she sputtered on I realized she was criticizing David for their past sex life, saying something to the effect that David couldn't perform and that he had cheated on her. I saw David becoming embarrassed and uncomfortable, his hands tightening on the steering wheel, knuckles whitening. Gathering my courage, I called out, "That's enough, Valerie!"

Valerie responded immediately, her voice turned to the low growl of a dog, "You better shut the fuck up, bitch, or else I'll shut you up!"

Overcome by fear, my immediate reaction was to get away. I reached over and wrapped my fingers around the car door handle, wanting to jump out, not caring how fast the car was moving.

All I knew was that there was a psycho sitting directly behind me, about to erupt, and there was no telling what she would do next.

David quickly leaned over and gently touched my hand as if to say, *be patient.*

He then pressed his foot down on the accelerator; the car picked up speed, as David tried to get to Valerie's apartment as fast as possible. Meanwhile the rain was pouring down even harder, as Valerie continued to vent her anger. It seemed there was no stopping her.

David, trying to avoid getting Valerie any angrier, began agreeing with everything she said, replying in a pacifying tone, "Yes, Valerie, I know, Valerie." Paul also tried to calm Valerie down, but with little success.

I was so upset I was shaking and kept my lips firmly pressed together.

Finally we arrived at Valerie's apartment; David stepped on the brakes and pulled to a stop.

"Get out of the car, Valerie!" David said, in a firm, angry tone.

Valerie yelled back at David, "I'm not going anywhere." She half rose from the seat, pounding on David's back. We all quickly jumped out of the car into the pouring rain and slammed the doors shut.

Valerie slid across the back seat to the other side of the car, trying to open the car door to get out. Paul, his brother and David ran quickly to the other side of the car, trying to hold the car door shut, as Valerie began screaming and kicking. Somehow, she wedged the door open.

I stood in shock, drenched in the pouring rain, as I watched Valerie get out and begin chasing David around the car, with Paul and his brother running behind as they tried to catch and hold Valerie back.

"David," I yelled, "get in the car so we can get out of here." Just as David made his way to the driver's side door, Valerie caught up to him, and with a closed fist, she punched David in the side of his head. Moments later Paul and his brother grabbed and held Valerie back, as David and I jumped in the car. I began yelling at David, "Please, let's get out of here fast." As the car tires slid on the wet pavement, I turned and looked out the back window in horror as Valerie, yelling, began chasing the car, like some wild rabid dog.

Then I turned and looked at David's head where Valerie had slugged him. It was swollen and had turned an angry red.

"Oh, my God," I cried. I broke down in tears as David kept apologizing over and over.

"I'm so sorry you had to witness such an ordeal." He then went on to tell me Valerie lied about him sneaking out, that her accusations were nothing more than that of a jealous vindictive ex-lover.

It was a subdued Christmas that came and went that year.

Shortly after the New Year of 1994 arrived, Los Angeles was hit with a powerful, pre-dawn earthquake. When daylight broke, David, the kids and I went to his studio to check if there was any damage. A few things had been tossed around from the shaking, but for the most part the studio seemed to be fine.

Just as we were leaving the studio, the phone rang. David, answering it, was short and curt and quickly hung up the phone.

"It was Valerie," David said. "She's in a panic because of the earthquake. She wants me to come over."

"David," I began.

He looked in my eyes, "Donita, I have absolutely no plans to see or talk to Valerie."

Not long after that, David began to work on a movie he had written and planned to direct. "Parts of the movie," he said, "are going to be filmed in Romania this coming spring. I'll be gone for a few months." Though I was sad that we'd be parted, I decided to use that time to fix up and paint the house.

Towards the end of April, David left for Romania and I began the repairs on the house. The kids and I spent our weekends visiting David's parents; Dianna and I slowly became closer. She realized how deeply in love I was with David, as she observed how much I missed and talked about him.

While David was away, I went over to his studio to pick up the mail and check his phone messages. One day, there was a message left by the phone company issuing a past due notice on a phone bill. They warned of a disconnection if it was not paid by a certain date. Confused as to why they were calling, as I had kept up with all the payments, I called the phone company to find out what was going on. I was told David's name was on an account that had been opened five years ago. The phone number of the account was not his old apartment or the studio.

I wrote down the mystery phone number and left the studio. I decided to call the number from a pay phone down the street. An answering machine soon picked up. "Hi, this is Nikki; please leave a message and I'll get back to you soon."

I realized immediately that it was Valerie's voice, but why was she using a different name? And, it didn't make sense to me that the phone was billed to David, as I had been told Valerie was a very successful interior designer. I reasoned that she should be able to pay her own bills. Not wanting David's credit to be messed up, I called David and told him about the phone company's call. He said he would deal with the problem when he got back and not to worry, that it was from a long time ago, before we met. I was frustrated that yet another problem stemming from Valerie had surfaced, after we had tried to put her behind us. I decided it was time to deal with her myself.

I called the number again and this time I left a message. "Nikki, Valerie or whatever your real name is, David and I have a family and home. Take care of your own bills and leave us alone!" I said in a stern voice and hung up.

Hoping I had made my message loud and clear, I tried to put the whole puzzling thing out of my mind and concentrate on fixing up the house. Time passed swiftly and soon it was the end of June. One day, while Sam and Jessica were playing with the hose in the backyard, I was chipping off old paint at the front of the house when I heard the phone ring. It was David, calling from Romania. He told me how lonely he was and asked how I'd feel about leaving the kids with his mother so I could fly to Romania for a week to visit him. It sounded wonderful. After being away from David for so long, I too was lonely and immediately said, "Yes!"

"Good," he said. "The company financing my movie will be happy to pay for your round-trip ticket, in return for your delivering a package to them."

Not thinking twice about it, I quickly replied, "Yes," as I had delivered things between studios for David many times before.

Shortly thereafter the plane reservations were made and David called to tell me, "Someone with a studio name-tag will meet you at the Los Angeles Airport to deliver the package in person."

The day before I was to leave, I turned my two excited kids over to David's mother, who they knew would spoil them rotten. The following morning I quickly finished packing my bags and then headed off to the airport. Running short on time, I rushed to the ticket counter to validate my ticket and then began looking for the person from the studio who had the package I was to deliver to David. Quickly spotting his name-tag, I practically ran over, since there wasn't much time before I had to go through the gates.

He handed me a brown manila envelope, which felt lumpy and heavy. He told me not to open it, saying, "There's $35,000 cash in there. Make sure David gets it when you get to Romania." He turned and quickly rushed off.

I stood there in surprise after being told the contents of the envelope. Moments later I heard my flight number over the intercom. I tucked the envelope under my shirt as I rushed to get to the appropriate gate.

As the plane leveled out to its cruising altitude, I unhooked my seat belt and made my way to the lavatory. Not knowing the protocol for bringing such a large amount of cash into a foreign country, I found myself becoming nervous, but it was too late to back out. Knowing there was nothing I could do about it now I loosened my belt and shoved the envelope down my pants, covering the bulge with my shirt.

Returning to my seat, I adjusted the seat belt to fit around my stomach. Soon afterward a flight attendant approached, passing out questionnaires that asked if we were bringing anything into the country that needed to be declared. As I slowly read it over, I came across a question asking if I had more than $10,000 to declare. I felt my heart pumping harder, as I nervously marked the answer no and passed it over to the flight attendant as she made her way back to retrieve the questionnaires.

Knowing there still were a number of hours ahead before I changed planes in Germany, I drifted off to sleep. The rest of the flight went smoothly. Once in Germany, I changed planes. There was one more stop in Vienna before we arrived in Romania.

On the last leg of the journey, wanting to look nice for David, I went into the lavatory and changed into a dress, putting the envelope into my purse. As the plane began its descent towards the airstrip in Bucharest, the weather got choppy. I felt frightened. I held tightly to the armrest as the plane tossed from side to side on an unsteady course, preparing to touch down.

As the plane slowed down to a stop, I looked out the window and observed several members of the military, armed with machine guns and attack dogs, standing guard on the airstrip. Following closely behind the other passengers exiting the plane, I got off and saw a van quickly approach to take us to the main terminal of the airport. As I got on the van my stomach, which had been flip-flopping because of the turbulence, calmed down. As we pulled up to the terminal, I noticed bullet holes in the airport windows. My nerves suddenly turned my stomach queasy again. Exiting the van, I found myself quickly surrounded by several Middle Eastern men wearing turbans.

They all began talking to me at once. Not understanding a word they were saying or what they wanted, I made my way through them and followed the other passengers into the airport where our passports were checked and stamped for entry. At the baggage claim, I noticed a bearded, dark-haired man holding up a sign with the name of the company David was dealing with, but David was nowhere in sight. The man motioned that he was there to pick me up. Walking toward him, I wondered if David had shown him a picture so he could recognize me. He told me David was unable to make it to the airport and that I was to come with him. After retrieving my luggage, we began weaving our way through the passengers towards customs. Looking ahead I saw a long table strung out with open-faced suitcases, followed by a long line of people. Watching custom officers open and rummage through every bag and suitcase that lay on the table, I felt nervous and clutched my purse tightly under my arm.

"Stay close to me," the bearded man whispered. Following his lead, I was whisked past everyone in line as we headed directly towards a customs officer. No words were spoken between the bearded man and the balding customs officer, as money discreetly passed from hand to hand. I was rushed off into another area of the airport where we met a military policeman shouldering an automatic machine gun. Glancing down, I once again witnessed money discreetly being passed from hand to hand. The bearded man was buying our way out of the terminal.

Walking outside to an open parking lot, I saw several men waiting next to another van. A tall dark-haired man began to approach me, as the others stood close by. Standing before me, he said, "Do you have something for me?" I knew it had to do with the money I was carrying, but I was reluctant to hand over the envelope I'd brought to him, without knowing if he was the right person. My bearded escort nodded and so opening up my purse I pulled out the envelope, handing it to the dark-haired man.

Then my escort told me, "Please get in the van." After I got in the group of men boarded it as well. Shocked at what I'd just experienced, I sat silently as we drove off into the countryside surrounding Bucharest, the men talking among themselves in a language I couldn't understand.

After a long drive we arrived at the hotel David was staying at. My escort told me to get out and he removed my luggage from the back. Then he got back in the van with the other men and they drove off, leaving me standing alone. I walked up the steps to the hotel and a doorman opened the front doors. I entered a long corridor, the floors covered with jewel-toned oriental rugs. "My name is Donita Woodruff. I am visiting David Allen," I told the clerk at the front desk. He called a bellboy to take my bags and me to David's room. When we got to the room the bellboy opened the door, brought in my luggage and left. Looking around at the sumptuous room, I saw no sign of David. I hung up a few clothes and refreshed my weary body, fixing my hair and reapplying makeup.

Bored and unable to sit through Romanian television, I made my way back to the front desk, where I asked where David was. I was told he was filming at the Black Sea and wouldn't be returning until later that afternoon. I wandered around the hotel for a while, exploring the plush surroundings, watching exotic-looking people come and go. Around a quarter to four, I went outside to wait. A van pulled up to the front steps of the hotel and David was one of the first to emerge. He saw me right away. We kissed, hugged and walked arm in arm and back to his room, where we could finally relax together.

Later we went to the hotel's lovely candle-lit dining room and had a romantic dinner. Happy to be together again, we talked into the late night. Finally, I asked David about the money, telling him how nervous and uncomfortable it made me to be a courier. David apologized for not telling me the contents of the package. "I brought $40,000 in cash when I came to Romania," David said, explaining the situation to me, "but more money was needed in order to continue production of my movie. In fact," he said, "red tape was slowing down production and this was the only way of getting the money into the country quicker." Although I understood that in David's mind finishing the film was paramount, I told him I never wanted to be put in that position again. "I can see how it would make you uneasy," David apologized. "I promise you it won't happen again."

The following morning David was going with the film crew to do some shots in a cave. "You're welcome to come," he said, "but I have to tell you it's a long drive and uncomfortable conditions." Tired from the long trip, I decided to stay behind at the hotel and read a new novel I'd brought with me. Toward noon the phone began ringing. Thinking it was David, I picked it up saying, "Darling?" The person on the other end immediately hung up. For a moment the thought that Valerie might be up to her old tricks crossed my mind.

Dismissing the call as someone dialing the wrong room number, I left the room to take a walk in the beautiful hotel garden, whose graceful foliage had been cut and artfully shaped. How lucky I was to be here.

My time in Romania with David went by too quickly; before I knew it, I had to pack my bags and head back to California. The memory of our loving mood was dispelled when, within a week after my arriving home, David called in a sort of panic, asking me to drive down to his mother's house and pick up a check for $10,000. "I need you to give the check to my secretary to cover some bills I forgot to take care of before I left. The creditors are hounding the office." David added something that sounded very odd: "Be careful about the money you spend."

What a strange thing to say, I thought to myself after hanging up. I wondered if David, who'd always treated money in a very off-hand way, was having financial troubles.

chapter five

Grains of Suspicion

In late August, a moody David returned home from Romania. It seemed that, having been away so long, David had reverted back to his bachelor ways of liking to have things absolutely quiet around the house. Any noise the kids or dogs made irritated him to the point where he would get up and go to another part of the house. I felt like I was walking on pins and needles as I tried to keep the peace. As the fall went by, David's behavior began affecting our relationship. He became less attentive in his affections towards me, slowly isolating himself. Worried, I tried to think of things I could do to help our relationship. One day while watching television, I saw an infomercial about a book on how to improve the physical and emotional togetherness of your relationship. *Maybe it would help ours,* I thought. I picked up the phone and ordered the book.

When it arrived in the mail, I quickly started reading it, finding many suggestions about being more considerate, trying to understand where your partner was coming from and fighting fairly. I tried them all. Another suggestion I decided to try was meant to revive a warm sexual relationship: discreetly drop a pair of sexy panties under the table by your lover's feet, acting like you unknowingly dropped your napkin, as you excuse yourself to go to the rest room. Feeling shy and uncertain but willing to try anything to make things work with David and me, I decided to go to Victoria Secret and buy the sexiest pair of panties I could find. The day I went to the store, I dressed extra inconspicuously, wearing all dark clothes. Looking around, I saw the tables were full of thong panties of every color and material, but since Christmas was coming, red and green predominated. I avoided being helped; too embarrassed to ask for assistance, I shrugged off store clerks with a "just browsing." Nevertheless, I spotted a see-through pair of red panties with lace embroidery on them. They were so naughty-looking, normally I never would have bought them for myself. Keeping my head down and avoiding all possible eye contact, I quickly purchased the panties and made my way home to put my plan in motion. I wanted to go out alone with David and try the idea I'd read about, but those days we were going out very seldom. Finally, Jennifer and Jim, our neighbors down the block, called and asked us to join them for dinner. I was so anxious to try to mend our relationship I didn't want to wait any longer. I didn't know how long it would be before David and I would go out again due to his unpredictable mood swings. I told Jennifer about my situation and what I had planned for David. She laughed and said, "If it works with David, I'd like to try it with Jim."

The night we were to have dinner with them, we all decided on a nice Italian restaurant just around the corner from where we lived. The hostess seated us at a nice table for four. While waiting for our food to arrive, we talked about current events and kids' activities. Nervous and unable to keep my mind on the conversation, I excused myself to go to the ladies' room. Just before I got up, I reached down to grab my purse and planted the scandalous panties. Then I stood up and, trying to look innocent, knocked the napkin off the table near David's feet where the panties lay. My idea was that David would bend down to pick up my napkin and spot the panties. As soon as the plan was set in motion, I made my way straight to the ladies' room. Not sure of what to expect upon returning to the table, I could only hope my plan worked. But when I returned I looked down at the floor and noticed the panties were gone, but David didn't look any different than he did when I left the table.

Confused, I felt things must be really bad between David and me, because my plan didn't work: he didn't even react. He didn't think I was sexy anymore. Shaking my head I glanced out of the corner of my eye at the kitchen door, where three busboys stood next to each other with huge grins on their faces. One of the busboys held up the red panties, as all three looked straight at me. I was mortified. One of the waiters must have seen the napkin drop and when he picked it up also found my red panties next to David's feet. Never had I been more embarrassed and at the same time I was disappointed that my plan hadn't worked.

After we dropped the neighbors off and pulled the car up in front of our house, David and I sat in the car talking. I told David about my little plan to try and make our relationship better. As I explained about the panties a smile came across his face, "Were they clean?" he asked, as he grinned jokingly, then got out of the car. I felt both furious and hurt at the same time as I made my way inside the house. After that things got even worse. David hardly talked to me and we seldom made love.

A very quiet Christmas came and went. When New Year's Eve arrived, David and I went to a local Irish pub. Looking around the pub, I saw happy people having a good time, yet David and I both sat quietly, with little enthusiasm for the partying going on around us. As the clock struck midnight, David slowly leaned over and gave me a hug, saying, "Happy New Year," with a low-toned voice.

Looking around, I saw the other people jumping up in excitement as balloons, confetti and the rasp of noisemakers flooded the air, followed by happy voices singing "Auld Lang Syne." At that moment I felt a deep sense of sadness. All that I had done to enhance my relationship with David seemed to be of no avail. I didn't know what else to do and began to think we were growing apart.

That night I decided to put whatever extra money David would give me into a private bank account, saving it up to get the kids and me an apartment if we did separate.

As spring approached, I had just enough money saved to live on if we had to move out on our own, when, out of the blue, David began to change for the better. Becoming more loving and attentive, he seemed to be trying to make up to the kids and me for his odd behavior. By this time, however, I was afraid to trust him again. But I wanted to so badly that I waited a few weeks to see if David's change in behavior was real or just temporary.

To my surprise and happiness, things between David and me got back on track, enough that I felt comfortable to stay.

When spring arrived, David's son Andy came down for a visit. While David was off filming, Andy helped me put down new flooring in the laundry room and helped plant some trees in the yard. It was hard work, but he seemed to enjoy the family spirit. One day on a work break, Andy and I sat at the patio table in the backyard talking, mostly about his activities and interests. Soon, Andy brought up Valerie. Without letting Andy know of the prior problems I'd had with her, I sat quietly and listened.

He told me he didn't like Valerie, that in the past when he came down to visit he always found Valerie at the house. Then he began telling me about these strange feelings he got when he was around her, although he never could quite figure out what it was. I wanted Andy to know he wasn't the only one who felt this way about her, but also didn't want to involve him in the past problems his father and I had had with her, so I sympathized but was guarded in my responses.

Shortly after Andy returned home, David told me he had been asked to work on another movie, which would take him back to Romania, but to a different location. David said, "I need to leave in May and I'll try to return sometime in July." I sighed and tried to be understanding but I felt upset. It would be another three months away from David. I could not help worrying, hoping our relationship wouldn't end up strained, as it had the last time he returned from Romania.

When May came, I helped David pack his bags and I tried to be upbeat, though I was sad to see him leaving. I told myself everything between us had gone so smoothly the last few months, surely we'd be okay when he returned.

Driving David to Hollywood, I pulled the car into an open parking lot where he was meeting up with other crew members and parked. As we sat in the car, David turned and gave me a kiss and a hug. "I love you, Donita," he said with feeling. "I love you, too," I replied as he got out. I sat teary-eyed and watched from the car as David began putting his luggage into the van that was taking him and the film crew to Los Angeles Airport.

While David was away, I kept myself as busy as possible with the kids. I tried not to dwell on David's absence though I missed him terribly. Taking the kids out to lunch one day, I ran into my old friend Bob as he was delivering packages near the house.

We happened to start talking about David, and Bob said, "I was standing across the street and I saw a good looking black woman dressed to the nines come out of the studio with David." Then he added, "But there was something really funny about her." I knew right away that he was referring to Valerie. He mentioned that this was a long time ago, before I'd met David. But he couldn't shake the image. Bob jokingly chuckled, "From far away, she seemed to stride out like a man."

I started laughing out loud. The idea of Valerie being a man was absolutely ludicrous. After all, although I too felt there was something strange about her, I had seen her up close; she had been in the women's rest room with Carolyn and me, talking about menstrual cramps! "There is something strange about Valerie all right, but there is no way that David would be with a man." Bob and I both continued laughing as I said goodbye and walked back to the car.

I took the kids to a restaurant where David often took us. Ginny, the same hostess who always took care of us, seated the kids and me and asked where David was. "He's in Romania, filming a movie," I told her. As the kids and I sat eating our lunch, I became more and more curious if the hostess had ever seen David bring Valerie into the restaurant.

At the end of the meal, while the children were having dessert, I walked over to Ginny and trying to act nonchalant, described Valerie to her. She knew right away who I was talking about. She told me, "David used to bring her here, but he stopped after he met you." She added that she was glad David met me, because I was much nicer than Valerie and together we made a happier couple.

Ginny said Valerie seemed odd, that there was something not quite right with her. But just like Andy and me, the hostess could not put her finger on what it was about Valerie that seemed strange.

As the next few days passed, Valerie's unknown origins raised my curiosity more and more. I decided to take a drive down to the Los Angeles County Courthouse to see if I could find anything on her. No luck, but by then I was too curious to stop. I went to the Burbank Courthouse and only found a document about the car accident Valerie had been involved in.

I found myself thinking crazy thoughts, wondering if the strange feeling I had about Valerie had any connection to the comment Bob had made.

Pondering over my concerns, I began to come up with a wild idea. What if I wrote Valerie a note? What if I said something to the effect that I wanted to forgive her and invite her over to the house? When Valerie arrived on my front porch and knocked at the door, I could call up the police and tell them there's a crazy man dressed as a woman at my front door, harassing me. Then the police would have to come over and check to see if she really was a woman. But then I started thinking rationally. What if Valerie really wasn't a man? I could get in trouble for making a false call to the police; I could face a harassment charge, because of the note I sent tricking her and, worse yet, I could lose David over this.

It was too much of a risk to take. And the more I thought it over, the crazier the whole idea sounded. Whatever it was that made me uneasy about Valerie, it didn't involve her sex; it had to be something else.

When summer arrived, my curiosity about Valerie faded, though, from time to time, I still remembered others' comments and my own strange feelings towards her. She had left David and me alone for so long, I didn't see any point in looking for trouble.

Moreover, though we were separated by thousands of miles, David and I kept in constant touch by phone. He always professed his love for me, telling me how much he missed me. Before too long he was making plans for me to visit him in July.

While David was away time inched slowly by, but in July he sent me a plane ticket to join him. I spent most of the fourteen-hour flight thinking about my relationship with David. We had been together almost five years and we had our ups and downs, but I completely loved him and was hoping that someday soon we'd marry.

I felt my nerves grow strained again as the plane circled in descent and finally landed at the Bucharest airport. Through the airplane's small portal I could see David waiting for me at the gate. We headed out of Bucharest, driving until we reached the gates of the private hotel the production company had rented. It looked more like an army compound from the outside, with high walls surrounding the hotel and military police standing guard along the walls and at the gate.

David said he was anxious to show me around the hotel grounds but first took my luggage to his room and let me clean up a bit from the flight. He excitedly walked me out through the main entrance of the hotel and onto a dirt road that led to an old golden-domed mausoleum. As we walked toward it, I glanced behind us to find two military policemen shouldering machine guns and snarling attack dogs following our steps. It seemed surreal that such a dark and ominous presence would be strolling through the beautiful grounds.

On my second day in Romania, David had to film in a rural location, far from the reach of civilization. I wanted to spend as much time as I could with David, but I didn't want to be stuck out in uncomfortable conditions for who knows how long. So I told David I'd stick around the hotel until he returned. Alone at the hotel, I called home to check on the kids and then spent some time resting from the jet lag I was still feeling. I fell asleep and somehow had a strange dream about Valerie.

As dusk set in, David and the crew finally returned. For dinner that night we went to the hotel's sumptuous dining room, decorated with ornate details and lavish design. I felt I was in a fairy tale setting. But I noticed David seemed to be somewhat preoccupied. He didn't talk or eat much and appeared to be someplace else the entire dinner. When he sat down on the bed afterwards, I felt a rather odd feeling quickly come over me. Before I realized what it was, I shocked even myself when, from nowhere, I blurted out, "David, is Valerie a man?"

David jerked back, looking at me with a surprised expression on his face. "No," he replied in a disbelieving tone, "I'm shocked that you would even ask such a thing."

But again, as if I had no control, I found the same strong urge come over me; finding myself possessed by it, I pressed the question more demandingly.

"David, I'm going to ask you again: is Valerie a man?"

David looked at me as if I was crazy, asking where I could have come up with such a wild notion.

I couldn't stop myself; once again the same question flew out of my mouth. Again and again, David denied Valerie was a man.

I kept pressing the question and then asked one last time, making David look at me, dead straight in the eyes. "David, you have to tell me, is Valerie a man?" I asked, one last time.

David's face slowly changed from an expression of denial to one of total horror.

"Yes," he replied in a defeated tone.

I swiftly turned towards the window in complete shock and tried to regain my breath. I was weak at the knees, my heart pounding hard from total disbelief. As I slowly turned around, not wanting to face the bizarre reality I was now in, David looked up at me, from where he sat on the edge of the bed.

"I thought you knew," he said, his voice quivering.

I couldn't stop whispering my horror. "Oh, my God, I can't believe this is real," I said in shocked dismay, as I crossed my arms and rocked myself back and forth to calm my rattled nerves.

David slowly got up off the edge of the bed and walked towards me. As I looked at him coming close, my shock quickly turned to hysterical anger.

"Stop! Keep away from me!" I yelled angrily.

David returned to the bed and sat down. "Please," he begged. Still in a stunned daze from the news, I found it difficult to collect myself, let alone understand David's words, as he pleaded for me to listen.

David began his story by saying, "I met Valerie in 1984, when I answered a personal advertisement in the newspaper that was placed in the 'Female Looking for Male' section."

I stared at him. "Go on."

"I believed it was a woman who placed the ad, so I answered it," David explained, with desperation in his voice. "We talked over the phone several times before I eventually drove down to San Bernardino, where Valerie was living, to meet her in person." Swearing up and down, David said he had dated Valerie for three months before she confessed she had once been a man; "She had already had a sex change operation," he told me.

Begging and pleading for me to understand, David said that by the time he found out Valerie was a transsexual she had already obtained phone numbers and addresses of his family and friends and told him that she or he would use them as blackmail if he didn't help her financially.

Continuing his story, David said that he knew it would devastate his mother if any of this was exposed, adding that it was one of the reasons he and Valerie had violent fights in the past. "When we first began dating, Valerie wanted me to introduce her to my mother, as my girlfriend." David then told me that upon his discovery that Valerie had once been a man, he wanted out, refusing to allow Valerie near his family, and that was when Valerie began her blackmailing campaign.

Once I came into the picture, David explained that Valerie became extremely jealous and violent. She began making more demands, threatening him with blackmail unless he introduced the kids and me, taking more control over David's life.

"Remember the note you put in my car? Remember I told you Valerie was with me when I got the note?" David asked.

As I stood there, my head still spinning, David went on to say that I became a big threat to Valerie. When he spent money on the kids and me, Valerie felt her security was being taken away from her. "I was forced by Valerie to play along or she said she would ruin my life," he whimpered.

Practically in tears, David exclaimed, "Do you have any idea what it's like to have someone control your life, to have someone threaten you all the time? I had no idea, even with Valerie being so violent with me, what she would do to the ones I love."

"David you have to stop talking. I have to think about all this," I snapped, as thoughts started rushing through my mind. Confused, upset and uncertain of what to believe I quickly ran out of the room. I made my way down the front staircase and all the way outside to the back door. In a blurred daze I strolled through the hotel's garden. I looked around; my life as I once knew it had suddenly changed, as I felt the full force of gravity weigh down on my shoulders. Never in my whole life had I felt so deceived.

I thought back to the first day I met Valerie. I recalled that strange feeling I had when I was around her, that feeling I couldn't pinpoint. My doubtful memories came back to me now. How Andy expressed his dislike for Valerie and the strange feelings he got from her, what the hostess had said at the restaurant and Bob's innocent, joking comment about Valerie being a man all flashed through my mind and from that moment on, I refused to see Valerie as female. Behind that feminine mask, I was sure now, was a violent man. Nearly overwhelmed, I sank into a chair on the hotel's patio.

"This can't be real," I said to myself, continuing to have flashbacks of my past with Valerie. It all began to make sense now, as I recalled the change in her voice the night of the Christmas party, her strength in tossing three grown men off the car door and when she sucker-punched David in the side of the head with a closed fist, just like a man.

As I sat there in a fog of confusion, David, who had followed me, slowly crept up and sat down across from me.

I knew he was there, but so many thoughts were crowding into my head that I couldn't speak. I could hear the tension in David's breathing, as I watched him open up his hands and bring them up to his forehead, then pass them in a downward motion over his face and to his chin.

"I know this is a very big shock, Donita, but please believe me when I say, I'm a victim too. I've been trying very hard and very carefully for years to get Valerie out of my life, but once she found out about you, she became even worse to deal with," David said nervously.

I looked at David as he repeated himself, telling me again how threatening and controlling Valerie was, how she had used his family, friends, colleagues and now me, as tools to get what she wanted.

As sick and pathetic as the whole situation sounded, David somehow made sense.

I knew his mother well enough to know that if she found out
something like this it would cause her a great deal of emotional pain,
if not affect her fragile heath. I took into account other things as well,
that David had once been married and had Andy, and how he told me
that I was the girlfriend about whom he dreamed, the one he never
had. I recalled the two separate occasions when David came over to
my apartment with cuts and bruises on his face and head and the
hang-up calls Valerie made to David's apartment.

Trying to think through it and make sense of everything that happened in the past, along with what David was telling me now, I found
myself slowly beginning to match up the current situation with the
past. Suddenly all I could remember was Valerie.

As the information started sinking in, I felt that maybe David was
telling the truth, that in fact he was a victim of blackmail.

"Oh, my God," I said as David paused in frustration. My feelings
slowly changed from being angry and upset at David to being enraged
at Valerie's cruel and controlling ways. Feeling like a huge ocean
wave had come crashing down on me, I was starting to realize how
conniving Valerie was.

I remembered David telling me he was scared of what Valerie
might do, if we went past a certain point in our relationship. Now it
made sense to me why David had first stalled about the idea of our
living together.

Thinking back to the discussions David and I had about it, I
remembered feeling he was using Valerie as an excuse. Now with his
new explanation of the circumstances, I found his reason for stalling
made sense. David recalled how he once told me he didn't want to
risk any trouble from Valerie and how he changed his mind, risking
everything in order to be with the kids and me.

"I'm going to kill him when I get back!" I said, angrily. David
stared at me, never having seen me so furious.

I was trapped in Romania, but then again I was glad I was there. I honestly felt if I had found all this out back home, I would have totally lost control.

David tried to calm me down, telling me my actions wouldn't solve anything, but only make the situation worse. I exploded at David, telling him I wasn't really going to kill Valerie; it was only a figure of speech! "But I am going to put a stop to Valerie making your life as miserable as possible." David, backing down in relief, agreed something had to be done about Valerie, but carefully.

Angry that I had been played for a fool, I told David not to dare refer to Valerie as a "she" around me.

David put his hand up in a motion of agreement. "Yes, yes," he said, "I completely understand."

In trying to calm myself down, I began asking more questions. "What's his real name?" I asked in a determined, low tone.

David looked at me with confusion. "I don't know," he replied helplessly. "I've only known this person as Valerie Taylor."

"What about identification? Have you ever looked at his driver's license or anything?" I asked in frustration, wanting to know who Valerie really was.

"I did once see an identification card. It said Valerie Taylor on it." Recalling my findings about the car accident, I concluded David could be telling the truth, as I myself did not find anything with another name, but only that of Valerie Taylor.

"Where did he come from, David?" I asked, still upset, although I was trying to remain calm.

"I don't know! Look, Donita, please, you have GOT to believe me when I say that I myself have tried very hard to find out who Valerie really is in order to put a stop to all this blackmailing. I swear to you, I don't know much more than you do. All I know is that her—I mean his—parents are dead and that's ALL I was told from Valerie about her—I mean HIS—background. I don't know where he came from or his real name. Please believe me; I would NEVER have a relationship with someone like this. I was tricked and lied to," David replied in obvious annoyance.

"Wait, something doesn't make sense, David. How did Valerie end up living with you?" I asked.

"The same way as everything else: blackmail," David replied.

"Why didn't you just tell the police?" I prodded.

"Because I wanted to handle it myself," David explained. "Look, it was embarrassing enough that I had believed this person to be a real female. To go to the police and explain my situation would be even more embarrassing, not to mention the embarrassment it would bring to my family."

With no other information to go on and not knowing where Valerie came from, I knew it would be difficult to find out who Valerie Taylor really was. Nevertheless, I knew Valerie needed to be exposed in order to put an end to the blackmailing.

Feeling truly scared of what I might do if I cut my trip short and confronted Valerie and knowing I needed time and perspective to calm myself down enough to deal with the situation more rationally, I decided it was best to continue my stay in Romania.

During the remainder of my visit, my feelings about David drifted back and forth. On one hand, I felt he was weak for not standing up to Valerie when he found out that she had once been a man, but on the other hand, I found myself feeling sorry for David for ending up in such a cruel circumstance.

I spent the majority of my time alone at the hotel, thinking over what I had learned about Valerie. My real concern was how I was going to handle the situation when I returned home.

Needing to think, I took long walks through the forest near the hotel, though my privacy was limited, as two military policemen always followed closely behind me, watching my every move. One day, when they were so close I could feel their breath on the back of my neck, I let them know their company was not needed or wanted.

I turned around and gave them both the dirtiest looks I could muster. Quickly getting the message, they turned around and walked off to a more discreet distance.

David returned to the hotel at the end of each day of filming, but he was becoming so deeply depressed it was affecting his work. One evening David said he was able to take two days off, which were mostly spent with him following me from spot to spot around the hotel grounds. We hardly spoke to each other. David said he was becoming more and more concerned, not sure of what I was going to do.

In fact, I was not sure either. My feelings switched from anger to sympathy for David and the situation he was in. I tried in a desperate effort to put the whole thing out of my mind, pretending that everything would be okay during those few times I went to downtown Bucharest with David or visited the studio near the hotel.

When my trip to Romania was about to end, I swiftly packed my bags as David called for a taxi. He joined me in the car as we drove to the airport.

As we got near the airport, I forced myself to speak. "David, I have a lot of thinking to do when I return home." He nodded grimly.

Upon arriving at the airport, I found out my flight had been delayed three hours and suggested David return to the hotel. His head down, he agreed.

I spent most of the flight home in the lavatory, crying. At the house, the sight of Jessica and Sam helped take my mind off what had happened in Romania. I tried to be upbeat for their sakes and not convey how upset and badly shaken I really was. Days and nights somehow passed.

David, noticing I hadn't telephoned or left any messages for him at the hotel, called the house. I kept my conversations with him short, telling him I wasn't sure of my feelings yet—or what I was going to do. I could tell from the sadness in David's voice that he felt he might lose me for good.

That night I called Gayle and told her the shocking news about Valerie and how she'd blackmailed David. After that, Gayle called nearly every night after the children went to sleep, trying to console me.

David continued calling me from Romania, but I found it hard to talk to him without breaking down crying. David said, "Donita, I'll do anything it takes to make you happy."

Not sure how David was going to handle Valerie, I backed off, hoping David would have the strength to put an end to their relationship and her blackmailing.

As I thought over the situation David was in, a fearful thought quickly entered my mind and I wondered what kind of life Valerie had led before meeting David. The sudden fear of AIDS entered my mind. Not wanting to panic, I tried my best to remain calm and picked up the phone to make an appointment for an AIDS test.

Later that same day, David called to see how I was doing. I told him of the appointment I had made. He kept reassuring me there was no reason to fear such a thing, as he had himself tested after discovering Valerie was once a man and that the test was negative. Nonetheless, I knew it was something I had to make sure of, no matter what David said.

After taking the test, I was told I would be called to come back in and find out the result, as it would not be given out over the phone. During the next couple of days, as I waited anxiously for that one phone call to tell me that the results were in, I found myself becoming more and more nervous, wondering *what if?* The phone rang and the time for learning the truth was scheduled.

After a short stay in a sterile waiting room, I heard my name announced over a loudspeaker and was taken to a room where someone would be coming in to meet me and tell me my results. What was only minutes felt like hours on end, until a heavyset gray-haired woman entered the room with my test result.

She first told me the result was sealed and that she herself did not know what it was. I anxiously waited, wanting to know up front what my fate was, but now I was fearful, as I wondered if there was a reason she held back before telling me.

"Before I open this and tell you if it's negative or positive, I need to ask you a question," she said. It seemed like a form of torture. I was now becoming scared, as if she did know the results and was keeping them from me.

"What do you mean you need to ask me something?" I replied, my eyes tearing up from fear.

"I need to know, if your test is positive, what you plan to do when you leave here," she asked, with a concerned look upon her face. I was becoming restless with anxiety, but felt if I didn't keep myself calm, she would not tell me what I needed to know. I sat quietly for a moment, thinking of my children and what I would miss out on if the test was positive. I wondered what effect it would have on their lives, thinking of all the important moments I wouldn't be there for.

Dark images filled my mind. I thought of Sam and Jessica's high school graduations, which were still years in the future, and seeing them off to college. I would never meet or know my future son- and daughter-in-law or have the joy of someday holding my grandchildren in my arms. Not wanting to fill my mind with fear of "what if," I gave the woman the answer she was waiting for so I could put my mind at rest. "I'll go home and deal with it in a calm manner, then take it from there," I replied. I sat quietly, as she pondered my answer with uncertainty.

"I'm going to open it now," she told me. My heart began beating fast as I sat frozen stiff in my seat, watching as she unsealed the results, reading them and then looking up at me.

"Negative," she said, with a comforting smile.

Shutting my eyes tight with a sense of relief from the dark outcome I had painted in my mind moments earlier, I took a deep breath, then stood up, thanking her as I exited the office.

Later that day David called home. I told him the result of the test and the fear that had awakened in me while I was waiting to hear it. David tried to console me by telling me again, "I told you, you had nothing to worry about."

"David, please, I need to know you're telling me the truth about everything, I need to know. I have a right to know. I'm very confused," I said, still shaken from what I had gone through earlier in the day. David, with a sad desperation in his voice, pleaded with me to believe him.

"Donita, please, listen to me. Valerie's made my life a living hell. I've tried very carefully and cautiously in the past to get her out of my life, but threats about my family, my career, you and the kids are brought up every time she's in contact with me, and the blackmailing starts all over," David replied.

"I want to know how you plan on dealing with Valerie when you come back," I said. "I'm going to say the truth, that you know every-thing now and as embarrassing as it is, if I have to, I'll tell the police if the blackmailing doesn't stop."

As the days passed, David called me as often as two times a day. He told me the movie he was working on was going to wrap up by the end of July; then he would be returning home.

As I listened, David said in a soft and loving voice, "Donita, we've been together for almost five years now and I want you to know that I love you very much, more than you'll ever realize. Why don't we just get married and make a whole package?"

Shocked, and totally caught off guard, I almost dropped the phone.

Before these last revelations about Valerie came to light, I had waited so long for David to ask me that question I had almost given up hope, but the timing couldn't have been worse. My reaction was dulled in response. I told him, "I will think about it, but getting Valerie out of our lives should be first and foremost."

David, agreeing, stated, "I am going to risk it all and deal with Valerie when I return home." However, he did not want to get off the phone until I gave him a straight "yes" or "no" answer to us getting married. Uncertain of my feelings now, David continued to try and convince me he'd get Valerie out of his life for good. He kept repeating how much he loved me and that he never wanted to lose me. My heart spoke and I told David, "I love you too, but you don't know how much all this is hurting me."

Torn about what to do, I paused to think. I was confused but decided that David was a victim in all this. Punishing him for it didn't seem right.

"Yes." I finally replied.

David, sounding extremely happy with my answer, said he wanted us to get married soon after he returned from Romania. He said he'd be calling his mother about our engagement and would ask her to help set up the wedding. David then went on, "I'll call you back with a list of friends and colleagues I want to invite to the wedding."

After getting off the phone with David, I stood, questioning whether I had made the right decision. I walked out to the backyard and sat down at the patio table. Tears began flowing down my face. I wasn't sure of the decision I had made to marry David. All I knew was that I loved him.

As soon as I went back into the house the phone rang. It was Dianna calling to congratulate me; David had wasted no time in telling her. His mother, sounding ecstatic, quickly hit me with an onslaught of wedding ideas and asked me to come down with the kids the next weekend to shop for a wedding dress. Later that night, David called back with a list of names of people he wanted to invite. Before I knew it, we had a wedding date set for the middle of August. With money being tight, we planned to have a small ceremony in the backyard of David's parents' house. With Dianna keeping my every waking moment busy with wedding and reception plans, I found my mind had finally wandered away from Valerie.

Hoping to have as nice a wedding as possible with the budget we were under, I felt David's mother would know best how it could be done with the amount of money we had to spend, although she took more control than I really wanted to relinquish. Not wanting any tension between us I tried my best to compromise. When I mentioned wedding rings, Dianna began telling me how she had never had the wedding she wanted. Then Dianna showed me her wedding ring. Since we didn't have the money to buy the type of ring I'd like to have, she suggested I wear hers and buy David a simple gold band. As soon as David returned home from Romania I measured his finger to have his ring sized just right.

At first I let Dianna help with plans—after all, we were using her home for the ceremony—but Dianna soon took over the affair. I finally found a wedding dress I loved. Dianna wasn't too happy with it and suggested we keep on looking, but I had had enough. I put my foot down and insisted on getting the dress I liked. Dianna shrugged her shoulders and slinked off to the other end of the store as I got fitted. Despite the drama we really did have a good time together, tasting wedding cake and picking out floral arrangements.

At home I began working on the invitations and rushed to the post office to mail them out the following day. One invitation I would never send out would be Valerie's. Most of the guests who were going to attend were on David's side; his family and circle of friends were much larger than mine. The best part of being home was that even with all the wedding preparations, I had some time alone. The kids were in summer camp, David was still in Romania and I finally had time to think.

At the end of July, David returned home. Although the kids and I were happy to see him again and I was excited about our impending marriage, I wanted to make sure he was going to deal with Valerie. "I promise you, Donita, Valerie's days of blackmailing will be over," he assured me and told me not to worry, to keep my mind on the happier times ahead. "We'll soon be husband and wife and we all will start a new life together."

Trusting David would keep his word, I forced my mind to stay on the wedding, as it was fast approaching. David and Sam got fitted for their tuxedos and Jessica got a cute white dress to wear. I found myself secretly trying on my wedding dress, making sure it still fit perfectly. The mail was a steady stream of RSVPs from our guests; we excitedly opened each one to read the responses. We met with disc jockeys and band leaders, florists and caterers and before I knew it, the big day arrived.

The ceremony and the day were perfect. Returning from the beauty salon, the bridesmaids and I got ready at Dianna's neighbor's house. My maid of honor was an old friend from Los Angeles and my bridesmaids were my sister and David's two nieces, while Jessica was the flower girl. I felt so spoiled having all my friends and family tend to my every need; I truly felt like a princess for one day. Maybe the best of all, I was able to patch up my relationship with my father. He was proud to walk me down the aisle and give me away to my husband. David and his groomsmen looked dashing in their black tuxedos. Sam seemed to enjoy dressing up in such fancy clothes and got a kick out of being the ring bearer. Never had I seen David so happy. I think his smile was wider than ever. It was contagious; the whole wedding party had huge smiles on.

I can fondly remember the ceremony, watching David stand nervously before the priest as the groomsmen and bridesmaids made their way down the aisle, my father squeezing my hand as he gave me away, the words "you may now kiss the bride" echoing in my mind.

The weather was gorgeous and Dianna's backyard was filled with white flowers, tables with ornate centerpieces and rows of white folding chairs. There was an outside dance floor, a disc jockey and a bar, and when the sun set the backyard came to life with candles and Chinese lanterns. We danced well into the night and laughed and celebrated with our closest friends. I remember my first dance with David as husband and wife. Looking into his blue eyes I felt so secure.

I think both Dianna's and my dreams of a wedding collided somewhere in the middle, making it even more special.

Before heading off for the long weekend honeymoon, David and I drove down to a small restaurant on the waterfront, where we toasted each other with the champagne David brought. Still in our wedding clothes, we received congratulation after congratulation as we sat at a table by the windows. Only staying a short time, we soon began walking towards the front door when David stopped, telling me he needed to use the bathroom. Not wanting to wait inside, I continued on to the limousine. David took longer than usual, and when he came out and got in the car, I asked what had taken him so long.

He said some old drunk at the bar had grabbed him by the arm on his way out, telling him to be a good husband to me. David went on to tell me, "The old man told me never to lie or keep secrets from my wife or I would end up like him, no wife and no life." I laughed, saying it was good advice; David chuckled, as we drove off to our hotel.

We spent the next few days in Monterey and Carmel, taking in the beautiful sights of the California coast. We enjoyed elaborate dinners and sunsets over the Pacific. Our nights were filled with passion and love, and though I was hesitant about David's abrupt proposal and short engagement, the honeymoon couldn't have turned out better. During the day we strolled arm-in-arm through the quaint streets of Carmel, taking in all the art galleries and crafts shops. David surprised me at every corner with a kiss or a tiny gift, re-establishing our bond of love that had been under so much tension in the last six months. I was sad to see our trip up the coast end and I still don't think there is a more beautiful experience than looking out over the cliffs of California with someone you love, watching the sun dip below the Pacific.

chapter six

A Shocking
Discovery

A few weeks after David and I were married, we were sitting at the kitchen table together, drinking coffee and discussing plans for putting a swimming pool in the backyard when I noticed David wasn't wearing his wedding ring. When I asked him where it was; he told me he had lost it in the bedroom somewhere, that "it had slipped off." Although I found his answer strange and had had the ring made to fit David's finger perfectly, I didn't comment on his explanation. We headed to the bedroom together and began searching for the ring, but we were unable to find it.

The loss of his wedding ring saddened me greatly. David promised me he'd look for it again when he returned home from work that evening, but I couldn't help obsessing about the loss. Perhaps thinking it was a bad omen, I decided to search the bedroom thoroughly. I went over it section by section, but no ring turned up. Frustrated, I called David at work, asking, "Can you remember where you last saw your wedding band on your finger?" Once again, David said he last saw it in our bedroom.

"We'll look together all this evening," he promised. We did, but
to no avail.

After a week of intensely searching the house, we stopped.
Although I was upset, I tried to keep occupied with other things, hoping that one day soon I'd come across his ring when I least expected
it.

It helped that the children were thrilled by the idea they would
soon have a swimming pool. And David said, "Let's go ahead and do
it. It will help get your mind off the ring."

The following Monday the pool builder came over to take meas-
urements in the back yard. I followed him around the yard as he ham-
mered long metal stakes into the ground and roped off the area with
white string, marking an outline where the pool would go. At the
backyard wall, he suddenly leaned down to the ground and picked
something up.

"Did someone lose a gold ring?" he asked, holding up a partially
dirt-encrusted object.

"That's my husband's wedding band! I've been looking all over
for it!" I replied. "I don't know how to thank you for finding it."

Although I was overjoyed, I could not help but wonder how
David's wedding band ended up all the way in the back of the yard,
when he said he had lost it in the bedroom. Maybe he was embarrassed to tell me that he didn't know exactly where he'd lost it.
Despite my trying to push it away, a bad feeling began to develop
deep in my stomach. Something wasn't right. Could David have
deliberately thrown his ring back there? I called David at the studio
to tell him the pool man had found his ring at the far end of the yard
when he was measuring for the pool. I couldn't help myself and
blurted out, "It's awful strange. Do you have any idea how it got
there?"

David said he was confused himself. "I have no idea," he told me,
then tried to change the subject. But things between us would never
be the same after that. I found myself trusting him less, often

questioning many of the things he said. It hurt that I couldn't believe the man I loved, the man I had married.

By the end of October, David's behavior had gotten so strange that I started to wonder if Valerie had anything to do with his moodiness. However, with us being newlyweds, sending the kids back to school again and keeping busy decorating the house, I had put the problem with Valerie out of my mind most of the time. But now I began to think I had made a mistake. One night as David and I sat in bed watching the news, the phone rang. It was Valerie on the other end, asking to speak to David.

"Why? What do you want?" I asked, angrily.

"Give David the fucking phone, now!" Valerie replied, in an enraged voice.

In shock, I turned and looked at David.

"Who is it?" he asked.

"It's Valerie. How did he get our number?" I whispered, while covering up the receiver.

"Here, give it to me," David said in frustration.

As I listened, David calmly repeated the word, "Yes," over and over again. As I lay in silence, I became suspicious, realizing things were not as I thought them to be. In rethinking the situation, I started to wonder about all that had happened over the past few months and years with both Valerie and David. I was now more determined than ever to find out who Valerie really was and the real connection David had with him. Finally, David hung up.

Stunned at this new realization, I slowly rolled over. We both were silent as David turned out the light.

Not being able to sleep, I soon got up and I paced the living room floor for most of the night. Suspicions flooded my mind. Had David thrown his wedding ring away because of Valerie? Was she threatening him again? Was she threatening me and my children? Had I made a terrible mistake in marrying David and, if so, what was I going to do now?

Somehow, early the next morning, I got the children off to school while avoiding any conversation with David. Silently I watched as he poured coffee into his mug and left for work.

With Sam and Jessica at school for the day, I decided to continue my interrupted search for Valerie's real identity. My first stop would be the Burbank courthouse to see if I had missed anything.

Returning to the same place where I had obtained the document on Valerie's car accident, I was surprised to see the same clerk who had helped me the first time I had been there. "I'm still checking on Valerie Taylor," I said, "and I haven't had much luck. Please, could you look again?" The clerk asked if I was only trying to find information through traffic documents.

"No, I want anything and everything I can find on this person," I said.

Seeing my helplessness and frustration, the clerk told me, "Look, you have to go to each division in the courthouse to see if there are other documents on the woman. My area only covers traffic." She went on to say, "You should try the civil, criminal and superior court for further information. Tell them Rhonda sent you." Then she told me where the other offices were located. Walking down the corridor, I first headed to the civil court window.

"Do you have any documents on a Valerie Taylor?" I asked nervously. "Rhonda sent me."

"I'll take a look." I watched the clerk walk away and soon return with a document in hand.

Before even looking over the document that had just been handed to me, I anxiously rushed up the stairs to the superior court window where I hoped to find more documents on Valerie.

As I got near the top of the stairs, I slowed my pace and began skimming the first document given me. It was a civil lawsuit against Valerie, involving the car accident I'd already known about. What I hadn't known until then was that several people Valerie hit had sued. Reaching the very top of the stairs, I stopped and turned the page over. At the top of the document was typed "Valerie Nicole Taylor AKA Freddie Lee Turner."

A rush of shock quickly hit me, my eyes blinking in a flash of disbelief. Finally I had found out Valerie's real name. Feeling like I was going to pass out as my breathing quickened, I leaned limply against the wall, trying to regain my composure. After resting there a few moments I told myself I needed to go on; there could be more. My next stop was the superior court. I walked there as quickly as I could. Stammering, repeating that Rhonda had sent me, I asked the clerk for any documents she could find on both Valerie Nicole Taylor and Freddie Lee Turner.

By now I was shaking and agitated. I began pacing the floor while waiting for the clerk to return. It seemed like an hour, but only minutes had passed when he came back to hand over a decree for a name change. Quickly walking over to a corner of the room, I began reading the name change document. The first page read both names, Freddie Turner and Valerie Taylor, the first being changed for the other.

The second page showed a small newspaper clipping, stating, "All persons interested in the said matter involving Freddie Turner changing his/her name to Valerie Taylor should appear before the Burbank court and show cause why the application for a change of name should not be granted."

The third page asked for "the nearest living relative of the petitioner who is changing names."

Freddie had his father's name listed as the closest living relative. Another shock, since David had told me both of Valerie's parents were dead. What was going on here? Who was lying? What was the truth? Trembling, I continued to read the city, state and address of Freddie Turner Sr., Valerie Taylor's father.

There was more, adding to my shock. The document further stated, "The petitioner has undergone a sex change operation and has changed his sex from male to female."

Reading along to the near end, I saw where Freddie was requested to sign his real name on two different pages. The signatures on both signed documents flowed evenly and neatly, except for how he signed his last name, Turner. Both times it had been handwritten sloppily, so as to be almost unreadable.

With the shock of obtaining the name change document, I realized I hadn't looked at when it was filed. Quickly turning back through the pages I found the date.

Another jolt: I was dating David during that time! It didn't make any sense to me: David had told me in Romania that he and Valerie had met seven years before and that Freddie had already had the sex change. If that was so, why would Freddie wait so long to change his name? My heart pounded. Had David been lying? Was he an innocent victim or a willing participant in this masquerade?

Had I only been lied to once or was I played for a fool all the while? With the documents in hand I swiftly made my way down the stairs and out of the courthouse to the parking lot, where I jumped into the truck, put the documents on the seat beside me and sped off to David's studio. When I arrived, I grabbed the documents and barged my way in. I rushed up the stairs and found David, sitting alone in his office. I threw the recently discovered name change document in his lap.

"You must have known all along! You must have known all along what his real name was too! I bet you even helped him change it, didn't you?" I yelled, erupting into rage.

David looked down at the name change document in his lap, and then looked up at me, as he slowly leaned back his chair. Then, still staring at me, he put his fingers together underneath his chin.

"You just had to go digging, didn't you?" David replied, calmly.

At that very moment I realized from David's demeanor that I had hit the core of the truth about the relationship between him and Freddie.

"I can't believe this! Did you pay for Freddie's sex-change too?" I asked, as I stood stunned, waiting for his reply.

"Yes. Yes, I did," David, replied calmly.

"Oh, my God, David. You're gay?" I asked, my voice rising in pitch.

David immediately snapped back, "NO!" with an offended look upon his face.

"Then you're bisexual!" I said firmly, standing my ground.

"No! I'm not that either," David replied.

"Then what the hell are you?" I asked, angrily.

"I'm neither!" David replied, without explaining.

"This is very serious, David. You owe me an explanation," I said in a demanding tone.

But David kept on mumbling, "This isn't the way it was," and other gibberish that made no sense to me. Flustered because I wasn't getting straight answers from David, I told him to meet me at the house, because I didn't feel comfortable talking about this at the studio.

I left his studio and got into the truck. In a daze, I slowly drove the truck home through traffic and parked in the driveway. Turning off the engine, I sat in the truck for a few moments while thoughts continued racing through my mind. All of a sudden it hit me! I should record everything David was going to tell me; that way I wouldn't forget anything because of the state of mind I was in.

Quickly jumping out of the truck, I ran inside, throwing my purse and keys on the table and began tearing through the house, looking for the tape recorder David kept, knowing I had to move fast, as David's car was going to pull up in the driveway at any moment.

Once I found the tape recorder and microphone, I raced downstairs to our bedroom and planted the tape recorder underneath the bed. Then I pulled the microphone up behind the headboard, slipping it between two pillows. After making a quick test to be sure the

tape recorder was working, I ran back to the living room and waited
for David to pull up in the driveway.

Within a few minutes, David pulled his car into the driveway. I
knew he always took the time to rearrange the work papers he needed
for the evening before getting out of the car. Quickly running back to
the bedroom, I got down on the floor and reached under the bed to
push the record button. I raced back to the kitchen before David
reached the front door. Sitting down, I took a deep breath and tried to
regain my composure, hoping not to draw suspicion to my behavior.
I felt the more civil but curious I acted, the better my chances were of
getting information from him.

As I sat there, I realized I needed an excuse to get David into the
bedroom and thought one up. A few moments later I heard the key
turn in the lock and David's footsteps in the living room. When he
entered the kitchen where I was waiting, I sprung my plan, saying,
"I'm not feeling too well. I need to lie down on the bed. We can talk
in there." I knew I must have looked harried and upset enough for
him to believe me. As David followed me to the bedroom, I carefully
but quickly made sure I lay on the bed in a position that would allow
the microphone to pick up our conversation. Knowing it would be
hard, I told myself to remain calm during the onslaught of questions
I had for David. It was difficult not to show him how angry I really
was with him. I felt I had been deceived by him for five years and I
deserved answers to every question I had.

"David, I don't want to upset you or have a fight, but there are
things I need to know."

First, I asked when Freddie had his sex change; where it was
done and who the doctor was that performed the operation. I was not
sure of his willingness to tell this information, but I asked anyway.

There was silence for a minute or two, then David surprised me.
"The sex change operation took place while Freddie was living with
me." Trembling, I recalled that that was the same year David had
been nominated for an Academy Award. Suddenly I remembered

his mother telling me she had been upset that David had not invited her to the event and his relating that he took Valerie as his date to the Oscars. I had completely forgotten about it until then.

David then told me he had flown Freddie to Trinidad, Colorado, where a doctor named Frank Barken performed the surgery on Freddie, adding, "I cared for him during his recovery process, after he returned from Colorado."

Feeling sick to my stomach that David had lied to me all along, I continued asking more questions; the true details of this horrific ordeal began to unfold. I was becoming angrier and it was hard not to scream out as David tried to make everything sound so normal, telling me I was the one who needed to accept his revelations. He kept on making excuses. Finally, knowing my anger was about to explode, I stopped asking questions. For a few more minutes, I kept quiet, just listening to his meaningless speech. Then, knowing I could take no more, I sat up and got off the bed. "David," I told him, "you need to pack your things and leave. I will be filing for divorce." David seemed to realize there was no going back this time. He gathered some of his things and left the house, and I turned the tape recorder off. Falling onto the bed, I broke down crying, confused and sickened at all the lies and the discovery of the long-term relationship David and Freddie had been having together.

I wanted to get David and his things out of the house as quickly as possible. I began cleaning out his desk drawers, collecting his papers into a filing box. Soon I came across a credit card receipt from a local pharmacy. Curious as to what it was for, I read over the receipt and found it was a bill for an expensive drug prescription. David didn't take prescription medicine; even his asthma inhaler was purchased over-the-counter.

Shrugging my shoulders, I tossed the receipt into the box with all the other files and papers and continued cleaning out his things. I gathered his dress clothes out of the closet and gently placed them on the bed. All the while, I kept staring at the box of papers, wondering

what the prescription was for. It was probably nothing, but I had to
know. David had filled our relationship with deceit and lies; I had to
know how far it went.

I grabbed the receipt and drove over to the pharmacy. I walked up
to the pharmaceutical counter and waited patiently until someone
helped me. Quickly making up an excuse, I told the pharmacist, "My
husband and I are trying to get some of our bills together and we don't
remember what this prescription was for." I discreetly slid the receipt
over to him.

"It's a prescription for female hormone supplements," he said,
looking skeptically at me.

I thanked him and tried to remain calm as I quickly exited the pharmacy. Getting into my car I realized that Freddie's apartment was only
a few blocks away. It was becoming more and more apparent how
deeply involved David was in helping Freddie change his appearance
as thoroughly as possible.

Knowing I had to pull myself together with the kids about to
return home from school, I began fixing an early dinner for them.
Then I remembered it was Halloween. How could I get through it?
Nevertheless, I got their costumes ready and called our neighbors to
see if the kids could go trick-or-treating with them. Luckily, they said
it was fine. It would be the first Halloween I had ever missed taking
them trick-or-treating, but I was in no shape to go anywhere. For a few
moments I broke down uncontrollably; then, not wanting the kids to
know something was wrong, I went to the bathroom and splashed
cold water on my pale face, thinking it was apropos that I looked like
a ghost. I put on some makeup and told myself I would have a good
cry later.

Just as the kids sat down to dinner, Gayle called. Right away she
could tell something was wrong. I told the kids to finish eating while
I talked on the phone in the bedroom. "I'll be back in to help you with
your costumes," I promised. Closing the bedroom door behind me, I

sat on the bed and began to cry, as I told Gayle what I had found at the courthouse and that David admitted he had paid for Freddie's sex and name change. Gayle was in shock.

"I'm so sorry, Donita; I know how much in love you are with David. This must really be tearing you apart," Gayle said, as she tried to console me.

Gayle sounded just as confused as I was.

"So David's gay, then. But it doesn't make sense why he would be with you, if he's seeing a transsexual," Gayle said.

"I don't know, Gayle; there's a lot I don't know yet, but you can sure bet I'm going to find out," I replied angrily. "At least I know now why David tossed his wedding band in the backyard, not to mention why he continued the deception and mountain of lies."

The following morning, November 1, I sought out a divorce attorney I'd heard of, Sam Carter. I made an appointment to see him that same day. Sitting down in his comfortable office, I struggled to tell him what was causing me to want to file for divorce. It was even more difficult than I expected.

"Now let me get this straight. Your husband had a sex change?" Carter asked, running a hand through his thick gray hair. He adjusted his glasses, with a puzzled look on his face.

"No," I replied. The room went quiet. As he looked up at me, I felt a sense of hopelessness. "Listen, I spent five years of my life with this man. My kids and I trusted him. I believed he loved me and my kids; that we were a family, but all he did was lie. Behind my back he had a relationship with someone who was born a man, but he helped him change into a woman." I was practically yelling as tears welled up in my eyes.

Nodding his head up and down with understanding, he arched his eyebrows and then began to rub his nose with his fingers, while thinking quietly to himself. Taking a pen in his hand, he started talking out loud as he wrote.

"From what you've told me, and I'm going to be honest with you, it doesn't look good." As soon as I heard him I started shaking my head in disbelief. He continued, "But—"

"Yes?" I interrupted.

"But, you could take him to civil court and sue him for damages," he said.

"I'm not going to do that, because David works in the movie business. It could draw even more attention," I told him.

"Even better reason to do it. He might be willing to settle out of court, but you have to get the paperwork together to show him you're taking this seriously," he replied.

"That's not what I meant. I can't do it because it would draw attention to my kids and me, and I can't have that. I don't want them to know. Do you have any idea how much hurt and ridicule it could cause them? All the kids teasing them about their stepfather being involved in this... I don't even know what to call this! No! I can't have that."

"Yes, I see what you mean."

"There's nothing you can do, is there?" I asked.

"With the short amount of time you were married and not having anything to hold him to on paper, there really isn't much, unless..." he trailed off.

"Unless what?" I said, jumping in.

"If the date you and David separated is later than you said, it might help," he finished saying. "When was it you and David separated?"

"Last night. Right after I found the legal name change document on his boyfriend, Freddie. I confronted David about it and he didn't even try to deny it. Nice Halloween trick, huh? Then I kicked him out of the house," I said, almost laughing at the bizarre story that had just come out of my mouth.

Taking a pen in his hand, he began writing, telling me what tactics he was going to use to claim emotional damages. As we talked over my shocking discovery about David's true relationship with Valerie or Freddie or whatever else he called himself, Mr. Carter looked as dazed as I felt.

"And I thought in my long career, I'd heard everything. I'm really sorry for you, Mrs. Allen. What a ghastly situation." I nodded, not trusting myself to say anything.

When I left Mr. Carter's office, I headed back to the house and called David at the studio.

"I just thought I'd let you know you'll be served divorce papers soon," I said angrily. I knew it was childlike on my part to want to retaliate, but I couldn't help it.

"Okay, if that's what you really want," David said, as if it weren't a big deal.

"If that's what I want? What did you think I'd do? Stay with you?" I replied in shock. I quickly hung up the phone.

Later that day, I went back to searching for the full facts about Freddie Turner. I studied Freddie's name change document closely, noticing the name of an attorney, Gary Moore, on it. Picking up the lawsuit document stemming from the car accident I reread it thoroughly and noticed Gary Moore's name on that document as well. It quickly became apparent to me that Gary Moore was Freddie's lawyer.

I got out the yellow pages and found Mr. Moore's name with a small advertisement, listing him as a criminal attorney. I wondered why Freddie would use a criminal attorney for a name change. Besides the car accident incident, could Freddie have something else in his past? I had to find out. I took a shot in the dark. Having found out the city where Freddie's father lived and thinking that could be where Freddie was from, I sat down and wrote a letter to the Greenville, South Carolina, police department, requesting any criminal records on Freddie Turner be sent to me. After all, they were in the public domain. Anyone could get them and I wanted them if they existed.

Meanwhile my own emotional condition deteriorated. I broke down continuously, couldn't sleep and constantly replayed in my mind the discovery of David and Freddie. I couldn't stop thinking of it and my own heartbreak. I knew I had to stop for Jessica and Sam's sake, but if I were to be strong for them, I needed help getting through the situation. I took out the yellow pages once again and started looking for a mental health professional to see.

Feeling more comfortable with a female doctor, I located and called Dr. Sue Ashford, a psychotherapist, only to get her answering service. Without giving the details of my circumstances, I left a short message, saying it was important that she return my call as soon as possible. When Dr. Ashford did return my call, I felt myself choking up, while I tried to explain my situation. Dr. Ashford gently tried to calm me down. Realizing it was a serious situation, Dr. Ashford asked if I would be able to meet her at her office at ten o'clock the next morning.

After getting the kids off to school, I grabbed the documents on Freddie and drove over to Dr. Ashford's office. Dr. Ashford introduced herself to me. As we sat in her cozy office, which looked almost like my living room, with its needlepoint embroidered pillows and comfortable couch and chairs, I started to fill her in on my relationship with David. I began telling my story, starting with how David had introduced me to a friend of his named Valerie, who I felt was rather strange though I could never pinpoint what it was about her that unnerved me. Then I revealed the shocking truth I had recently discovered surrounding David and Freddie. And though I had told the story many times by then, the pain was no less.

Dr. Ashford felt I needed help to get through the divorce. She asked that I come to see her twice a week, more if needed. She paused for a moment, then went on to say she'd like to see David as well, adding that he needed help too. Agreeing with Dr. Ashford, I called David later that night, telling him that I had gone to a therapist who wanted to see him as well.

David exclaimed, "There's nothing wrong with me. I don't need any therapy."

"David, you know I filed for divorce because of what I found out about your strange relationship with Valerie."

"That's your interpretation," he responded, becoming agitated. He agreed to see Dr. Ashford, but for only one visit.

The following week David and I met at Dr. Ashford's office. She called David into her office first. I sat nervously trying to figure out what he was saying to her in the discussion going on in the next room. After an hour passed, David emerged from the room, didn't even glance at me and rushed from the office. Dr. Ashford then came out, asking me to come with her. Making it clear that she had to respect patient/doctor confidentiality, Dr. Ashford refused to discuss her session with David, only saying that he wanted us to stay together and make our marriage work. Her face impassive, she went on, "David has no intention of continuing therapy. He feels there is nothing wrong with him." In disbelief, I frowned and shook my head, realizing at that very moment that David had tried to play Dr. Ashford, as he had me.

"Look, Dr. Ashford," I explained, "the most important thing to me is to get help dealing with my divorce so it won't affect Jessica and Sam. I don't want the truth about David tainting their lives." She calmed me down and said she felt she could help me out and work through the problems together.

Later on in the day, I started gathering the rest of David's things. While going through the closet, I found an old briefcase of David's tucked away in the back behind some clothes. I knew the kids would be coming home from school soon, and I had told them he had to go on another long trip to a far off place to make a movie on locale. I didn't want them to see me rummaging through David's stuff, causing them to question why I was packing all his things.

Nevertheless, I wanted to know what was in the briefcase. Not wanting to get caught by the kids, I went into the bathroom, locked the door behind me, put the briefcase on the floor and sat down. I tilted it up and popped open the latches. The first thing I pulled out was a book titled *How to Pick Up Women*. Chuckling in confusion, I pulled out a small green piece of paper with a flight schedule from San Francisco to Burbank written on it. Recognizing Freddie's handwriting, I turned it over, finding David had scrawled on the other side, "Women make you crazy, then they write you off as a weirdo."

I recalled when David told me he had a dark side; I remembered ignoring his remark, thinking he was just scared of commitment. Now I thought of where I was, how revelations about David kept getting weirder.

Hearing the kids come through the front door, I quickly tossed everything back into the briefcase, ran out of the bathroom and threw the briefcase back into the closet.

I continued my sessions with Dr. Ashford. I kept her informed about my findings on David and before I realized it, Thanksgiving was only a couple days away. I had completely forgotten that David's family was supposed to be spending the holiday at our house. I found myself confused as to what to do and rushed to the phone to call David.

"David, did you tell your family we're getting a divorce yet?" I asked.

"No, no, I didn't, why?" David asked.

"Well, your whole family is going to show up at the house in a couple of days for the holiday," I said miserably.

"Yeah, that's right; I forgot," David said.

"Well, what do you plan on doing about it?" I asked, angrily.

"I don't know. What do you expect me to do? It's the holidays and my mom is too fragile to be told why we're suddenly getting a divorce," David said.

"You're the cause of this divorce. I can't believe you're putting me in a position like this!" I yelled, frustrated and angry.

I didn't want innocent people getting hurt. And I had to think about Jessica and Sam. I could explain that David was coming back for the Thanksgiving holiday, but I wasn't ready to tell them about the divorce. I was going to do it slowly as they adjusted to his not being in the house anymore. Making an impulsive decision, I decided to let things be and have Thanksgiving as planned.

"David, listen to me very closely. I'm crazy for even doing this, but since there are two families that are going to be affected by this, we're going to go ahead with Thanksgiving, but you are going to HAVE to face your family soon and tell them, because after Thanksgiving, that's it!" I said in a stern tone.

"I understand. That's fair," David replied.

Just before the holiday arrived, I went to see Dr. Ashford and explained the situation about David's family coming to the house for Thanksgiving. Dr. Ashford was in disbelief that I was going to try to pull off a holiday dinner in the midst of my divorce. Explaining that there were too many people who would be hurt otherwise, I told her I would make it through the meal somehow.

Then Dianna called to invite herself to stay a whole week, from Thanksgiving Day on. As if it weren't bad enough that David and I were lying to his family during Thanksgiving, now David was going to have to stay at the house the whole time his mother was there.

Thanksgiving Day, David's family began arriving one by one. Dianna was the first to arrive, as David and I began the act of happy newlyweds. As Dianna began explaining that David's father was under the weather and had decided to stay home, David's brother and his wife showed up at the front door.

I tried my hardest to avoid David, staying busy in the kitchen cooking, so as to not have to act lovey dovey in front of his family. Several times that day I ducked out of sight into the bathroom, turning the sink water on to avoid letting them hear me cry.

Later in the evening, as I made my way towards the back porch, David looked at me. I could tell he was uncomfortable with the charade, just as I was. He told me he had a headache. Playing the part of a caring wife in front of David's family, I offered to get him some aspirin. Walking into the bathroom, I opened up the medicine cabinet and grabbed two pills from the bottle. After filling a glass with water, I returned to David and gave the pills and glass to him, wanting to throw the water in his face.

David paused as he looked down at the pills.

"What are these?" David asked in a suspicious tone, before taking them.

Knowing no one was close enough to overhear me, I leaned towards David, mischievously.

"It's cyanide; it'll kill ya," I said, smiling, and walked away, leaving David bewildered.

I was glad when the evening ended, although Dianna was staying for an entire week. I didn't know how I'd get through it. Nevertheless, I knew it wasn't her fault, so I tried to make my mother-in-law's visit as pleasant as possible. The nights when David returned home after work were the worst. Having to sleep in the same room with David so as not to cause suspicion was the hardest part.

On the fourth night of Dianna's stay, she asked me when I was getting a job. I knew David must have initiated this idea and was doubly angry at him. Dianna, having no idea what I was going through, not knowing the emotional state I was in due to David, could not guess the real situation. David wouldn't admit he was the cause of my distress; he turned around and trailed off into the next room like a coward. Finally, having taken too much, I snapped, "Well, probably sooner than you think." I came close but didn't spill the beans on David.

As soon as I could, I ran to the bathroom, locked myself in and broke down in tears. Eventually becoming enraged, I stormed out of the bathroom in a fury, ran downstairs to the bedroom and once again locked myself in. Retrieving David's and my wedding pictures, I spread them out across the bed. Crying hysterically, I began tearing the wedding pictures up, one by one.

chapter seven

Dark
Days

A dreary December arrived. One cold, wet day, Sam and Jessica sat in the living room watching a movie as dark clouds hung outside, drenching the streets with rain. After going outside to retrieve the mail from the mailbox, I began shuffling through the bills when I came across an envelope postmarked Greenville, South Carolina. Immersed in my visits to Dr. Ashford and keeping the children stable, I had totally forgotten the request I sent to the police department, asking for information on Freddie Turner. But seeing the envelope made my curiosity rush back. What more, if anything, would I learn about my husband's strange lover's past? I ran back inside the house and to the bedroom, closing the door and locking it behind me. I slowly sat down on the bed. Nervously I ripped open the envelope. To my surprise I looked at what appeared to be a list. Looking closer I saw it was a two-page criminal list on Freddie, along with a mug shot of him.

"Oh my God!" I cried out loud, taken aback by the shock of what Valerie Taylor had once looked like. There was no doubt about it: Freddie was a man. As I began reading I saw that he had left quite a trail of crime behind him.

The earliest arrest shown was nearly twenty years before. Based on his appearance in the mug shot, Freddie seemed to be in his late teens, leaving me to assume this was the start of his criminal life.

The list named each charge for which he had been arrested. The first was indecent exposure, followed by disorderly conduct, then contempt of court and giving false information to police. After that his record showed solicitation for immoral purposes and resisting arrest. The list went on and on like an encyclopedia of bad behavior.

Sitting there, list in hand, my mind revolved back to my early meetings with Valerie and the uneasy feelings I had around her. From the first time David introduced us, I thought she was strange, but I had to admit to myself in no way would I ever have guessed something like this.

The following day I received another envelope in the mail from the Greenville Police Department. This one contained two more mug shots of Freddie. Along with the mug shots came detailed official reports of the arrests listed on the criminal dossier I had received the prior day. Another paper caught my attention and immediately stuck out from the rest. It told that Freddie had been suspected of assault with a deadly weapon and that the victim had been Freddie's girlfriend. She had jumped out of the moving car they were in together after Freddie had threatened her with a deadly weapon. Suddenly, the night of the Christmas party flashed into my mind. Shaking, I recalled how close I had come to jumping out of the car due to Freddie's temper.

Reading over the page again, I noticed it didn't state what weapon was used; even more confusing was that Freddie had had a girlfriend.

Expecting David to drop by the house that day to pick up the rest of his things, I thought I'd share Freddie's past with him, not knowing what he knew himself.

David arrived later in the day and I followed him as he collected his things.

"David, I think there's something you should see," I said. David stared at me, curious.

"What's that?" he asked. I handed him Freddie's mug shots. He looked at them for a moment, then back at me.

"Who's this?" he asked.

"That's Valerie, David. Or actually, Freddie, but you already knew that from the get-go," I said sarcastically, and then handed him the list of Freddie's criminal arrests.

"I've never seen Valerie look like that; it's not how I know her," David said, taking little interest in Freddie's arrest list. David said he didn't know anything about Valerie's past life before they met. According to him, Freddie was nothing more than a stranger in his eyes. But I had to know the truth.

The following week during my session with Dr. Ashford, I showed her Freddie's mug shots and criminal list. Dr. Ashford seemed both confused and taken aback by the information I had obtained on Freddie. I explained how frustrated I was at David's refusal to see the arrest list.

I knew if I was to get through this without losing my mind I would have to know everything that was being kept from me, in order to understand why David had been lying to me. As I continued, I told Dr. Ashford about Thanksgiving and what a disaster the visit with Dianna had been. Some days I felt like my sessions with Dr. Ashford were doing some good, but others I felt like they did nothing. At times it seemed as if I felt just as bad leaving as I did coming in.

A couple of days after seeing Dr. Ashford, I received a phone call from her. "I've been doing some thinking about our last session," she said. "Donita, have you ever seen a movie called *The Crying Game*?"

"No, I haven't. Why?" I replied.

"I really think you should see this movie, Donita. It reminds me of David and the situation he's in," Dr. Ashford replied. "Please watch it carefully."

I said I would get it as soon as I could.

Dr. Ashford went on to tell me that she would be out of town for the next couple of days, "Call my answering service if there is any emergency. Another doctor will be available to see you if you need immediate help."

Curious as to what Dr. Ashford meant by saying the movie reminded her of David, I went to a nearby video store and rented it the following day. That night after the children went to sleep, I put the film in the VCR. The beginning of the movie didn't seem much like David's story, but then came the scene with a black transvestite in it. Soon following was another scene where the transvestite undressed in front of a man, who had not suspected his date was a transvestite. Stopping the movie on that particular scene, I called David at the studio, asking that he come over to the house. I hoped that one last effort would help to wake him up to reality; this scene might do it. When David arrived at the house, I asked him to follow me into the living room, then pushed play on the VCR.

David stood silently watching the movie, while onscreen the transvestite unrobed and the unsuspecting date ran into the bathroom and threw up.

I blurted out, "That's what you've been with, David; that's what Freddie is—a man!" I tried to convince David one last time of how he'd deceived himself.

"No, Valerie is a female," David said, obviously irritated. Without another word he walked toward the front door.

When David walked out, closing the door behind him, I realized that he was completely hiding from himself who Valerie really was.

In a daze I sat down and pushed play, watching the remainder of the movie.

After it was over, I sat there weeping. Later that evening I lay in bed recalling scenes in the movie, which caused flashbacks of the first few months David and I began dating. In my mind scene after scene played again, transposed with similar moments I had spent with David. Suddenly one of the last scenes in the movie flashed into my mind. In this one the transvestite shot a woman to death. My mouth dropped open, as a stunned feeling crept over me. I began connecting the murder scene with what David had told me late one night when I thought he was talking about the dialogue of a character in one of his movies. I remembered his words just as he had spoken them that night. They were seared into my consciousness.

"I know someone who killed someone and got away with it," David had said.

"Was it a man or a woman?" I remembered asking.

But he hadn't replied and I thought he had just fallen asleep; maybe what David once said to me was real and Freddie was a killer!

Now other dark thoughts came rushing in. I recalled Freddie's violence with David and the assault against Freddie's girlfriend. *Could I be on to something?* I asked myself. I tried to tell myself I was only imagining things. There was no mention of Freddie being a wanted suspect and no mention of murder on the dossier. Still, my gut had been right before. Valerie had not been what she seemed. In fact, he was something far worse. I wasn't about to deride my feelings now. If anything, I was more committed to finding out the truth and I knew what I had to do.

Somehow I had to think of a way to get David back to the house. I had to find out if what he had told me that night so long ago was true and whether Freddie could be the killer David had mentioned.

Deciding to use the excuse that I needed to talk to David concerning our divorce, I waited until the next morning after the kids left for school. I called David and cajoled him into coming to the house. When he got there, I fixed us each a cup of coffee, then asked David to sit outside on the front porch with me, so we could talk. As we sat, quietly sipping our coffee, I mulled over how I was going to ask David if what he had told me that night years ago was real and if it concerned Freddie. I realized there was no way to approach the question other than just to come right out and ask it. Carefully putting my coffee cup down on the porch table, I turned towards David. Somehow despite the horror of it all I was sure I had to find out once and for all.

"David, is Freddie the one who killed someone and got away with it?" I asked.

David glanced over at me with a surprised look on his face. "What? Killed someone? What are you talking about?" David replied suddenly, as if I was crazy.

I told myself, *You must stick with it like a pit bull, Donita; don't let up.* So I asked in an even more decisive voice, "David, is Freddie the one who killed someone and got away with it?"

"I don't know what you're talking about or where you got such a crazy idea," he replied, continuing to give me the same skeptical look. I had gotten to be much more apprehensive about David and a good deal less trusting in these last awful months than I had been in all five years we were together. It was now easier for me to tell if he was hiding something. I closely watched his body language, down to the movements of his eyes. David's secrets were becoming more visible to me. Gazing at him, I felt like I was peering through a sheer curtain.

Softly, carefully, I phrased my next inquiry. "David, you told me something strange, years ago when we first met, that I recently recalled. You said you knew someone who killed someone and got away with it. I didn't think it was real, what you said, but knowing Freddie's violence, it's making me wonder if what you said is really true. Now, I'm going to ask you one more time. Is Freddie that someone you said killed someone and got away with it?" I asked my question in a low, stern voice. Keeping my eyes in direct contact with David's, I could see that it was making him feel uncomfortable.

"No! You're crazy for even thinking such a thing," David replied.

"Okay. I hope you're telling me the truth, because I'm going to dig until I find out," I said, standing up and grabbing my coffee cup.

"Fine, do all the digging you want; there's nothing to find," David replied, calmly.

Although David was confident with his answer, it wasn't enough to fool me as he had done so many times before. Whatever he was hiding, I felt I was only a grasp away from knowing.

"Okay, David. But remember, one way or another, I'll find out," I called out as I opened the front door, walking into the house.

David soon followed silently, passing me in the kitchen as he headed to the bedroom to collect his remaining things. Nervous and frustrated but knowing I had to forge forward, I walked into the living room and stood staring out the window, thinking what my next move should be. No matter how David thwarted me, I wasn't going to stop. I had to find out if Freddie did or didn't kill someone. But at that moment I had a gut feeling, and if I had to bet, I would bet he did.

Within a few minutes, I heard footsteps coming towards me. David walked through the kitchen in my direction. Turning away from the living room window, I scrutinized David. It was obvious he was agitated; he moved with an anxious shuffle and his forehead had broken out in a nervous sweat. As he neared me, David took a deep breath. I could tell from the way he was acting that something intense was about to happen.

"Donita, you better sit down; I have something to tell you," he said. When he brought his hand up to his forehead, I could see it shaking.

My heart began beating hard, as I knew David was about to confess something big to me. I told myself to stay calm and be quiet, not to interrupt and to let him say what he had to say.

He motioned to me to sit down on the couch, then David sat at the other end.

"Okay, I'm listening," I replied, in a soft voice.

The room was silent. David put his hands together, rubbing them back and forth. Once again he wiped the sweat from his forehead.

"You're right, Donita. Valerie's the one; she's the one I told you killed someone and got away with it," he said, rubbing the sides of his mouth with his hand.

My heart felt as if it had stopped beating. David had confessed the truth of my biggest suspicion. Knowing I needed to stay calm, I kept from making any moves that would make David stop talking. I fought to keep my expression blank and told myself, *If I keep composed and refer to Freddie as Valerie, David may be willing to tell me more.*

"How did you find out Valerie killed someone?" I asked with an emotionless face.

"About three months after I started seeing her," David said, "we went for a walk one day and I guess she felt she could trust me enough to confide in me and she told me she'd once killed a man," David explained.

"Why after only knowing someone for a few months would she admit to having killed someone?" I asked, in confusion.

"I don't know. Look," David replied, "I'll tell you what I know, or what I was told from Valerie about what happened." He was so jittery he could barely sit still.

"Okay, go on," I said. "I'm listening." I forced my voice to be reassuring, even though I felt like I was going to detonate at any moment.

"Well, from what I remember her telling me, it happened late one night. She and a guy she knew were in a motel room and it was raining hard," David replied.

"Do you remember the person's name?" I asked.

"Yes, but I was only told his first name, Billy. Anyway, I remember Valerie had this huge breakdown while telling me this story—almost hysterical—and, before I knew it, I found myself feeling very sorry for her, that she was in that situation," David replied, as he continued.

"What happened between Valerie and Billy that night, David?" I asked.

"Well, she said there was some sort of fight; in fact it was a pretty big fight, but I don't know what it was about, or I've forgotten. Nevertheless, like I said, there was this fight and Valerie said she feared for her life when Billy came at her. According to Valerie there was a gun on one of the side tables next to the bed and she grabbed it and pointed it at this Billy person, to keep him from coming at her. Then she shot him in the chest, I think she said two times. And then Valerie became hysterical again as she told me the next part. She said Billy then fell to the floor and that he was bleeding a lot, so she sat on the floor and held him. But she said he died quickly and she freaked out and ran," David replied.

"I find it hard to believe, having seen Valerie attack you and now knowing Valerie's violent past, that she killed this man in self-defense," I said, staring at David suspiciously.

He looked off into the distance. "Yes, well, maybe you're right; I don't know, but I do recall her telling me at a later time that it was a relief killing Billy, that it was revenge for all the men who never accepted her as a real female," David replied. He looked back at me. "I wonder," he said, his voice trailing off.

I felt he was wondering at that moment whether Valerie's story of shooting Billy in self-defense was true. I was not about to let this recognition go.

"Where did the murder happen, David?" I asked.

"I don't know. Valerie said it was in a small town, but that's all she said. She never told me the name of the town or what state it happened in," David replied. "I wish now I knew more."

But I felt he probably had repressed some of the things Valerie had told him, not wanting to know. I pressed further.

"When did this happen, David? What year was it?" I asked.

"I don't know that either; Valerie never said and I never asked," David replied. I watched him closely. His lips were pressed together in a thin line. He was still hiding things from himself, unresolved questions, memories and insights. I wasn't willing to let him use that charade anymore.

"Didn't you realize what you were doing by helping a fugitive change identities, David? Not to mention letting her live with you?" I asked.

He nodded slowly, as if seeing mental images and considering this for the first time. "Yes," he finally admitted. He paused for a moment and then went on, "And I knew there was a risk involved in my helping Valerie, but I felt sorry for her and wanted to." I could see that he was defending himself.

If what he said was true, I felt he had made a poor choice, but I was not about to compound it by allowing the truth to disappear. But getting David to open up was going to take time and effort I could only hope I had. I took a deep breath and continued.

"Where was Valerie living when she told you about the murder?" I asked.

"In a house in San Bernardino," David replied.

"Do you remember where the house is?" I asked.

"Oh, I imagine I could find it if I wanted to. Why?" David asked, suspiciously.

"I want to go. I'm curious. I want to see it," I replied.

"Right now?" David asked.

"Yes, right now," I said.

"Donita, why do you want to see where she lived?" he demanded.

"It will help me understand; I just want to see it, okay?" I said softly.

"All right, but I still don't see the point; it's just a house like any other," He said.

Secretly I hoped seeing the house again would revive some of his repressed memories. David had locked all this away too long. He ought to deal with it and I knew I had to.

As I drove towards San Bernardino with David sitting next to me, I noticed he looked unnerved and agitated. I had to handle David delicately. Somehow I had to find out who this Billy person was, and when and where he was killed. To do all this I knew I needed David's help. I decided for the time being not to ask any more questions that had to do with the murder, hoping David would tell me more on his own with the help of the stimulus of the house he had once lived in with Valerie.

"So, who was Valerie living with in the house in San Bernardino?" I asked, calmly.

"An older man named Bart she'd met, just someone who took her in. I met him a few times when I went down to see Valerie. He seemed like a pretty nice man," David replied.

The rest of the hour drive to San Bernardino was mostly silent. David seemed to be in deep thought, except when he was giving directions. I concentrated on keeping a mental picture of the freeways he was having me take. Finally, he told me to get off at the next exit ramp.

"Turn right at the exit," David said.

"How far is the house from here?" I asked.

"A few blocks down," he replied.

The further down the main boulevard we drove, the worse the area became.

"Turn left at the next street," David instructed me.

As we turned off the boulevard, we drove deeper into a neighborhood where old couches and trash were strung along the sidewalks. Graffiti covered abandoned buildings and security bars covered the windows and doors of the houses and businesses.

"Slow down; we need to make a right at the next street," David said.

"This place is making me nervous, David. How much further?" I asked, as I locked the doors and rolled up the windows.

"I don't remember it being this bad," David replied.

"Where's the house?" I asked nervously, as I drove slowly past a few men gathered on a street corner, selling drugs.

Trying not to make eye contact, I saw the men staring at David and me as we drove past them, knowing we didn't belong.

"Turn left here. I know it's around here somewhere. I remember that an empty field was across the street from the house. I know we're close to it," David said.

"Let's hurry. This area is making me uncomfortable," I said.

"Turn down here; this looks familiar to me," David replied. "Now turn left and drive slowly; it's one of the houses on the left." A few yards later he called out, "Stop here; that's the house Valerie lived in." He was pointing to a yellow bungalow.

"There's someone standing by the house. Is that Bart, the man you told me about?" I asked.

David quickly scanned the guy standing out front. "No, that's not him. Bart was tall and lanky. That guy's too short. But it doesn't look good that we're sitting in front of their house. I showed you; now let's just go," David replied.

Driving home on the freeway, I didn't want David to question what I was going to do with the information he gave me about Freddie, so I changed the subject and asked about his work. He began to tell me about the movie he was shooting as we made our way back to Burbank.

When we got back to the house David said he had to get back before five. Although he still appeared jittery, he didn't ask what I was going to do with the information he had given me, nor did he say anything more about showing me Valerie's house. After he left I went straight for the phone and called Dr. Ashford.

I hoped she had returned from her trip. I waited anxiously as the phone rang.

"Hello. Dr. Ashford speaking," she answered.

"Dr. Ashford, thank God you're there," I said, taking in a deep breath.

"What is it, Donita? What's wrong?" she asked, with concern.

"You're not going to believe this, but remember that *Crying Game* movie you asked me to watch?" I asked.

"Yes," she replied.

"In the movie there's a murder scene at the end of the movie where the transvestite kills someone," I said rushing to explain the connection.

"Yes, what about it?" she asked.

"Well, you're not going to believe this, but there's a murder in my situation too!"

"Oh, Donita," Dr. Ashford said, with a doubtful tone.

I tried to convince her that what I was saying was true, but hearing myself go on and on, even I had to admit how bizarre it all sounded. Worrying the one person from whom I needed help the most would question my mental stability filled me with anxiety. What was I to do now?

Getting off the phone with Dr. Ashford, I sat down at the kitchen table and began crying. I thought about reporting what David told me about Freddie to the police, but felt they too would think I was nuts. Having no idea where and when the murder happened and not knowing the last name of the victim would ensure that they would dismiss my revelations. And telling them the killer had a double identity would be just as hard to believe. If Dr. Ashford had doubted me, the police surely would. I was left with the feeling that I couldn't call them until I had proof.

I had to talk to someone who would believe me and sympathize. I called Gayle. Both frustrated and agitated, I began talking so fast that Gayle was hardly able to get a word out. Soon I started crying again.

Gayle broke in with, "Slow down and calm down. I don't understand what you're saying."

"Oh my God, Gayle. David told me Freddie murdered someone!" I blurted out. Then slowly I went over what David said.

"Donita, are you sure? How did you get David to tell you that Fred murdered someone?" Gayle asked.

"I couldn't stand it. It's been swirling around in my mind. Finally I asked him if Freddie had murdered someone, but he denied it. Then I told him I had to know. I wasn't going to give up until I found out the truth. A few minutes later he told me to sit down, that he had something to tell me, and that's when he admitted it to me," I explained. The tears were flowing freely now.

Gayle seemed to know I needed to get my frustration and agony out and was silent while she let me vent. Then when she thought I was calm enough, she let her own feelings show.

"Donita, remember when David told you that he knew someone who killed someone and got away with it, and how you found it odd?" Gayle asked. "I've never forgotten you telling me that."

"Yes, but I didn't think it was real. But now I know it was true after all! That movie Dr. Ashford asked me to watch triggered my own memory of that night. I just called her to tell her what I found out, but she seemed to doubt that what I told her was true and that made me more upset as to what to do next," I said.

"What movie?" Gayle asked.

"Not long ago Dr. Ashford asked me to watch this movie called *The Crying Game*. She said it reminded her of David and the situation he was in with Freddie. I think David told her that, like the guy in the movie, he didn't know his girlfriend was a male. But something else in the movie really jarred me. At the end of the movie, the transvestite kills someone. That scene made me remember what David told me, so I took a chance and confronted David about it," I explained.

"Donita, you're amazing when you get those gut feelings. You don't give up and I guess David realized that and confessed," Gayle said. "Don't worry. I'll stand by you no matter how unbelievable the situation is. I know you must have gotten to him for him to disclose the real truth finally. But at the same time, Donita, I have to tell you I am fearful that you could be in great danger as you continue your search into Freddie's dark past."

I knew she could be right. "But I have to go on," I insisted. "I can't give up now."

After we hung up, I spread out the documents and mug shots I had obtained on Freddie. Starting with the name-change document I began writing down dates, trying to make a timeline of events that took place in hopes of piecing together what would help lead me to when and where Billy was killed.

Knowing the murder took place before Freddie met David, I wrote down that it had to have happened at least twelve years ago or more. After compiling all the data I had, I reread it. There was no doubt I'd need more information. I started thinking up ways to obtain it.

Still, I was worried at the danger Gayle had voiced not only for me, but for the children. The following day, I called David and asked if he had told Freddie that I now knew about the murder he committed.

Although David said he didn't tell Freddie, he did say Freddie was aware that I'd been doing some digging around and had discovered his real name. When David said that, I realized Freddie wasn't the only one who knew I was digging. By my sending out for Freddie's criminal record, the police in South Carolina might think I knew where Freddie was. Maybe that was the reason they sent me his criminal records, but there was no mention about the murder. I felt more nervous. My name and return address were on the envelope.

I told David, "Maybe the police think there's some connection that will lead them to capturing Freddie." *If they just happened to show up, then I wouldn't have to worry about them not believing me*, I thought to myself.

David quickly grew concerned, not so much for Freddie or me and the children, but more for himself. He wanted to call an attorney and explain the situation to see how it should be handled. Although I no longer trusted David, I felt it wouldn't hurt to talk to an attorney. I told David to go ahead and find one and that I wanted to go to see the lawyer as well.

The following day he got an appointment with Mike Paton, an attorney he'd heard of. We drove there in separate cars. Neither of us knew what to expect. Sitting at his desk Paton listened patiently as David began explaining the involvement he had with Valerie Taylor/Freddie Turner and the situation he was in because of it.

When David finished his side of the story, Mike Paton glanced over at me with a helpless look on his face. "I can see how hurt and angry you are. You have every right to feel that way," he said to me. Then he turned and looked at David with concern, telling him, "You fully aided and abetted a fugitive."

He glanced back at me. "However, Mrs. Allen, because you had knowledge of a murder, and didn't report it right away, you too can be in some serious hot water," he said.

In shock at his disclosure that I could be in trouble as well, I leaned forward.

"Who was I to tell? Who in their right mind was going to believe me? Why would the police believe such a wild story if I had no facts or proof?" I asked, angrily.

While trying to calm me down, he partially agreed with me that having no proof posed a big problem. "However, your husband has gotten you involved," he said. "Why don't you tell me why you're here and I'll see how I can help."

David interrupted, saying, "The reason why we're here is because Donita decided to do some digging into Valerie's past."

I was past angry now. "Everything you tell me is a lie, David! I did it because you seemed to be hiding something and I felt I had to know what it was! I had no idea it would involve murder," I said disgustedly.

David rubbed his chin for a moment. "Yeah, well, Valerie lives in a dreamy kind of world. I don't know that she really killed someone. I just told you what I was told. Many stories she's told me in the past have had discrepancies in them," he replied.

"David," Paton shook his head, "discrepancies or not, this seems like a very serious situation you both are in."

David sat stupefied, scared and tense as Paton went on.

"Mrs. Allen, maybe when some time has passed, if you haven't heard anything from the police, we can conclude they don't know Freddie is wanted for murder or that he's responsible for committing one, for that matter. However, to be honest with you, this isn't my line of expertise; I mainly do family law. My advice would be for you to see a criminal attorney about this matter. I assume you'll be divorcing David?" he asked.

"Yes, that's in the works," I replied.

Walking out of the office into the reception room, I quickly found my feelings of irritation and anger turning into a sense of helplessness and fear. David, on the other hand, looked relieved.

Later that night, as I lay in bed, agitated thoughts spun round in my mind. *What if it's true that the police don't know Freddie killed someone? How could I just forget it?* Yet I didn't want to take the risk of discussing the matter with Dr. Ashford and being told as I had been by Mike Paton that it was best to leave it alone. Although I was worried that I could be in some hot water for having knowledge, I began to wonder: if Freddie killed someone, what was my real responsibility? Yet what if he hadn't? And what if he harmed someone else? Murder was too serious of an accusation to make up for it not to be true. I felt at that moment there was no sense in going to a criminal attorney, as I would most likely be told the same thing I had already heard. Yet I couldn't let what I had found out go. I couldn't forget. I could never be at peace until I knew for sure, but proving it was going to be tougher than I had imagined. Still, I knew myself well enough to realize I had to go on—to find out the truth.

chapter eight

Pinpointing
a Murder

After digging through drawers and finding a United States map, I laid it on the kitchen table, alongside the documents and mug shots of Freddie that I had obtained. Since my suspicion was that the murder probably happened twelve years ago or more, I wrote down 1983 as the last suspected year. Freddie had last been arrested in Greenville in 1977. I used that date to start, feeling the murder had to have happened somewhere between those two dates. The question that came to mind was *where*? I hypothesized it happened in a small town somewhere in South Carolina. Grabbing a pen, I drew a circle around a hundred-mile radius of Greenville, the epicenter from which I would begin my search. Then in the margin I began writing down all the names of the small towns spreading out from Greenville.

Now, I asked myself, how was I going to get the information I needed without disclosing my real identity and opening myself up to the charges Mr. Paton mentioned? Since my search only involved small towns, I felt the police in those areas would have good records of any unsolved murder cases. I paused to think. I had to come up with an excuse as to why I was inquiring about unsolved murders. Suddenly a believable white lie came to me: I'd say I was writing a book about unsolved, small-town motel murders. I was ready. I would make up a false name for myself and start searching for a motel murder involving a gun and a victim whose first name was Billy.

I paused again, my thoughts overwhelming me. Perhaps I ought to see Dr. Ashford, but she had doubted me before. Deciding it was best to withhold most of what I was doing from her, I decided Gayle would be my only confidant. I knew I could trust her and she would support me.

Next I dialed information for several of the small towns, writing down the phone numbers of the police departments I planned to call.

With all the effort I'd put in, I thought it would lead to some instant results, but it didn't take long to find out how difficult it was going to be. I continued, only to find endless frustration and roadblocks. After being put on hold, transferred countless times and laughed at when the police heard my justification for wanting information on unsolved murders, I realized I was getting nowhere. Finally I gave up and went back to the drawing board. I had to come up with a better plan. While looking over the name change document, I found myself drawn to Freddie's father's name. Perhaps this was a better bet to get information. Once again I had to figure out an excuse. I decided, if asked, I would say I had met Freddie in Carolina years before and was trying to locate him. I called information and got his phone number.

I took a deep breath and began dialing.

"Hello?" A man with an aged, crackling voice answered.

"Mr. Turner?" I said.

"Yes," he answered.

"Mr. Freddie Turner Sr.?" I asked.

"Yes, this is he," he replied.

Suddenly, I found myself at a loss for words. I recalled David telling me at one time that both Freddie's parents were dead. Obviously it was one more cover-up in a sea of lies, but whose lie was it? Gathering my courage I pressed on with my inquiry.

"Do you have a son named Freddie Lee Turner?" I asked.

I heard a sharp intake of breath then silence. I wondered if he would hang up on me. But to my surprise, he answered.

"Yes, I do," he slowly replied.

"When was the last time you saw or talked to him?" I asked, as my heart pounded and my hand tightened around the receiver.

Silence again. I waited for a response, wondering how far I could go before he'd hang up on me, or at what point he would ask why I was requesting information. But once again, to my surprise, he answered my question with willingness.

"About nineteen years ago," he replied.

"Do you know where he is or where he lives?" I asked, easing my questions in.

"No. The last I heard, he was living in New York," he replied.

Realizing he didn't know anything or wasn't willing to tell a stranger if he did, I thanked him and quickly ended the call. Then it hit me. Mr. Turner never once asked who I was or why I was calling. This was especially odd to me since he said he hadn't seen or talked to Freddie for nineteen years.

Nineteen years. Mentally I subtracted the date. I added that to my conjectured timetable of when the murder might have happened. A sigh escaped. My thoughts darted off to another subject. I would have to come up with a new plan. I decided to take a short walk. It would help me think. As I opened the front door, I saw the mailman walking over to the next house. I walked down our drive and pulled the mail he'd left at our house out of the mailbox. Shuffling through it, I came across a heavy white business-sized envelope. I noticed it had no writing on it, not even a stamp.

I called out to the mailman, asking if he had delivered the unmarked envelope. He called back, "No." I quickly grew suspicious of its contents, hesitating to open it. A dark thought crossed my mind. What if the children had gotten the mail that day? Another thought hit. David had told me Freddie knew I found out his real name and might find out I knew about the murder. I panicked and wondered if it was Freddie who put the envelope in the mailbox. Through my mind passed the thought of the dark sedan I'd seen so many times stopped in front of the house. Terrified, I held the envelope up to see if I could ascertain its contents. I couldn't. Although I really wanted to know what was in it, I felt opening the envelope was too risky. I decided to take the letter straight to the police department. I would tell them I received this mysterious letter which had no postmark and the weight of the contents inside the sealed envelope made me concerned.

I quickly drove over there, walked into the police department with the envelope in hand, approached the front desk and quietly told the officer on duty that someone had put an unmarked, heavy white envelope in my mailbox. While I was explaining that it had made me feel somewhat concerned, the young blond officer's eyes widened. He stood up, putting up both his hands in a stop motion at me.

The officer's behavior made me grow even more concerned. In a nervous yet soft-spoken voice, he told me not to put the envelope down, but to hold it carefully and not put any pressure on it. "The police department has just gotten new procedures on how to handle suspicious packages and envelopes," he told me.

Standing there helplessly, I grew more and more agitated. I felt that the situation was fast getting out of hand. But I had no choice, I had to wait. The officer telephoned his sergeant and was told to call the bomb squad immediately. As he hung up the phone, he told me not to move, to stand still and to extend the envelope outward in the palms of my hands. The people who were standing near me had overheard the officer. In fear they made a quick exit out of the police department.

I stood there, shaking, with my arms extended. The officer told me to walk slowly out the front door of the police department. He continued to give me instructions as he followed me, "Now walk along the side of the police department and around to the back parking lot, where the bomb squad will be meeting us." When we arrived at the designated spot, the officer told me to stop and not move.

Talking back and forth to his sergeant on a handheld radio on what to do next, he began asking me questions, "Do you know anyone that would want to harm you or want you dead?" he asked.

My mind was filled with dread. I immediately thought of Freddie, but I had no proof to back up such a claim. Realizing there was no way I could explain my situation and fearing that I wouldn't be believed, I stammered, "No," and swallowed hard.

We continued to wait. I was unable to speak or even move.

Noticing I was becoming tired the officer radioed his sergeant, asking "Can she put the envelope on the ground?"

He was given permission and I was told to slowly, carefully lay the envelope onto the pavement. Finally the squad came. I was told to go home, that they would call me once they found out what was inside the envelope.

A combination of disgust, fear and anger swelled within me as I drove home. Immediately I called David, telling him what happened, and my suspicion that the letter might be from Freddie.

"This has got to be the worst day of my life," David said, as if his world was falling apart around him.

"David," I said annoyed, "why are you worried about yourself? I am the one who found the envelope."

David then began to tell me that Freddie had just called him a few days prior, worried about what I might find out. He said he had told Freddie not to worry, that I had stopped digging around. "I believed this to be true as well," he snapped. Feeling it was best to keep quiet so that David and Freddie would think I had stopped snooping, I didn't comment on his words, but said I was still concerned about the envelope, where it had come from and what was in it.

After getting off the phone with David, I sat waiting for the police to call. Thoughts swirled in my mind. Never had I felt so alone. I sat there dazed. Startled, I jumped when the phone began to ring. It was the officer who I had talked to at the police station.

He told me the bomb squad had opened the envelope after searching it for explosives, only to discover it contained a set of pictures of robots, adding, "You can come down and pick them up." After retrieving the pictures, I called David, telling him what the police found. Suddenly David remembered someone from his work was going to drop off some pictures he needed for a job involving robotics. "Not knowing we were no longer together, he must have put them in the mailbox at the house," David said.

"David, do you know how scared I was for the children and me?" I yelled.

Although I had let my mind run rampant worrying about the envelope and it had turned out to be nothing, I knew there still was a real risk in continuing my search for evidence about the murder. Now I tried to go over the situation slowly and logically, asking myself, *If Freddie didn't murder someone, then why would he be calling David, worried I might find something? Why would David be telling Freddie not to worry, that I had stopped digging? And why would David act so worried, if there isn't something to hide?* I continued going over everything I'd learned piece by piece, questioning myself and formulating a new direction as I thought it all out.

Thinking back to the day David revealed the story of Freddie and the murder, I came to the conclusion that David knew more than he was willing to share. I felt the only way I was going to be able to get down to the truth and get the answers I needed was to act like I was cracking under the pressure, which was close to the truth. David might fall for my act and want to comfort me.

In addition, if I could make David feel I had become so unhappy with our living arrangement that I wanted him back he might ask to come. Knowing David was miserable living at the studio, it would be one more added reason to get him to move back into the house. I felt the more time I had with him, the better the chance he would talk about Freddie.

Later that night, I told Gayle my plan. "It's risky, Donita," she said, taken back by my determination to find the truth when I'd always been so shy and tentative about confronting problems. Nevertheless, seeing she couldn't dissuade me, she said, "I have to admit it might be worth a try." Talking to her only increased my determination. I decided to act on my plan.

After taking some time to think up the right words to persuade David to move back into the house, I picked up the phone and called him. I found it easy to cry on cue since I really was upset. Using my emotional state to my advantage, I told David I loved him and didn't want to lose him, adding I was scared and needed him. Although it took some convincing, my plan worked. David agreed to move back into the house late the next day.

Now with my plan set in motion, I knew I would have to continue my sessions with Dr. Ashford in order to deal with my conflicted emotions. Although I felt she still doubted my story, I was sure, at some point, I would be able to prove to her that my suspicions were correct. Freddie Turner had committed murder. I got an appointment for the following morning and told her my plan.

Dr. Ashford was amazed that I asked David to move back into the house. I explained that it was the only way to find out more about the relationship between him and Freddie. After my session with Dr. Ashford, I followed my usual routine; I ran some quick errands, cleaned the house and finally started dinner. Soon after, David pulled in the driveway. When he entered, I somehow managed to smile and hug him.

I couldn't believe David was falling for it, but after being played for a fool for so many years, I felt using the same method on him that he used on me was just what he deserved.

I watched David closely, looking for clues as to his real feelings. David seemed to enjoy the thought of having control again. I told him I regretted digging around and had no further interest in causing Freddie trouble. When the time was right I'd start innocently asking questions about Freddie. I'd have to use the name Valerie, as that seemed the only time David was willing to be more open with me.

As the days passed, I found it harder and harder to act like the loving wife David perceived me to be. I didn't like behaving in such a deceitful manner, but under the circumstances, I didn't know any other way. All I wanted was the truth.

A few nights later I found an opportunity to talk to David. "You need to explain to me the situation you are in with Valerie," I said. I told him it was the only way I could understand and felt it was the only way I would be able to put the whole thing behind me.

Not wanting to hit David with questions that would scare him off, I decided to ask how Valerie got another ID in a non-threatening tone. I took a deep breath, knowing if David got up and walked away, my effort would have proven to be a waste of time. Instead, David began telling me that he found a person in the San Fernando Valley who made fake IDs, adding that he took Valerie there to have one made up.

With numerous questions passing through my mind, I wasn't sure what to ask next. I was worried I would ask something that would cause him to close up on me. Still, I went on. One thing I was curious about was who had performed the other operations on Valerie. I already knew the name of the doctor who had performed the sex change in Trinidad, Colorado, but there was never any mention of who performed the other procedures, including the breast augmentation.

Trying to sound innocent yet curious, I slipped the question in, asking David who had done that surgery.

"Dr. Paul Anderson," David said.

I got away as soon as I could and added the doctor's name to my growing list.

That Friday night, David brought home a large box of files to begin preparing his taxes. As I began cooking dinner, I noticed through the kitchen window that David had walked outside and was throwing several files into the trash can alongside the house. Curious as to what the files contained I decided I'd better wait until Monday morning, after David left for work, to see what he had thrown away.

When Monday morning arrived, I got Sam and Jessica ready for school. I kissed and hugged them goodbye. Peering through the living room window, I proudly watched my kind and decent children as they walked off to school. I was glad they knew nothing of the sordid events I was trying to unravel. Knowing it would only be a matter of time before David would be leaving too, I sat patiently sipping a cup of coffee, waiting for him to finish breakfast and go to the studio. Soon enough he got in his car and drove away. I watched until the car was out of sight. Then I quickly made my way to the backdoor and outside to the trash can.

Opening the first lid, I saw the files and began pulling them out, not sure what I would find, if anything. Taking them inside the house I began filtering through them. Soon I came across an old phone bill from the studio house. I checked the date. Realizing it was from the time Freddie had lived with David, I began scrutinizing the calls that had been made.

There were multiple calls to Trinidad, Colorado, the place where Freddie had his sex change done. Further down I also found a few calls to Greenville, South Carolina. Knowing it was the same city Freddie had come from, I assumed he had been keeping contact with someone in his family. But his father said he hadn't been in touch with Freddie for nineteen years. Had he hidden the truth or was Freddie in touch with someone else? I put the phone bill aside and was searching through other files when a small piece of paper fell out. As I bent down to pick it up, I saw a phone number in David's handwriting on it.

Looking back at the phone bill from the studio, I noticed the number had the same area code as Greenville, South Carolina, but none of the numbers on the phone bill matched the one David had written down.

I recalled David telling me he didn't know where Freddie came from, so how could this new piece of the puzzle fit in? David had to have known where Freddie was from, as the phone bill was in his name. I quickly decided David must have been lying about this as well. It was becoming more and more obvious that David did in fact know more than he led me to believe.

Taking the phone bill and papers, I placed them along with the other information I had already obtained in the large yellow envelope and slid it back under the mattress.

A few hours later, David called me from the studio. He asked me to go into his desk and get his check binder. "Look through it and you'll find a copy of a business check that my accountant needs for a tax write-off."

After searching and finding it, I looked in the very back and found, tucked away, a receipt for a cashier's check in the amount of $1,000.00 that had been made out to Valerie Taylor. The check was written in July of 1994. That month was around the same time David had called me, asking me to get $10,000.00 from his mother, to cover some bills. Suddenly I remembered how David had asked me to be careful with grocery money, which I had found odd for him to say.

Now I understood the hang-up call I'd received in the hotel room when I went to visit David the first time in Romania. "It must have been Freddie calling to ask David for money," I murmured to myself.

David had all along been giving Freddie the phone numbers to the movie locations he was at, as well as the number to the house. But something didn't make sense. If it was David Freddie wanted to talk to, then why did he taunt me by making hang-up calls to David's apartment before we moved into the house? And why did David tell me Freddie was blackmailing him but later change his story?

The more I thought about the whole confusing situation, the more bewildered I became. If the relationship between David and Freddie was intense, it made no sense for David to continue a relationship with me, when he had had plenty of chances to break it off.

Trying to make sense of it made no difference now, but what did make a difference was the fact that a man's murder was going unsolved. What kind of person would turn his back on the knowledge of this horrible event, as if a human life didn't matter? It was unconscionable.

I knew if I didn't try to find out who Billy was, it would be like a cement weight on my conscience for the rest of my life. Even though I was torn between the emotions of what I was personally going through and those of David confessing to me that Freddie had killed Billy, I still knew I had to do what I felt was right. I had to find out who Billy was and where and when he was killed. In my mind I went over the facts and suppositions I'd learned so far: I was sure I had discovered the right state where the killing occurred; all I had to do was find the small town in which it happened. Frustrated that my earlier attempts of calling around to police stations failed and knowing Greenville was a large city, I felt I had to come up with a different approach. Meanwhile, I didn't want to blow my cover and have David find out what I was doing behind his back. I returned his call, telling him I had found the check he needed, and kept quiet about the cashier's check I had discovered. Feeling I needed to give David enough time to think things were totally back to normal, I impatiently waited through the rest of the month of January.

During this time I kept in close contact with Gayle. We desperately tried to think up different ways to get evidence of Billy's murder.

One of our ideas was for me to go to a pay phone and call the numbers found on both David's old phone bill and the piece of paper with David's handwriting. But I ran into yet another dead end. So much time had elapsed since the murder that all the numbers had been disconnected or were no longer in service.

As February approached, I became increasingly frustrated, as I tried to get David to talk more about Freddie and he continued to shy away from the subject.

Since my new attempts with David were getting nowhere, I decided to try a different approach, hoping David would be sympathetic.

A few nights later after putting the kids to bed, I went to talk to David. I found him lying on the bed in our bedroom, watching the news on television. I lay down quietly beside him. My whirling thoughts about the murder drowned out the news broadcast. Telling myself to be calm I said, "David?" in a cautious tone.

"Yes?" he replied distractedly.

"I really want to talk to you about something," I said softly.

"What about?" he asked.

"Before you say anything let me explain," I said, calmly.

David sighed deeply, as if he knew it had to involve Freddie. "Okay, what did you want to say?" He bit his lip.

But I couldn't stop. "Listen, maybe Billy was no angel, but his family has a right to closure and you're keeping that from them for your own reasons. I mean, listen: what if someone killed a member of your family? How would you feel if years later you found out someone had knowledge of it all along and didn't do anything about it?" I asked.

"Well, I would assume that person would have some responsibility in divulging that information," he replied in a monotone, as if he was mouthing platitudes.

But they weren't platitudes to me. I believed in our responsibility for others. "Then why aren't you?" I asked passionately.

"Because the situation I'm in is very complicated, that's why," he replied, in a frustrated tone.

At that moment, I realized there was no sense in battling it out. We were coming from two very different places.

Toward the end of February, I began receiving hang-up calls in the same systematic way I had while living at David's apartment. I knew the calls had to be coming from Freddie. During the next two days, I became more and more nervous as the calls started coming more frequently and a dark sedan was again appearing at odd times in front of our house.

Once again I called the phone company, asking that *69 service be placed on the phone, but this time Freddie had thought ahead. He had fixed the system so that his calls were blocked. Not willing to give up, I got caller-ID, only to find that also failed, as his number would not show up when the phone would ring.

Each time it was the same thing over and over, "Hello... hello... hello?" I'd say and hear a click from the phone being hung up on the other end.

Finally I had enough. I told David that Freddie must be stalking me, making hang-up phone calls again. David brushed my words off. "The stalking is your overactive imagination. The hang-up calls are probably coming from one of Sam or Jessica's friends," he said matter-of-factly.

Disgusted that David would put this off on the kids and not take me seriously about it being Freddie, I could keep silent no longer.

I blurted out, "I really want to know something, David! Why? Why marry me? Why did you carry on this fake relationship with me all these years?" My voice rose with the frustration and anger I'd felt for so long. It all came pouring out.

David stood silently, as he had when I confronted him about Freddie's name-change document.

"You were used as a front by Valerie," David finally answered, looking briefly at me, then at the floor.

I knew right then that Freddie wasn't my only problem. David had used the kids and me as a front, so his family wouldn't know about his secret life. It all made sense now. As David and I stood silently, each locked into our own private thoughts, I remembered what his mother had said to me about David finally bringing a girl home; she hadn't seen him with a woman in so long she was starting to wonder if he was gay.

It was clear we couldn't go on living together even though I needed to find out the whole truth about Freddie. Disgusted at David's behavior and his reason for marrying me, I told him to leave the house at once. Adding to my fury was my realization that by his silence David was literally helping a murderer escape. This only heightened my own determination to find the evidence that would seal the killer's fate and finally make my family safe.

chapter nine

Dangerous Moments

The next morning, still feeling uneasy because of all that had happened, I jumped when the phone began to ring. Picking up the receiver I wearily said, "Hello?" only to hear that same familiar click as the phone was hung up. Two more hang-up calls followed. The next time the phone began to ring, I slowly picked up the receiver, and without saying hello, I instead listened nervously, holding the receiver close to my ear, sure Freddie was on the other end of the line.

This time the person didn't hang up; he stayed on the phone, as if lying in wait. Then an echo-distorted voice called, "I'm coming to get you." Not knowing what to do or what to say, I kept silent for a few minutes. But when the caller didn't cut the line off, I felt it was now up to me to make the next move. I began to speak, slowly.

"Freddie? Freddie Lee Turner?" I said, in a low, questioning voice.

No one spoke, but I could hear a sharp intake of breath, almost as if Freddie were in a panic. Quickly I hung up. Standing there, my eyes widened with fear. Nervously I began pacing the kitchen floor. *Freddie must know I am on to him.* His hoax was up. I had forced his hand. The question was, what would he do next?

I found out that afternoon. I looked out the window and saw a dark sedan stopped in front of the house. I rushed outside to confront the two shadowy figures in the car, but before I could do anything it peeled away in a screech of tires. Suddenly I remembered David had said he told Freddie I was trying to find out about the murder. There was no time to waste.

I needed somehow to catch Freddie making the calls to the house in order to prove to the police that I was not just a hysterical woman. I pondered different plans but ultimately decided they were all too dangerous, especially since, above all, I had to protect the children. I needed the advice of a professional. Turning to the yellow pages of the phone book, I started looking for private investigators that did civil and criminal investigations. I saw an advertisement with a logo saying *specializing in difficult and unusual cases*. Ryan Kelly was both bonded and licensed. I called, explaining someone was constantly calling my house and hanging up. I asked if a tap could be put on the phone to catch the person.

Investigator Kelly said, "It's against the law to tap a phone." An overwhelming feeling of helplessness came over me and I broke down crying.

Recognizing my desperation, Kelly asked me to explain my situation in more detail. Between sobs I said, "I'm afraid you'll think this is crazy."

"Don't aggravate yourself. I am a retired police officer who was in the homicide division. I have seen and heard it all. Now take a deep breath and slowly explain to me what is going on. It sounds more ominous than just a few phone calls."

"You're not going to believe me," I said, in desperation, while trying to calm myself down.

"I won't know until you tell me," he said.

"Trust me. I can guarantee you that you haven't heard a story like this before," I said.

"You sound pretty upset and the only way I can help you is if you tell me what's going on. First off, tell me why you wanted your phone tapped," he asked.

I took a few moments to gather my thoughts and then began to explain the strange circumstance I was in, still fearful the private detective wouldn't believe the incredible tale I was about to reveal to him.

"For the last six years, I have had a relationship with a Hollywood special effects supervisor and director. He was nominated for an Academy Award. I married him six months ago. Before and maybe after we were together, he was involved with someone else. They had and have a very explosive relationship," I paused.

"And is this the person you think has been calling and hanging up on you?" he prodded.

"Yes," I sighed. "Its been going on for years off and on and recently I started digging into his past and I just found out my husband told him about it. He's dangerous and he is, I think, stalking me. There are hang-up calls all the time. In fact his calls are nonstop, not just in the morning, like he used to do, and," I took a deep breath and rushed on, "it's the rest of the story that makes me sure my children and I are in danger."

"What did you learn?" he asked in a concerned tone.

"This is the part you're not going to believe, and trust me, I wanted to tell the police, but I didn't think they'd believe me either, unless I had proof. This person has two identities; he's a transsexual now with another name, but when he was a man he committed a murder and," I choked up then went on, "I recently found out it was my husband who paid for his sex change and helped him change his name, knowing all along that he killed a man."

"You're in serious danger," Kelly said in a stern voice. "Whom did he kill? What's the person's name and where did the murder take place?" he prodded.

"That's the thing; I don't know who he killed, where or when it happened. All I know, from what my husband told me, is that the victim was named Billy and he was killed in a small town, in a motel one night. I have a pretty good idea the murder happened somewhere in South Carolina. That was the state this man lived in at one time. I also found out his father lives down there. But I don't know what small town the murder happened in or when he committed it! I don't even know if the police know he did it," I replied, in frustration.

"Where do you live?" he asked.

"I live in Burbank," I replied.

"Look, I have a friend, Ted Kamon, who's a homicide detective at the Burbank Police Department. I think he can help you," Kelly said firmly. "Listen to me, let me have your name."

"Donita Allen," I replied.

"You're obviously in a real bad situation here. Let me call Ted. I'll explain what you told me and I'll call you right back about what to do next. Don't be scared. We're going to take care of this," he said in a fatherly manner as he continued to try and calm me.

Still feeling anxious, I gave him my phone number, then hung up, feeling some sort of relief that he might be able to help me.

Agitated, I paced the kitchen floor while waiting for Mr. Kelly to call back. Then, the phone began to ring "Hello?" I answered quickly. An eerie silence filled the air, as there was no response.

Freddie was taunting me again, but what he didn't know was that I had just taken the first step in stopping his unvoiced but certain threats.

"What do you want from me?" I yelled, and when there was no answer, I hung up the phone.

The second I hung it up, the phone began to ring again. Thinking it was Freddie, I began shaking, but when I picked it up I felt immediate relief. It was Ryan Kelly returning my call.

"I'm sorry. I thought you were Freddie calling again. He just did after we got off the phone," I said.

"Calm down. Everything's going to be okay now. I called my friend Detective Kamon. He's in his office right now. Now I'm going to give you his number and I want you to tell him everything you told me," he said.

After the call ended I clutched the phone to my chest holding the paper with Det. Kamon's number in my hand. I was scared, but I began dialing his number.

"Homicide. Det. Kamon speaking," he answered.

"Det. Kamon, this is Donita Allen. I believe Mr. Kelly called about my situation," I said, in a whimpering voice.

"Hello, Mrs. Allen. I've been expecting your call. You have a murder you want to report?" he asked.

"Yes, and did Mr. Kelly tell you why I'm so concerned?" I asked.

"From what I was told, a murder was committed by a man who's had a sex change since. The victim's name was Billy and your husband is somehow involved, right? Am I correct so far?" he asked.

"Yes," I replied. He sounded so competent and immediately got to the point, making my spirits rise.

"What's the name of the person who committed the murder?" he asked.

"His real name is Freddie Lee Turner, but the one he's using now, that he had it changed to, is Valerie Nicole Taylor," I replied.

"Do you know where the murder occurred?" he asked.

"From what I've learned, it happened in a small town, I'm guessing somewhere in South Carolina. That's the state he once lived in. I found it on his name-change document. But I don't know when the murder happened or what Billy's last name is. That's why I held off on telling the police. I didn't think they'd believe me." I paused; my heart was racing even faster than my thoughts. Steadying myself I went on, "It's such a crazy story, and not having any proof, I didn't know what to do, so I called Mr. Kelly hoping he could help me."

I did what the detective asked, beginning my story from the day I was introduced to Valerie. I spoke slowly, trying not to forget anything important.

As I continued my story, telling Det. Kamon about David's role in helping Freddie change his identity, David came up behind me, catching me off guard. Intent on my conversation, I hadn't heard the front door open.

Unnerved by his unexpected presence, I began shaking, realizing David had overheard me.

"My husband just walked in!" I whispered into the phone, in a panic.

David's eyes widened.

"What are you doing?" David called out, obviously shocked by what he'd overheard. Stunned, I just stood there clutching the phone, not knowing what to do next. For a few moments both of us stared at each other.

"Let me see who you're talking to," David demanded.

Almost involuntarily I extended the phone to him.

"The police—talk to him. Tell him!" I replied, anxiously. David reached out, taking the receiver from my shaking hand. His angry eyes stayed locked on mine, as he covered the receiver with his other hand.

"I can't believe you did this," David hissed. His teeth were clenched. I felt frozen, unable to move. I felt my body tensing up, not knowing what was going to happen next, as David brought the receiver a slight distance from his ear so I could still hear.

"Hello?" David said, in a gruff, questioning tone.

"Mr. Allen?" Det. Kamon asked.

"Yes, this is he," David replied, tensely.

"I've been informed by your wife that you have some information about a possible murder that's been committed," Det. Kamon said. David flashed me a look of fury.

As David was being questioned by Det. Kamon, he kept his gaze riveted to mine. I knew then there was no turning back. Finally, the real truth about Freddie Turner's violent past for which I had searched for so long was going to come out.

"How soon can you and your wife come to the police station?" Det. Kamon asked.

David paused for a moment.

"It's not possible for me to come there right now. What about tomorrow morning at 10:30?" David asked, stammering.

After Det. Kamon agreed, David hung up the phone, and then turned towards me.

"I don't think you realize the position you've put me in by calling the police," David said, as he began pacing the floor nervously.

I stared at him for a moment.

"You should have thought about that before you helped a murderer, David! I only wish I had done this when I first found out! Now, Freddie's stalking me and my family. I had to call someone!" I replied, my voice rising. I glared at him.

"That attorney we saw told you to leave it alone!" David said, in a frustrated tone.

I took a deep breath, shuddering. "Knowing that Freddie committed a murder, doing nothing was not an alternative my conscience could bear," I said. "And now that he knows I know, I have to put my children's safety before anything—to say nothing of my safety as their sole guardian," I said. Anger filled me, but in that anger I became stronger.

David's conversation with the detective ran through my mind.

"Why did you tell Det. Kamon you couldn't come down right now?" I asked, suspiciously.

"Why do you think? I need time to talk to a lawyer. By the way, if you recall, the lawyer we saw said you hold some responsibility in this too, for not reporting the murder when you first found out," David replied, in an attempt to scare me.

"As you are aware, I had nothing concrete to report. But I'll call an attorney myself to see what is true and what isn't," I replied furiously.

"Fine, Donita, do what you feel you have to. I'm going over to the studio where I can speak to a lawyer privately," David shouted as he walked out, closing the front door behind him.

After David shut the door, I rushed to get the phone book and began looking up criminal attorneys. Finding a listing, I grabbed the phone and frantically dialed his number, hoping not to hear the same thing Mr. Paton had told David and me.

Unfortunately the first attorney I got hold of concurred with Paton that I could be prosecuted for withholding evidence that I didn't report to the police right away. Scared, I called another attorney, only to be told he wouldn't have anything to do with the case. He suggested I get another opinion.

For the next few minutes, I sat paralyzed with fear. Making one last attempt, I called one more attorney, only to be hung up on in the middle of explaining the situation to him. Frustrated and scared, I panicked.

Quickly rushing out of the house, I got into the truck and drove over to David's studio. Swiftly making my way to his office, I paused to listen at his door. I could overhear David on the phone explaining what was going on, and the person on the other end of the phone yelling though I couldn't distinguish the words. Opening the door I called out, "Who is that?"

"Warren Howell—he's a criminal attorney," David replied, disconcerted, pressing the phone to his chest.

When David brought the phone back up to his ear, I could hear Howell still yelling. This time I understood what he was saying, "What has your wife done!"

"What have I done?" I said, yelling back.

It was total chaos. David tried to calm Howell and me down at the same time, but I wasn't about to be quieted. I grabbed the receiver from David.

"What have I done? Do you even KNOW the whole story yet?" I screamed at Howell.

"Okay, okay, let's all calm down. I didn't mean what have you done to your husband in a bad sense, but that you went to the police before seeing any attorney to protect yourself," Howell said, lowering his voice.

"I don't think you have any idea what's going on here," I replied, angrily.

"Listen, is there another phone your husband can get on so we can all talk about this at the same time?" Howell asked. I waved at David to pick up another phone.

"Are you both ready to listen?" Howell asked.

"Yes," David and I replied.

"Let me explain what you both need to do. The police will probably be watching the house. It's important that you stay away from it and each other," Howell said.

"What do you mean, stay away from the house? I can't do that, I have two kids!" I replied, angrily.

"Okay, if you have to be there, but don't use the phone," Howell said.

"Why?" I asked.

"Because the police most likely are going to tap the phone, once they find you're not going to show up tomorrow," Howell replied.

"What? What do you mean—not show up?" I asked, confused.

"Please, Mrs. Allen, trust me. I've dealt with the police many times before and I know how they are. Once you go to the police department, they'll arrest both you and David for not reporting this murder when you were first told about it. If you listen to me and do what I say, I'll be able to protect you both," Howell explained.

"I can't believe this!" I said, in frustration, as I began to cry. I didn't know who to believe at this point. I wanted to do the right thing, but I felt I was caught in a catch-22.

"Mrs. Allen, there's something I need you to do the second you get off the phone with me," Howell said.

"What?" I asked.

"I need you to go straight to the house and gather together any-thing you have connecting you and David to this person you reported. Go through the house thoroughly and get the stuff out of the house and dump it somewhere, where no one can see you. Make sure noth-ing's left behind if the police come to search your house," Howell said.

Tension burned in my brow. Howell continued to talk. "Mrs. Allen, this is what I want you to do. Tomorrow morning at 10:00, I want you to find a pay phone and call Det. Kamon, but don't ask to speak to him directly. What you're going to do is leave a message say-ing that you're going to be running an hour late and will be arriving at 11:30 instead," Howell explained. He then told David and me to meet him at his office at 10:30 to explore the whole situation in detail.

I had felt comfortable with Ted Kamon's advice and believed he truly wanted to help me. Now I was distraught after the conversation with Howell. Quickly, I returned to the house and frantically ran into the bedroom. I pulled out the yellow envelope that contained all the information and documents I had collected on Freddie from under the mattress. I sat down on the bed for a few moments and decided to look at the envelope's contents. I could hear my heart beating loudly as I spilled them out, first seeing the arrest list and mug shots. Should I do as Howell had asked or not? What if he was really interested in protecting David and not me? Knowing how hard the documents had been to obtain I was unwilling to destroy them all. I put the most important ones, including the map I'd made, back and I gathered up the rest. Then I went out to the truck. With Howell making me feel paranoid, I slowly pulled the truck out of the driveway and onto the street, looking anxiously out the rear-view mirror for any unusual cars.

Driving around town looking for a trash can, I realized that too many people were around to see me and might notice my strange behavior. I found an unpopulated park. I was a nervous wreck and tried to calm myself as I stopped the truck. Getting out and walking around, I spied a trash can. Looking around me to make sure no one was watching, I picked up a few newspapers, and discreetly shuffled the information on Freddie between the pages and threw the whole mess out.

Returning home, I tried to remain calm, knowing Sam and Jessica would soon be home from school. A short while later I saw them from the window, walking towards the house. Shaking off the emotional turmoil I still felt, I went to the door, kissed and hugged them and asked how their day went.

I gave them some milk and cookies and slipped away from the room feeling overwhelmed. Entering the bathroom on the far side of the house, I shut the door behind me and quickly covered my tearful face with a towel.

Somehow I got through dinner and their bedtime but lay awake most of the night worrying. The next morning I woke the kids up and got them off to school. As I kissed and hugged them goodbye, they walked off, neither of them suspecting anything was wrong. Just before 10:00 I followed Howell's instructions and drove to a pay phone.

As I walked up to it, I found myself becoming highly nervous. Taking a deep breath, I began dialing the police station.

"Good morning, Burbank Police," an officer answered.

"Yes, I need to leave a message for Det. Kamon. I don't need to speak to him in person." I didn't like it, but I followed Howell's advice; after all, he was a criminal attorney and I had no experience.

"I'll transfer you," the officer replied.

"You've reached the office of Det. Ted Kamon. I'm not in right now. Please leave a message and I'll get back to you soon."

"Det. Kamon, this is Donita Allen. I just wanted to let you know we'll be running an hour late. We'll be there at 11:30 instead. Bye," I said, and quickly hung up the phone.

Returning to the truck, I got in, turned on the ignition, pulled out onto the street and drove off towards Howell's office. Glancing at the clock, I saw time quickly passing. As I opened the door to Howell's office, I saw David sitting in a chair. He looked as distraught as he had the day he confessed to me about Freddie's killing.

Howell's secretary asked if I was Mrs. Allen. When I said yes, she told me she'd let Mr. Howell know that David and I both were here. David and I didn't say a word to each other as we sat on opposite sides of the waiting room.

Before too long, Howell opened the door to the waiting room and introduced himself, asking us to follow him to his office.

Due to my feelings of anger and betrayal caused by David and Freddie, I opted to sit far apart from David, and remained quiet as David began explaining his side of the story. He told Howell he first met Freddie from the personal ads. David's story was sketchy and he was leaving things out, so I filled Howell in on the missing parts.

Howell looked more and more intrigued as I told him of detailed events, including what I knew of Freddie's past history before David met him.

Upon finishing the story of how I had come to discover the truth about Freddie and the relationship between him and David, I sat, head down, in the chair. Silence filled the office. Howell leaned back, his face covered with pure amazement.

"You two are going to be millionaires with this story," Howell said.

I looked at Howell as if he were crazy. "My interest is not to make money, but to get help in the situation David has put me in," I said adamantly.

Shaking his head, Howell buzzed his assistant and asked her to get Det. Kamon on the phone. All three of us sat silently. David and I stared at each other, both of us worried about what was going to happen next.

"Det. Kamon is on line one," Howell's assistant said, over the speakerphone.

Howell picked up the phone. He started off by introducing himself to Det. Kamon in a calm professional voice, "I am representing David Allen and his wife in the situation regarding Freddie Turner."

After a couple of minutes on the phone, Howell's voice became louder and more agitated as he argued with the detective about David and me coming into the police station to explain the situation concerning Freddie.

"I will not have them do that," Howell became even louder, angrily refusing Det. Kamon's request. "Look, let me speak to your lieutenant," he demanded. We sat and waited for the lieutenant to get on the phone.

Howell and Lt. Sims, the officer now heading the case, immediately became embroiled in a verbal battle over our not coming into the police station. When Howell threatened Lt. Sims with a lawsuit against the police department for harassment, I began to realize how out of control the situation was becoming.

They began going at each other again and an obviously irritated Howell gave Lt. Sims certain details pertaining to Freddie and the murder, while leaving out details concerning David's involvement in helping Freddie.

Finally the call ended with Howell slamming down the phone. He looked over at David and me. "Okay, this is the deal. First off, David, you're in more trouble than your wife," Howell said, in a stern and concerned voice.

David slumped in his chair, bringing both his hands to his forehead in a gesture of defeat.

Howell then looked over at me. "But you're in some hot water for not reporting it right away."

My mouth dropped open in shock. Howell had spoken the same words Mr. Paton, David's first attorney had told me. I was now convinced that I would somehow be implicated.

"The police are most likely obtaining arrest warrants for both of you as we speak. Now, Mrs. Allen, I know this is going to be upsetting, but as far as you're concerned, if they arrest you, they'll most likely take you to Civil Brand, a women's jail." He paused, then went on. "Your kids will be taken away from you," Howell said, spreading his hands, a helpless look covering his face.

"My kids taken away?" I cried out, as my body began shaking with fear.

"This is what the police can do in order to get what they want; they can go after what will affect you the most," Howell said.

Leaning forward I twisted around to face David. "This is all your fault!" I screamed, ready to implode.

"Yeah, yeah," David replied. "My scene is even worse because of you," he hissed.

"Because of me?" I shrieked, staring at him. I resisted a terrible urge to smack him.

"Look, you both have to calm down." Howell grimaced. "Listen to me, both of you. With me threatening Lt. Sims with harassment, they might back off. Just do everything I've told you and remember, don't talk about this over your home phone with anyone."

"But will that be enough?" David asked, "Lt. Sims sounded like he wasn't about to quit."

"Now, Mr. Allen, although I'll do everything in my power to protect you, there's not much I can promise. You out and out aided and abetted a fugitive to the extreme. If this Valerie person lied and there was no murder, then you have nothing to worry about.

"Now this is important—you hear me on this. If one or both of you should be arrested, you are to call me immediately. DON'T talk or give any information to the police," Howell's voice was stern.

"Now, go home. I'll be in touch with you as soon as I hear back from the police about Freddie." I left Howell's office, feeling sick with worry that Sam and Jessica could be taken away from me.

I desperately wanted to talk to Gayle, but I couldn't use the phone at home, so I drove around looking for a pay phone. I spied one outside a grocery store, but a woman was using it. With my fragile sanity unraveling by the second, I couldn't wait any longer. Getting out of the truck, I walked briskly towards the woman on the pay phone and pulled a twenty-dollar bill from my purse.

"If you get off the phone right now it's yours," I said, waving the twenty-dollar bill in front of her.

Looking at me in delighted shock, she asked no questions. "I have to go! Call you back!" she said, quickly hanging up the phone.

As soon as she got far enough away, I used my credit card to call Gayle's number. When she answered, I blurted out the situation. She grew very concerned for the kids and me and suggested I come back to Oklahoma and stay with her mom.

"I don't know," I said. "Maybe that's a good idea. I'll call you back tonight and let you know what I'm going to do."

As I drove home, a vision of Gayle's mom's farm, where the kids and I would be safe, passed through my mind. I pictured the old, red barn glowing in the midday sun and the kids' laughter echoing in the air as they ran in and out of the fields, my worries of Freddie stuck far away in the Los Angeles smog. It was perfect. Still, I didn't want to run. But whatever I wanted, protecting the children had to come first. I drove over to David's studio. I found David in an emotional fog. I stared at him, as he glanced up at me for a moment, then put his head back down, not saying a word.

"There's one thing I have to know," I said, my eyes welling up with tears. "What made you think I'd never find out?"

David looked up at me while slowly drawing his hands down his face. "I underestimated you," he replied in a weak voice.

Silence filled the room, as I stared at David's face, empty of expression. I turned and left. I didn't know what to feel. I had, at one point, loved this man enough to marry him and all he could tell me was he *underestimated* me, as if I was nothing more than a pawn in his and Freddie's twisted love triangle. Six years of heavy remorse sank in my chest; I could feel its weight slow me down. As I dragged my beaten spirit to the truck, doubt crept over me: what had I done with the past six years of my life?

Driving home I contemplated what I should to do next. With my life seemingly falling apart and fearful the police could show up at any time to put me in jail and take my children away, I made the decision to try and leave that night for Oklahoma.

Torn between feeling hurt that the person I loved and trusted had betrayed me and feeling angry that the kids and I had been used, I pulled the truck up to the house. I ran inside, picked up the phone and called David, demanding he get money out of the bank and bring it to me without asking any questions.

"Why the urgency?" David asked.

"Don't you even DARE ask questions, just get me the money and bring it to the house!" I said, angrily.

"Fine, fine, I'll bring it," David relented, hearing my fury.

Hanging up the phone, I quickly went to the bedroom. Grabbing suitcases from the closet, I tossed them onto the bed. Shortly after, David arrived at the house, with money in hand.

"Donita, what's going on? What's with the suitcases?" David asked.

"I'm not losing my kids over a murder you helped someone get away with," I replied recklessly. David stood nervously watching as I opened dresser drawers, pulling out clothes and tossing them onto the bed.

Realizing I was about to leave, David panicked and ran to the phone, while pulling Howell's card out of his pant pocket. As I continued packing David told Howell my plan to leave town. A moment later he turned to me, "Howell wants to speak to you."

"You're only going to make things worse for yourself if you leave town, Mrs. Allen. You could be charged with flight during an investigation," Howell said.

"What am I supposed to do?" I asked, terrified.

David, nervous, began pacing the bedroom floor.

"Calm down, Mrs. Allen, please. I have everything under control. Now, I want you and David back in my office first thing tomorrow morning," Howell said.

He went on to tell me the police were concentrating more on David than they were on me and that he was just giving me the worst-case scenario of what they would do, if I were to be charged.

"If you flee, the police may think you're guilty," he warned me.

"I'm not the one who's guilty," I insisted. "I'm the one with a conscience."

"I understand how you feel, Mrs. Allen," he said. "But you must be careful how things look."

As we were talking, David left the house and returned to the studio. Agreeing that I wouldn't leave town, I hung up and called Gayle, telling her that the kids and I wouldn't be coming out to Oklahoma.

Once again I found myself trying to keep control of my emotions around Sam and Jessica. I didn't want them to suspect anything was wrong until I could gently tell them as much as they needed to know. After getting the kids off to school the next morning, I drove over to meet David at Howell's office.

Soon we were ushered inside. Howell said he had had another talk with Lt. Sims. "The police are running an FBI background check on Freddie, to see if, in fact, he is wanted for murder," he told us.

At that point I didn't know whether to be glad or afraid, but I was relieved the police were finally on the scene. In my gut I knew I had been living with a very dangerous situation for too long. Still, the lawyer had made me worry; pushing for the truth had placed me and my children in danger in a way I'd never imagined.

I took a few minutes to try to compose myself and glanced over at David.

"Do you see what you've done?" he asked, sounding panicky.

I shook my head. "I know what I've done; what about you?" David sat in stony silence. "What's the matter, are you afraid to answer?" I said in disgust and aggravation.

"Look, you both have to stay calm," Howell leaned toward us. "Lt. Sims agreed to back off until the police know for sure whether a murder has been committed or not." Both mentally and emotionally exhausted, I left Howell's office and drove back to the house.

As the next couple of days passed, waiting anxiously to hear back from Howell, I found myself mulling over all that had been happening. Suddenly I realized I hadn't received any more hang-up calls from Freddie. The last ones had occurred the day I called the private investigator.

"That's strange," I muttered. Suddenly the phone began to ring. "Hello?" I answered, cautiously.

"Mrs. Allen, Howell here. I've got some news. I just got off the phone with Lt. Sims. Are you sitting down?" Howell asked.

"Why do you ask?" I said.

"Just do it," he said. For some reason I obeyed.

"Ok, I'm sitting."

"Well," he went on, "Freddie Turner is wanted for murder. Just as you suspected."

Even though I felt I was right about Freddie, hearing it confirmed was shocking. "Oh my God," I said, beginning to shake. "I knew it. I just knew it."

"Let me tell you some of the details Lt. Sims told me," Howell went on.

"Just a minute." I said, my voice quivering. "Okay go on." I quickly grabbed a pen and began writing down the information Howell was telling me.

"According to Sims the murder took place on January 6, 1979, in Gaffney, a small town in South Carolina. The victim's name is Billy Marshall Posey. The only other thing I was told was that the FBI had also been looking for Freddie," Howell said.

"I haven't told David yet. I wanted you to know first. I need you to get over to my office right away. I am going to ask David to meet us there.

After hanging up, I got out the map I had made of possible sites where the murder could have occurred. Gaffney was in the circle. Then grabbing my purse, I ran out the front door and headed over to Howell's address. When I arrived, David wasn't there yet. Following Howell into his office, I sat down. Sitting at his desk, he looked searchingly at me.

"Donita, you'd make quite a detective," he said, nodding his head in amazement. "I want you to brace yourself, because this story is definitely going to hit the news after Freddie is arrested. You need to prepare yourself for the media attention you're going to get. Reporters will be clamoring to interview you," Howell explained.

Not having thought that far ahead, I immediately thought of the kids, not wanting this to have a bad effect. "Look, that would be bad for my children," I said upset. "You have to tell Lt. Sims to keep my name anonymous."

Just then, David walked into the office and closed the door behind him. Sweating profusely, he sat down, obviously on edge. "What's so important?" he demanded.

Howell looked at him. "Freddie's secret is out," he said, and began to fill David in on what he had already told me.

He concluded, "This is where things stand: The Gaffney police have lost the old arrest warrant and they're going to have to get another one. Until a new one is issued, all we can do is sit back and wait." He paused, then went on to explain, "This is actually a good thing, because it buys us more time."

"What's going to happen to me?" David asked, trembling.

"Well, as I indicated before, there's a good chance, since you helped Freddie not only change his name, but his entire identity, the police will be focusing their attention on you too," Howell replied.

David's face was flushed with worry, as Howell explained the possible media attention David would have to face, since he was in the movie business. Continuing, he told David, "There is no way to get around it. You should prepare yourself." Feeling physically drained from the emotional tension and having to get home in time to be there for the children, I asked if I could go. When Howell nodded, I got out of there as quickly as I could, leaving David sitting stony faced.

In the following days, while we waited for the new warrant to be issued, there was a strange, palpable silence in the house. I badly wanted to call Det. Kamon myself but was afraid of the consequences. The phone hardly rang and no one came over. After a few days, I began to wonder if David had warned Freddie, or even worse, if David might have helped Freddie skip town, or was planning to. Each time I spoke to Howell, he said there was no news.

Finally unable to stand the waiting, I called David, asking him to meet me in front of the house. When he got there I was waiting out front and a light drizzle was coming down. David rolled down the car window.

"What is it you need to talk to me about?" David asked.

"I'm going to ask you point blank, David. You haven't by any chance called Freddie to warn him, have you?" I asked, in a suspicious tone.

David paused, taking in a deep breath. "No. No, I haven't, but I have considered helping Valerie get out of town, if that's what you're getting at," David replied.

I looked at him amazed. Hearing from David's own mouth what I feared could happen, I quickly made up a lie, hoping David would fall for it.

"I want you to know I just got off the phone with my divorce attorney, after explaining the situation to him. He told me the police are most likely watching Freddie's apartment until he's arrested, as well as monitoring the calls coming in and going out from his phone," I said.

"Well, that doesn't surprise me, with all the damage you've caused Valerie," David said.

I stood silently in the rain, staring at David in disbelief.

"There's something seriously wrong with you, David," I finally said. "You need to wake up. This isn't a scene in a movie. This is for real, David!" I said, looking him straight in the eyes.

"You're the one who doesn't understand, Donita. I don't know why you felt the need to try and destroy Valerie's life, not to mention mine," David replied.

I took a deep breath, trying to speak calmly but decisively. "Freddie killed a man, and because of you, he's got his attention set on me now! Why? Why did you even tell me about the murder years ago, if you didn't want Freddie to get caught?" I asked.

"I don't know why! But you can surely trust when I say that every day that goes by I regret ever telling you," David crossed his arms as if to shut me out, his handsome face drained of emotion.

I bent over and touched his arm so he would look at me. "David, I think deep down inside you wanted Freddie to get caught, but you've been so wrapped up in your little fantasy world you have no idea what's real anymore. You've been living a lie all these years and you made my kids and me victims of it," I said.

"I don't think I did you and your kids wrong. I always took care of you all, didn't I?" David replied, turning his face away from me.

I stood speechless, my heart a clenched fist, as he drove off in the rain. He seemed to have no guilt, despite the fact he had put me and my children in mortal danger by exposing us to a killer.

chapter ten

An Arrest

Though I tried to act normal around the kids, I found myself snapping at them, my nerves frayed almost beyond repair. The stress of waiting to hear if Freddie had been arrested grew. It had other effects on me as well. In the shower large clumps of my hair would fall out, clogging the drain with my stress. My appetite was endangered, limited to a few sparse bites of food a day, enough to keep me breathing. Needless to say, I lost weight fast, but this wasn't the healthiest diet. Sleep had abandoned me long ago with no sign of return; my body ached and shivers of pain rode me all day. Why hadn't I heard anything yet? A few weeks had passed and not a word from anyone. I called Howell, only to be told he hadn't heard anything either and that he found that strange himself.

Had the police already arrested Freddie but decided to keep it quiet? I was too scared to call Det. Kamon. Finally, I decided to find out on my own whether Freddie was still at his apartment.

Getting up my nerve, I drove over to Freddie's apartment and parked the truck across the street, away from the front of the apartment building. My heart pounding with fear, I got out and began walking towards the front steps of the building. Slowly, I crept up the stairs to the security door. Pointing my finger at the buzzer to Freddie's apartment, I quickly pushed it once, waiting for an answer.

"Who's there? You'd better tell me. Don't think I don't know where you are or that you're safe." A paranoid voice came through the intercom. It was Freddie.

In a panic I ran as fast as I could, quickly jumped in the truck and sped off.

Arriving home I pulled into the driveway and turned off the engine. Sitting with my head against the steering wheel, I tried to figure out what to do next. The first thing was to secure the kids. I called a friend who lived nearby and asked if Jessica and Sam could stay with her for a few days. I knew I could trust her.

Knowing I badly needed some rest and advice, I decided to fly out to Oklahoma to visit Gayle for a couple of days.

I left early in the morning and when my flight finally arrived in Tulsa, Gayle was there to meet me. On the drive out to her mom's farm, I was finally able to relax from the stress I had been under. Gayle and I talked into the night about what would be best to do next. The next morning I called to see how the kids were doing. After I talked to Sam and Jessica, my friend got on the phone.

"Donita, I don't want you to worry, the kids are doing fine, but…" she paused and silence came over the phone line.

"But what?" I asked in immediate concern.

"You'd better call Det. Kamon. There's been an arrest," she replied.

"Who?" I said, not knowing if she was referring to Freddie or David.

"Freddie got arrested yesterday," she said.

"The same day I left for Oklahoma? How do you know this?" I asked, in shock.

"Your attorney called. He said you left my number in case anything came up," she replied.

"I'm taking the first plane out. Tell the kids I love them and I'll be there tomorrow," I said, alarmed, then hung up the phone. Quickly, I called Howell, who verified what my friend had told me and after promising him I'd find out all I could, I called David.

"I guess you've heard the news," David said.

"Yes, I did. Did Howell call and tell you?" I asked.

"No, Valerie called me from jail," David replied.

"Good, he should have been arrested a long time ago!" I said, angrily.

"Yeah, well, I'm sure the news of Valerie being arrested makes you very happy," David said darkly.

"I think you know the answer to that," I said and hung up the phone.

Shaking, I walked back into the room where Gayle was and tried to pull myself together.

"What, Donita? What's wrong?" Gayle asked. "You look like you're going to faint."

"They got Freddie, Gayle," I said.

"When?" Gayle asked, as a shocked look came over her face.

"Yesterday, right after I left. I have to get back right away and make sure the media doesn't get to the children."

On the plane ride home I braced myself for what was ahead.

Shortly after returning, I got a phone call that raised more questions in my mind.

"Hello?" I answered.

"Hello, Donita, it's Rick. Is David around?" he asked.

"David doesn't live here anymore, Rick. You can reach him at his studio," I replied before hanging up the phone.

Knowing Rick was a friend of both Freddie's and David's, I couldn't help wondering if he had known about Freddie committing a murder as well.

I called David's studio. Point blank, I asked, in a demanding tone, "David, did Rick know Freddie killed someone?" As I waited for David to answer my question, an uneasy pause came over the phone. "David?" I said, becoming suspicious of his delay.

"Yes, Rick knew," David, answered.

"Oh my God, so that makes two of you who knew Freddie was wanted for murder! How many others knew, David? And how did Rick find out about the arrest?" I asked, in shock.

"Valerie called Rick from jail and they somehow believe I'm the one who ratted her out," David replied.

So Rick had kept the ominous secret from me as well. I recalled the night of the Christmas party and Rick telling me I made the right move by leaving the room after Freddie became enraged at Rick's comment about David and I someday getting married.

Fighting to keep myself calm, I tried to get more questions answered.

"Who else besides Rick has contacted you concerning Freddie's arrest?" I asked.

"Someone I don't remember meeting," David replied.

"Who?" I asked.

"His name is Roger Mills," David replied.

"And what part does this Roger play in this?" I asked.

"I don't know. I was only aware he'd been seeing Valerie for a while, up until she was arrested, but I don't know for how long. I guess Valerie wanted Roger to hear the news from her first, before it ended up on television and in print. Apparently Valerie told Roger if he wanted more answers about why she was in jail, he should call me. From what I understand, Valerie told Roger that she had once been a man but wasn't guilty of murder," David replied. "You know, Donita, I really shouldn't be answering any more of your questions after what you've done."

"What I've done?" I said, enraged and irritated. I ended my call in disgust and wrote down Roger's name for future reference, keeping it with the other information I was compiling on Freddie's history.

David quickly phoned back. "Do you have the television on?" he asked.

"No, why?" I asked.

"Turn it on. Valerie's story is on every news station," David replied, tension in his voice.

"I'll call you back," I said. Quickly hanging up the phone, I hurried to turn the TV on.

He was right. Freddie's arrest was the headline all the news stations were carrying. Changing channels, I noticed that the attorney defending Freddie in Billy's murder was Gary Moore. I suddenly realized he was the same attorney who had represented Freddie on the legal name-change and vehicle hit-and-run documents I had gotten at the courthouse.

As I continued changing channels, dramatic headlines on Freddie's arrest flickered in front of me.

"A man wanted for a seventeen-year-old murder has finally been captured, but he is now a she," one heralded.

Clicking to another station, "A fugitive for murder who eluded police and FBI for more than seventeen years has recently been arrested in the upscale neighborhood of Toluca Lake. But it's what this fugitive did to avoid capture that surprised even the police. Don't miss this incredible story on the Channel 4 news at ten o'clock."

On still another, a news reporter was interviewing a tenant who lived next door to Freddie. The woman said, "She was quiet. Pretty much kept to herself. She kind of resembles Whitney Houston."

On the eleven o'clock news, I saw the most comprehensive story of all.

"Freddie Lee Turner, a wanted fugitive for the 1979 Gaffney, South Carolina, murder of Billy Marshall Posey, has finally been captured. How did Turner escape capture for so many years? He became a she, Valerie Nicole Taylor. Burbank Police state they have their man, but Valerie claims they have the wrong person and that she never was a man, further stating she never knew or killed the person she's been charged with killing. Tell that to the Gaffney, South Carolina police, who claim Turner was a well-known cross-dresser back there, and was last seen with Posey after leaving a local bar. Later that night, police found Posey lying dead in a motel room with multiple gunshot wounds."

"Never a man?" I said out loud, baffled as to how Freddie thought he'd get away with saying this.

The next morning was Saturday. Worried about the children finding out, I told them not to turn on the television. Sam and Jessica had met Freddie with me the first time I was introduced to him through David. I didn't want to risk the kids seeing Freddie's mug shot plastered on the news. I sat on the living room floor, contemplating how I was going to keep the news from the children, or whether it was time to tell them as much as I felt they needed to know.

The phone rang. Startled, I jumped up to answer it.

"Hello," I answered softly.

"Donita! I'm in shock. You were right! I've been watching the news and I can't believe this!" Dr. Ashford exclaimed.

"I told you there was a murder," I said. "Now you know."

"Yes, yes, I do! It was just so hard to believe. Are you okay? How are you holding up?" she asked with concern in her voice.

"I'm nervous about my name coming out. I don't want the kids to be affected by this," I replied.

"You have to monitor their television until you decide how to handle this with them. Do you want to come to the office?" Dr. Ashford asked. "I'll meet you there."

"No, I can't, but you're right, I have to somehow make sure my kids don't see this on TV. I'll call you back," I replied, getting off the phone.

Only allowing the kids to watch cartoons and rented movies prevented them from watching the news. I waited until Sam and Jessica went to bed before turning the television on again, to see if the story on Freddie was still on the air. The next day, it hit the newspaper stands, front page. Freddie's story seemed to keep getting bigger and bigger, gathering more attention as the news media tried to find out who the tipster was that led police to the killer.

Wondering why Howell hadn't called the house yet, I decided to call his office to find out what was going on with the police.

"I need to speak to Howell, now!" I said.

"Mrs. Allen, I am so sorry. I was just about to call you," Howell exclaimed.

"What the hell is going on? Why didn't you call when this hit the news?" I asked.

"Listen, I've been in close touch with the police and it's getting a little more complicated now. I wanted to try and get things sorted out before talking to you," Howell said.

"What do you mean, a little more complicated?" I asked, suspiciously.

"Well, first off, you need to prepare yourself, because Freddie could possibly do a 'tell-all' interview from jail and your name might come out as a result of it," Howell replied.

"I didn't even think of that!" I said, beginning to shake with anxiety.

"Also, it's the Gaffney police that have a say in whether you'll be arrested and have charges brought against you for withholding information. They'll send someone out here soon. Right now, they're working on getting Valerie extradited to South Carolina and she's trying to fight it," Howell explained.

Shocked at learning that I could be dragged out to South Carolina, just as David could, I became flustered and hung up on Howell.

With Howell telling me once again that I could be arrested, but this time by the Gaffney, South Carolina, Police, fear coursed through me as though I were about to lose my mind. Not thinking rationally, I picked up the phone and called David at the studio.

"Hello?" David answered warily.

"David! Get the RV and get over here now! I just got off the phone with Howell. The South Carolina police will be coming out here to get Freddie any day now. Howell said there's a good chance I'm going to get dragged down with you both! I'm taking the kids and you're going to get us the hell out of here or, I swear, I'll risk everything and call the police again, right now!" I said, sobbing.

"Okay, I'll gas up the RV and meet you at the house in an hour," David said, hanging up the phone. Running into first Sam's and then Jessica's bedrooms, I packed some clothes for them. Taking the suitcase I went to my bedroom and threw in some things for me.

"Where are we going?" David asked, with a concerned tone when he drove up to the house.

"We're all going where no one can find us—the mountains," I replied, telling David to head north on the US 5 freeway.

Nothing but the revving RV engine could be heard as David drove to the base of the Los Angeles forest. We stopped off in a small nearby town to get supplies. Coming out of the store, I saw a newspaper rack with the *Los Angeles Times*. I quickly put in some change and grabbed one. We got back into the RV and headed up into the mountains.

Opening up the newspaper, I found yet another story on Freddie, saying the Gaffney police had received confirmation that Freddie's fingerprints matched those of the murder suspect responsible in Billy's death. Glancing over at David, I still felt he knew a lot more about Freddie than he was willing to tell me, but I didn't want to talk in front of the kids.

I only spoke to David while giving directions on where to turn as we headed off the main road into a rural part of the forest. After David parked the RV, I began setting up camp before nightfall came. After we gave the kids dinner and tucked them in for the night, I remembered something. There was a small television tucked away in the back of the RV. I called David over.

"I want to see if the story is still being covered on the news," I said. While flipping the channels and trying to get reception, I caught Lt. Sims's name in a caption at the bottom of the TV screen.

Standing outside the Burbank Police Station, he was being interviewed by multiple news reporters. Lt. Sims was confirming that Valerie's fingerprints matched those of Freddie Lee Turner provided by various police agencies. He gave details of Freddie's arrest. Lt. Sims then went on to say that the police didn't known what to do at first, and then decided to take Freddie to a local hospital to have a doctor examine him to make sure of his sex.

He further explained the police weren't sure what jail to hold Freddie in, but finally decided, due to the sex change, that Freddie be placed in a women's jail at the Civil Brand.

I shivered, remembering that Howell had told me it would be the same place I would be taken to if arrested by the Burbank police.

Turning the television off, I looked over at David.

"How could you even think of helping someone like that, David?" I asked, in confusion.

"You'll never understand," David replied, one eyebrow cocked in an expression of contempt.

Speechless, I turned away. David was right. I'd never understand why or how he could be involved with such a violent person.

The next two days we all spent in the mountains were quiet. I played and went hiking with the kids. David and I spoke very few words to each other. Although my mind was filled with worry, my heart was glad that Sam and Jessica were okay. I realized I had no control over the situation at this point. I decided it was time to sit the kids down and talk to them. Hoping enough time had passed and the news covering Freddie's story might have tapered off, I told David to take us back to Los Angeles so I could see what was going on. We packed up the RV and headed back to the city.

Arriving in Burbank, we took the kids over to my friend's house for a few hours. I cautioned her not to let them watch television. Going into the other room I turned on the television, only to find the news still carrying updates on the bizarre situation with Freddie. Tired, dirty and fed-up with the whole problem, I decided to take the risk and return to my house with the children.

I took the kids into the kitchen. With a heavy heart, I let them know David and I were getting a divorce and that someone we all had met with him was guilty of a serious crime, which was now being talked about on the news. I told them the news about Valerie, leaving out the vulgar details they didn't need to know. I found it a relief that they took my muted announcement better than I had thought and went back to the game they'd been playing. I knew I'd have to tell them the whole truth sometime in the future, but I wasn't ready to do that just yet.

With the media still covering the story on Freddie, I continued to monitor what Sam and Jessica were watching and kept them close to the house. I'd hoped Freddie's arrest would taper off in the news without my name coming into play.

Howell soon called, saying that he'd try to get me immunity if I was arrested by the South Carolina police.

Still worried, I went out to get the *Los Angeles Times* newspaper, to keep abreast of what was going on. "Transsexual plans to fight extradition to South Carolina," the headlines read.

The article said the Gaffney Police Chief was planning to ask South Carolina's governor to request California's governor to force Freddie to return.

I felt a call to the California governor's office might help in getting Freddie forced back to South Carolina. I called the governor's office and was able to get his secretary on the phone.

Without giving my name, I told her I was the person who had turned Freddie in and that Freddie's extradition papers might soon cross the governor's desk. Frustrated, I began explaining the situation, finding it hard to hold back the tears. I told her how and why I discovered the truth about Freddie, and I explained to her the predicament it had put me and my kids in, after I tried to do the right thing.

Sympathetic to the situation I was in, the secretary tried to calm me down, as I begged her to tell the governor to sign the extradition order. She promised she would personally talk to the governor regarding the case and would explain the circumstances surrounding it and the concern I had about Freddie Turner.

After our talk I got through the next few days feeling slightly less agonized. That Friday morning after dropping the kids off at school, I picked up a newspaper. Opening it up, I read the headline: *Judgment: Transsexual fugitive can be extradited to South Carolina*. The article went on to say that a governor's warrant had been ordered and the municipal court judge held a compliance hearing, where it was ruled that Freddie be returned to Gaffney, South Carolina to face murder charges in the shooting death of Billy Posey. A momentary feeling of joy spread over me. Finally, Freddie would be out of my life, across the country facing trial for the heinous crime he committed.

chapter eleven

Seeking Answers

The news about what the governor had done brought me some relief, revived my courage and made me more intent on pursuing my leads on Freddie. I was going to do all I could to make sure he would never be a threat again. I decided it was time I telephoned Det. Kamon. Feeling tense, I picked up the phone and dialed the police station, asking for him.

"Homicide, Det. Kamon speaking," he answered.

"Det. Kamon?" I said.

"Yes," Det. Kamon asked.

"It's Donita," I said.

"Are you all right?" Det. Kamon asked in a concerned voice.

"I got scared, thanks to our attorney, but I want to continue helping you. He said I could be prosecuted," I replied.

"Let me guess—he told you we could arrest you and take your kids away, right?" he asked.

"Yes, he did, as a matter of fact," I answered back, hearing Det. Kamon chuckle.

"Donita, you were never in any trouble. Attorneys tell their clients the worst scenario that could happen, in my opinion, to scare them. How do you think they get so rich?" Det. Kamon said.

"But why did other attorneys say the same thing—that I could be arrested?" I asked.

"Could and will are very different," Det. Kamon replied matter-of-factly. "We don't arrest whistle-blowers for coming forward and contacting the police unless they are criminals."

"How come you never called or came over to the house to tell me this?" I asked.

"Howell was your attorney and he was threatening to sue the department for harassment if we tried to contact you in any way. Remember, it's a South Carolina case; we didn't have jurisdiction, except to arrest Valerie," Det. Kamon explained.

"But what about David? He's the one who helped Freddie get away for so many years," I said.

"I find that kind of strange myself; but, as I said, it's up to South Carolina to file charges," Det. Kamon said.

My resolve to bring Freddie to justice intensified. "I'm ready to help in any way I can with the case against Freddie. What do I have to do?" I asked.

"Come over to the police department tomorrow morning and we'll discuss our next steps," Det. Kamon said.

"I'll be there; you can count on it." After agreeing to meet Det. Kamon, I got off the phone. Infuriated with Howell, I drove straight over to his office to confront him face to face. Taking the elevator up to the floor Howell's office was on, I found myself becoming angrier by the minute. When the elevator stopped and the door opened, Howell was standing there, waiting to take the elevator down. I stepped out in front of him, blocking his way.

"Mrs. Allen!" Howell said, startled by my presence.

I looked Howell straight in the eyes.

"I was never in any trouble! In fact, there was never any risk of my kids being taken away from me, was there, Mr. Howell?" I said in a low, angry tone.

"Well, you just never know how things work out," Howell replied.

"Well, just watch and you'll find out," I said, angrily.

Howell looked at me in a surprised yet confused manner, as I got back into the elevator and pushed the button, closing the doors between Howell and me.

I was extremely eager now to find the answers the police needed to get justice for Freddie's victim. Returning home, I began writing up a summary of events, making a timeline of things that had happened involving Freddie and David and filling in the court records, phone records, mug shots and audio tapes I still had, hoping the information would help the police's case.

Arriving at the police station the next morning, I was brought upstairs to a waiting room. Nervously rubbing my hands together and looking around, I noticed a tall, blond and extremely handsome man in his late thirties walking towards me.

"Mrs. Allen?" he asked.

"Yes?" I replied.

"I'm Det. Kamon. Why don't you come with me?" he said, smiling.

I followed Det. Kamon to an office where he introduced me to Sergeant Williams, who also was working on the case.

"Well, where would you like to start?" Det. Kamon asked, pointing out a chair for me to sit in.

I told Det. Kamon and Sgt. Williams, "I've already started working on a summary of events that I feel will help, and I'll have it finished soon."

Det. Kamon leaned forward in his chair and said, "We need anything you can tell us as we and the South Carolina police are still in the dark as far as details about Freddie, such as his whereabouts while he was on the run. Whatever you know or can find out that will help to make a solid case against Freddie and David is important to us."

At the end of our meeting, Det. Kamon said he'd be in touch with me, handing me his card to contact him if I came on something before finishing the summary of events. He also gave me another detective's name, Ethan McMurry, who was with the Gaffney police.

"I've mentioned you to him, but why don't you let him know you're working with us again?"

Agreeing to do so, I went home and contacted Detective McMurry the following day. He had a very young and soft southern tone to his voice. I felt he couldn't have many years under his belt as a detective but obviously took his job very seriously.

Happy that I could now cooperate in the case without the fear of being implicated, I told him I was ready to do whatever I could. Det. McMurry explained, "Freddie is refusing to talk." I let him know of the summary of events I was working on. "You'll be getting a copy of it soon," I promised.

A few days later, I received a Gaffney newspaper with a front-page article about Freddie from Det. McMurry. It was an interview with Billy's younger brother, Reverend Perry Posey. In it Perry Posey stated he didn't know who turned Freddie in, but he was grateful to the person who did and hoped to tell them one day. I resolved that one day we would meet.

One thing I wanted to know was whether Billy had known Freddie before the murder. His brother might have new information to add to my summary of events. I wanted to call Rev. Posey.

Picking up the phone, I dialed information, and obtained Rev. Posey's home phone number. I decided to call immediately. There was no time to waste if we were to shore up the evidence against Freddie.

"Hello?" A woman answered.

"Is Rev. Posey in?" I asked, trying to sound composed.

"No, I'm sorry; he isn't in right now," she replied.

"I'll try back later then, thank you," I said, and quickly hung up. Later that night I called again.

"Hello?" the same woman answered.

"Is Rev. Posey in?" I asked.

"No, I'm sorry; he's not home yet. May I please ask who's calling?" she asked.

I paused for a moment because I didn't want to give my name out.

"Are you Rev. Posey wife?" I asked.

"Yes, yes, I am," she replied.

"Listen, I know you might not believe me, but I'm the one who turned Rev. Posey's brother's killer in," I said.

"You are?" she asked curiously.

"Yes," I said. "You can believe me. The police will back me up." I explained that I wasn't comfortable about giving her my name yet. "I really want to speak first to Rev. Posey. I am scared of the press getting my name."

Mrs. Posey understood. She told me the media had been hounding their family for an interview ever since Freddie's arrest. "Rev. Posey should be home in about an hour."

"Let me call back when Rev. Posey is there and I'll explain to him who I am. I think it's best that way," I said.

"Okay, that will be fine. I know he'd be happy to know who turned his brother's killer in. We thought he'd never get caught," she said.

Letting a couple of hours pass, I made a third attempt to call Rev. Posey, hoping I'd reach him this time.

"Hello?" Mrs. Posey answered.

"Hi, Mrs. Posey, it's me again," I said.

"Okay, let me get him for you," she said.

Covering the receiver of the phone, I could hear muffled talking in the background. I wasn't sure what to expect when Rev. Posey took the phone.

"Hello?" said a man with a deep but gentle voice.

"Rev. Posey?" I asked.

"Yes, ma'am, this is he," he replied.

"I assume your wife told you I would be calling and what it's about?" I said apprehensively.

"Yes, she did, but I have to be honest with you; we've been tricked by reporters before, so I apologize if I seem reluctant to discuss this over the telephone," Rev. Posey explained.

Knowing I had to say something that would convince Rev. Posey I was legitimate and had good reason to talk to him, I told him something about which I knew the reporters had no clue.

"This is very embarrassing," I said, my voice breaking. "My husband was having an affair with Freddie Turner and paid for Freddie's transsexual operation."

I could hear him gasp. Then he quickly recovered. "Okay, you don't need to say another word; I believe you. The police told me about your problem too, and I know for a fact the reporters don't know," Rev. Posey said.

"I read about you in the newspaper out here and felt the need to talk to you. I'm really sorry for all the pain this has caused your family," I said.

"Please, you don't know how thankful we are the killer finally has been captured. I'm just sorry you got caught up in this mess yourself. I think it's terrible how your husband involved you," Rev. Posey said.

"I really think he's mentally ill. He doesn't seem to feel any guilt in this and he's not cooperating with the California police either," I said.

"Yes, that's what I've been told out here by the police too," Rev. Posey said.

Feeling more at ease because of his kindness, I said "I want to tell you my name; it's Donita Allen." We talked for a while longer and then he said, "Well, Mrs. Allen, let's keep in close contact. Putting this killer away finally after all this time is a huge task."

"I'm doing everything I can to help the police, but my lawyer scared me by saying that I could be implicated and have my children taken away."

"You poor dear, that must have frightened you," Rev. Posey said. "And after you were so brave in coming forward."

I broke in, "Rev. Posey, I'm sorry if I seem rude in asking this, but I'm curious to know…" I paused for a moment.

"Yes, ma'am?" Rev. Posey said.

"Did Billy know Freddie before the night this happened?" I asked.

He hesitated before saying, "Yes, ma'am. In fact," he went on, "I remember Billy bringing Freddie over to the house one time, but I was introduced to this person as Freda. We were having a family get-together. I remember getting a strange feeling while looking over at what I thought was a woman. But then Billy leaned over to me and said, 'It's not what you think.' I don't know what he meant, 'cause he never said anything more," Rev. Posey explained.

"So you too were tricked," I finally said.

"I never would have guessed it was a man, but I do remember a real uncomfortable feeling being around that person," Rev. Posey said.

"I had the same feeling, until I found out the truth," I told him.

Another silence followed.

"Huh, you know, it just came to me, a situation that happened between Billy and this Freddie," Rev. Posey said in a puzzled tone.

"What's that?" I asked.

"Well, Billy was married at the time this happened, although he and his wife were separated; they were expecting a baby. Anyway, his wife was sitting in the car and Billy was standing outside the car talking to her, when Freddie approached them. I remember there was a verbal fight between him and Billy. It was over Freddie being jealous after he saw Billy and his wife in town together. In fact, Freddie had an argument with Billy's wife, too," Rev. Posey recounted.

A cold chill passed through me as I recalled the night of the Christmas party when Freddie began screaming at David and me in a jealous rage. "Something very similar happened to me," I said slowly, sharing with Rev. Posey my memory of that night with Freddie.

"I believe Freddie killed my brother in cold blood. In fact, I know he did, because I was the one who had to go to the motel that night and identify his body, and what I saw—was no accident," Rev. Posey said.

"Do you want to talk about it?" I asked softly, prompting him.

His voice was almost inaudible. "It's something I'll never forget. I knew my mother was too fragile to identify Billy's body, so though I was only seventeen years old then, I agreed to do it. I walked into that room. His body was lying across the bed, blood all over and bone stuck out of his arm; it was obviously broken," Rev. Posey said.

"A broken arm?" I echoed.

He said in a ringing voice I would never forget, "Yes, that's how I know Billy's death couldn't have been in self-defense. How can a man with a broken arm fight someone holding a 44-magnum on them? There was a fight that night all right, but Billy was the victim, not Freddie," Rev. Posey.

"Where did the gun come from?" I asked. My mind was spinning.

"It was Billy's gun. Billy played pool for big sums, so I guess he carried it for protection. In fact, I have a picture of Billy posing with the gun," Rev. Posey added.

Already aware of Freddie's violent past and hearing Rev. Posey's account of what he found in the room the night of the murder, I was sure the story David told me of Freddie defending himself was nothing more than another lie.

With Rev. Posey and me promising to keep in close touch with each other, we hung up. I sat down to work on my summary of events. Returning to the Burbank courthouse, I obtained new copies of those documents I had thrown away, upset for tossing the tape I had of David telling me details about Freddie, such as the name of the doctor in Colorado who had performed the sex change operation.

The very day I completed my account, Det. Kamon called.

"Hey, I was going to call you tomorrow morning. I just finished writing up my notes," I said.

"Good, can you bring it to me right away?" Det. Kamon asked.

"Definitely, I'll be right over." I replied.

Det. Kamon came down to meet me in the lobby of the police station, asking me to follow him to a conference room. Kamon sat on the edge of the table, while I sat down in a chair in front of him as he began reading my account and the documents I'd brought.

As he thumbed through the pages, I watched Det. Kamon's expression change from serious to surprised. Chuckling, he shook his head from side to side.

"What?" I asked, curious about his reaction.

"Well, one time I was having lunch in Toluca Lake, right down the street from Freddie's apartment. Anyway, I was sitting at the very end of the counter, and I noticed this woman sitting on the opposite end. I got this weird feeling about her. This is what's so funny; I realized when we went to arrest Valerie, that it was the same person I had seen at the counter that day," Det. Kamon said.

"You've got to be kidding me," I said, surprised.

"No, it's true, and I thought it was a real female. She was attractive. In fact, she looked a little like Whitney Houston, but there just was something odd about her. She was sitting too far away from me to observe closely what it was that gave me that feeling," Det. Kamon explained.

"Was Freddie with someone?" I asked.

"No, she was by herself eating lunch," Det. Kamon replied.

"How long ago?" I asked.

"Maybe a year before the arrest," Det. Kamon replied.

"So I guess both you and I were fooled," I said.

"Yep, seems that way," Det. Kamon answered with a half smile.

After Det. Kamon made some copies of the materials I'd given him, I headed back to the house.

The next day I received a call from Det. McMurry in South Carolina, letting me know he had received a fax from Det. Kamon in reference to the account I had written up and the documents I found. "We're going to use them to try and get a confession out of Freddie," he informed me. I hoped he'd be able to accomplish that mission soon, because it might quiet the notoriety which I knew sooner or later would get to me.

The newspapers were still filled with the Valerie/Freddie story. I scoured them all looking for clues to follow up on. Later that day, I read a newspaper article stating that Billy had died from multiple gunshots wounds to the groin and leg. As I thought back to the several versions of the story David had told me, the first one, in which he claimed Valerie shot Billy in the chest in self-defense, didn't match up. Rev. Posey had told me that Billy also had a broken arm. Today's report on Billy's wounds, in addition to what David told me, that Freddie said it was revenge for all the men who had never accepted him as a real female, made more sense than self-defense.

As I continued reading the article, I found out more about what happened the night of the murder. According to this account, Freddie had called a taxi from a pay phone, then he ran back into the room where Billy lay dying, grabbed some clothes and the bullet shells off the floor and ran back outside.

Once the taxi arrived, Freddie jumped in the back, pointed the gun at the back of the taxi driver's head and told the driver he'd just killed a man and to start driving to Spartanburg. Unknowingly, in his frightened state Freddie accidentally dropped some of the bullet shells on the floor of the taxi.

Once they arrived in Spartanburg, Freddie jumped out of the cab and ran off into the darkness. The cab driver quickly called police, telling them a man dressed as a woman had just held him up at gunpoint, confessing he'd just killed a man and left him in the motel where the driver had picked Freddie up. Responding to the call, police found Billy's lifeless body in room number ten of the motel.

After the Gaffney police identified Freddie Turner as the alleged killer, the FBI and state agencies were called to help in the search. Several times they came close, but as other state agencies unknowingly kept releasing Freddie under different aliases for petty crimes, he skipped from state to state, eluding capture. As the weeks and months passed into years, Freddie seemed to have vanished. The FBI dropped its search in 1984 and the case became inactive, as cold and dead as Billy's body.

I continued gathering information. Wanting to know more of the history between Billy and Freddie, I called Rev. Posey to see what else he knew about Freddie's past.

"Hey, I'm glad you called. I remembered something after we got off the phone the other night," Rev. Posey said.

"Good, I was calling because I had a couple of questions I wanted to ask you. First, tell me what you remembered," I said.

"Well, this happened the evening before Billy's twenty-fifth birthday, which was the night he was killed," Rev. Posey said.

"What?" I said, surprised.

"This might have been why Billy was at the bar that night, celebrating, but I don't know for certain, because he went there often," Rev. Posey explained.

"Listen, I have a question, and please understand, I don't mean this in a disrespectful way. I'm just trying to help the police," I said.

"Ask anything you want," Rev. Posey, said.

"Was there a relationship between Freddie and Billy? I only ask this because my husband David, as you know, had one with Freddie," I said.

"No, I don't think so, but Billy told me how Freddie, who I think I told you I knew as Freda at that time, used to frequent the bar Billy went to. According to Billy, Freda, who I now know is Freddie," he sighed heavily then went on, "had a sort of crush on Billy, but Billy didn't want to be anything more than friends. How and why they ended up at the motel, no one knew or understood. Maybe Freddie followed or met Billy there," Rev. Posey said.

I took a moment to think over how I was going to tell him my next disclosure. "I think there's something else you should know," I said softly.

"What's that?" Rev. Posey asked.

"Well, the newspaper up here said that Billy was shot in the groin and leg. That doesn't match the first story David said Freddie told him. It does, however, match the story David later told me Freddie admitted to him," I said.

"What did your husband tell you?" Rev. Posey asked.

"He first said Freddie shot Billy in the chest a couple times in self-defense and that Billy was on the floor of the motel room, but then he later said Freddie admitted it was a relief after killing Billy, that it was revenge for all the men who never accepted him as a real female. Now that I know Billy wasn't shot in the chest, but the groin area, David's second account of Freddie's story makes more sense. You know what's so frightening about this is the fact that these are two similar situations. Both Billy and David were married, both obvious victims of Freddie's violent temper and Freddie's jealousy over Billy's wife and now me," I explained.

"You're right; that is scary!" Rev. Posey said.

"I'm working on a few things I still need to find out. I'll call you back, okay?" I said.

"Yes, please do let me know if you learn anything new," Rev. Posey replied.

Getting off the phone with Rev. Posey, I had more understanding of the psychological pattern Freddie followed with both Billy and David. Perhaps if I saw him and acted sympathetic, David might be willing to tell me other things he knew about Freddie's past. I took a risk and went to see him.

The door to David's studio was locked. After I knocked a few times, David unlocked it. He looked surprised to find me standing on the other side.

"What are you doing here?" David asked.

"I need to talk to you," I said.

"You couldn't talk to me over the phone?" He stared at me oddly and I sensed that my behavior puzzled him a great deal.

"No, please, David, just let me in," I said. David stood motionless, a concerned look on his face.

"How do I know you don't have a gun in your purse?" David said.

My heart began to pound. "If you want to go through my purse before I come in, you can," I replied, extending it.

"What's this about?" David asked.

"I'm not here to fight with you, David. I just want to talk to you, okay?" I said, looking at David searchingly. I could feel the tension between us.

David gave me a look of mistrust, then sighed and opened the door further, letting me in. We walked up the stairs to the second floor of his studio and sat down across from each other.

"You know, the more I try to understand what the deal is with Freddie, I mean his personality, the more confused I am," I said.

"What do you mean—confused?" David asked.

"Remember I showed you that list of Freddie's arrests?" I asked.

"Yeah, well, I had no idea she had such a long criminal history," David replied.

"Aside from murder, you mean?" I blurted out.

"Call it what you want," David replied.

Seeing him getting jittery, I changed my approach.

"I never showed you the paper I got on Freddie pertaining to the assault with a deadly weapon. It was another victim of Freddie's, his girlfriend at the time," I said.

David looked at me questioningly, as I went on telling him that the girl Freddie attacked feared Freddie so much that she jumped out of the moving car they were in.

"I'm aware Valerie has a temper. She attacked me in a car too," David replied.

"Are you referring to when we were at the Christmas party or the times you came over to my apartment with cuts and bruises on you head and face?" I asked.

David sighed. "Actually, there was another time I specifically recall."

"Why don't you tell me what happened?" I said softly.

He looked almost relieved as he began.

"Well, I was called up to work on a movie that was being filmed on location in San Francisco that required my staying there a couple months. Anyway, Valerie was living here at the studio house at the time and I remember getting these calls from her, saying how bored she was from sitting around the house and that she couldn't go anywhere. I felt bad for her and flew her up to San Francisco to visit me."

"And then?" I asked.

"Well, I picked her up at the airport and, as we drove off in the car, she went into this sort of neurotic state, then started repeatedly punching me in the leg," David replied.

"Why, what caused it?" I asked.

"I don't know. I'd had several incidents like that with her, even at the studio, which is why I had to move her out and into her own place," David replied.

"David, don't you see Freddie is a sociopath with a long history of violence to the point that he killed a man?" I said, as I looked at David in desperation.

"Yeah, well," David, said, tilting his head, as if not to accept the truth.

"Tell me, David, did Freddie ever tell you anything else about his past while he was with you?" I asked.

Now that he had begun opening up, he almost seemed to want to go on. "Well, when we first met, Freddie told me a story about when he was a young teen, living at home with his mother, father, sisters and brother. Freddie was in his mother's bedroom, standing in front of a full-length mirror, looking at himself while wearing his mother's panties. Suddenly Freddie's brother walked into the bedroom, catching him. Yelling at Freddie, he asked why Freddie was wearing their mother's panties. Then when he didn't answer, he just pulled on some jeans and shrugged, Freddie's brother began hitting him and chased him out of the house and down the street. Freddie didn't go back."

"He really must have been very mixed up," I said, trying to sound sympathetic. Then I picked up on something David had told me earlier.

"How did Freddie support himself after he moved out of your place?" I asked. David said Freddie continued placing personals in the newspaper; then he admitted that Rick and Freddie had once been lovers and that Rick had helped Freddie financially.

"Why do you want to know all this anyway? What's the point?" David asked.

"Interest, David. So Rick and Freddie were lovers too, and he also knew about the murder. Does Carolyn know about all this?" I asked.

"No, I don't believe she does and I don't see any point in her knowing. I'm sure she's shocked at what's happened as it is," David replied.

"I'm going home now; I'll talk to you later," I said, standing up and grabbing my purse.

Arriving back at the house, I grew more and more curious as to what Carolyn did or didn't know, as David had lied to me so much already. Deciding to find out, I called Carolyn.

"Carolyn. Hi, it's Donita."

"Oh my God, isn't this crazy about Valerie? I can't believe it's true!" Carolyn said breathlessly.

"Carolyn, I have to ask you something. Did you know Valerie was a man?" I asked.

"No! And I was shocked. We were all in the bathroom with her that one night at the restaurant when she complained about getting bad menstrual cramps too, remember?" Carolyn replied.

"So you had no idea at all?" I asked, again.

"No, none whatsoever!" she replied.

"Did Rick tell you he knew?" I asked.

"I asked him, but Rick said he didn't know," she paused, the silence came over the line.

"Are you still there Carolyn?" I asked.

"Yes. There's something else you should know, Donita," she said.

"What's that?"

"Valerie used to call here drunk, yelling how she was going to get you out of the picture," Carolyn replied.

"When was this?" I asked shivering.

"It went on for quite a while, until all this started coming out," Carolyn replied.

I bit back my fear and anger. "Did you know Rick and Freddie were lovers at one time?" I asked.

"Rick told me that was when they first met, but he said Valerie wasn't his type of girl, so they just stayed friends," Carolyn said.

Just as I was getting ready to ask Carolyn more questions, Sam and Jessica walked in the door from school.

"Carolyn, I have to go; my kids are home," I said. I swiftly hung up the phone.

After I settled the kids down with their homework, I threw myself down on my bed. Feeling sorry for myself, I cried over how my life had turned upside down. I let the tears pour out for a while, then, telling myself I had to pull myself together for my children's sakes, splashed cold water on my face and took a walk around the block in hopes of helping to clear my mind. Entering the front door, I heard the phone ringing. I picked it up.

"Hello?" I said.

"There is a collect call for David Allen," an operator said.

"Where is the caller from?" I asked.

"Gaffney, South Carolina, Police Department," she replied.

Stunned, I slammed down the phone. I couldn't believe Freddie still was brazen enough to try and call David at our house. Didn't he know David had moved out? Or was this just Freddie's attempt to let me know he knew just where to find me if he ever got out?

chapter twelve

Truth
Unfolds

The next morning, determined not to stop my own search for evidence that would help the police convict Freddie, I looked over the documents I still had. Soon, I came across the paperwork on his hit-and-run accident and a name caught my attention, Robert Carnes. The name sounded familiar. Searching my memory I realized I had been introduced to Robert at the luncheon to which David took the kids and me, when I first met Freddie. What was the connection with Freddie, I wondered? I decided to try and track him down.

I called information, obtained his phone number and gave him a call.

"Hello?" a low-pitched man's voice answered.

"Is this Robert Carnes?" I asked.

"Yes it is," he replied.

"Do you know a Valerie Taylor?" I asked.

"Yes. Who is this?" Robert asked.

Goose bumps rose on my body.

"Then you know that Valerie has been arrested and who she really is," I went on.

"Who is this?" Robert asked again, his curiosity obviously piqued.

"My name is Donita. I'm David Allen's wife. We met at Valerie's apartment years ago," I replied.

"Yes, I remember," he replied.

"Robert, I'd like to ask you a couple of questions. If you don't mind," I said.

"What do you want to know?" he asked.

"Well, I'm sorry if this seems forward, but did you know Valerie was a man?" I asked.

"No, I didn't know until I turned on the television one day after getting home from work and saw the story of her being arrested for murder," Robert replied. "I'm still trying to deal with it. Valerie seemed to have a lot of secrets."

"Well, you may not know this part then. David is the one who paid for Freddie's sex change and helped him change his name. What really got me is that David knew about the murder the whole time," I said.

"Do the police know this? I didn't see David's name in the news when they showed the story about Valerie," he said.

"Yes, they know, but they haven't arrested him, yet. Did Freddie ever get violent with you?" I asked.

"No, but she did financially ruin me. I had to file bankruptcy because of her," Robert replied sourly.

"Since you're leveling with me, let me tell you something," he continued. "I have some pictures I took that day at Valerie's apartment. Valerie has her arms wrapped around one of your kids," Robert said.

"What! I don't remember any picture being taken with my kids and Freddie. Where was I when it was taken?" I asked.

"I think you were in the bathroom or outside taking a walk," he replied. "I remember it got sort of emotional inside."

"Listen, Robert, would you be willing to meet me somewhere and bring those pictures you took? Maybe I can answer some questions you might have about Freddie, as well," I said.

"Yes, I can do that," Robert replied.

Robert and I agreed to meet later that night at a restaurant called Baronies, on top of a large hill, a halfway point between us.

Later that night, after getting a baby-sitter, I drove over to the restaurant to meet Robert. Giving my name to the hostess, I was taken to the table where Robert was seated. Recognizing me he quickly stood up, pulling out a chair for me.

"Would you like to order drinks before dinner?" the waitress asked as she gave us each a menu.

"I'll just have a glass of water, please," I replied.

"A Coke for me," Robert said.

To avoid having the other customers hear us, I leaned toward him.

"Robert, I hope you'll understand if some of my questions seem forward, but I really need to get some answers. David's been very secretive about Freddie," I said.

"I had a feeling David had something to do with this. He and Valerie seemed pretty close," he said.

I nodded. "Would you tell me how you and Freddie met?" I asked.

"A personal advertisement in the newspaper," Robert replied.

"Let me guess; female looking for a male?" I said, giving a nervous laugh.

"Actually, yes," Robert replied.

"Yeah, that's how David met Freddie too," I said.

"I think most of the men Valerie met were through the personals," he said.

"How long have you known Freddie?" I asked.

"I met her not long before that luncheon she had at her apartment," he said. "By the way, I brought the pictures with me."

Robert handed them across the table, as the waitress approached with our drinks.

"Are you ready to order?" she asked.

"I'm sorry; I haven't even looked at the menu yet," I said apologetically.

"We'll need another few minutes," Robert said, casually waving her away.

When the waitress walked away, I looked down at the photos. The first picture was of Freddie, Robert, Sam and Jessica. Freddie's arms were wrapped around Sam as Jessica stood next to him. Chills ran through my body.

"It almost looks like a family photo." Robert's words may have been the most frightening I had ever heard. Just thinking of Freddie raising my children made me want to go over to his apartment and settle things for good.

"You didn't take these pictures, Robert; you're in both of them," I said.

"I forgot I was, until I looked for them to show you. Valerie must have asked someone to take them, but I don't remember who it was," Robert replied.

"Can I keep the pictures, Robert?" I asked.

"Yes, but I want to be cut out of them. I don't want to be associated with Valerie in any way," he replied.

"I understand," I said. "I wish David had made that decision. Do you know about his situation with Valerie?"

"Well, I do know David was financially helping Valerie for a long time," Robert replied.

"David has done more than his fair share of helping Freddie," I said pensively.

Robert abruptly changed the subject, obviously having questions of his own on his mind.

"How long ago was it that Valerie had the sex change?" Robert asked.

"About ten years ago, then he got his name changed. By the way, do you remember Rick Cooper?" I asked.

"Yes, I met him a few times; in fact he was at that luncheon at Valerie's too," Robert recalled.

"What do you know about Rick?" I asked.

"Just that he's someone Valerie met from the personals also," Robert replied.

"Rick knew all along, Robert. About the murder and Valerie's sex change," I said.

Robert looked down at the table; shaking his head in amazement.

"Who else do you know of that might have met Freddie through the personals?" I asked.

"Well, I remember Valerie had quite a few dinner parties at her apartment that I attended. There was a new guy who showed up last year," Robert replied.

"Do you remember his name?" I asked.

"Yeah, Roger something. I think his last name was Mills," Robert replied.

"Do you recall David ever being at any of these dinner parties? I mean around the same time this Roger came into the picture?" I asked.

"Yes, and, although I didn't ask, it seemed to me you weren't in the picture anymore. David was acting like a single guy," Robert replied.

"Was this after August last year that you saw David act this way?" I pressed.

"Yeah, I think it was. When did you and David get married?" Robert asked.

"Last year in August," I replied, angrily.

"Donita, I'm sorry this happened to you. I realize now from what you've told me, David can be just as manipulating as Valerie was." Robert spoke with a concerned look of sympathy on his face.

"I'm sorry for you too, Robert," I said sadly.

Robert seemed innocent, vulnerable and clueless as to what and who Freddie really was.

As I sat there finishing dinner with him, my thoughts were already spiraling inward. I began wondering about Roger; had Freddie also taken him for a ride? I turned the question over in my mind, deciding I'd contact Roger next.

Soon the waitress brought over the check. I asked Robert if he would mind if I got in touch with him again. He said that would be okay. We said our goodbyes and headed off in different directions.

The next morning I made an appointment with Dr. Ashford to see her later that day. After I had filled her in on what I had discovered so far, she became concerned.

"Donita, you could be putting yourself in a dangerous position by meeting these men who are involved with Freddie," Dr. Ashford said. "You don't know anything about them except they were involved with a sociopath and that could mean they're psychotic personalities too."

"Robert's okay," I replied.

"Yes, but what about this Roger Mills person you want to talk to? They all may not be like Robert," Dr. Ashford said.

"That's a risk I'm willing to take, Dr. Ashford. For five years I was manipulated and used. If I'm to help the police get enough evidence to keep Freddie in jail for a long time, and get through this myself, I have to do all I can. Otherwise he may not be convicted and I'll be in danger and never be able to heal the damage David did to me," I replied.

"You're gutsy; I'll say that," Dr. Ashford commented.

"Look, at least Freddie's in jail now. He was my major worry," I said.

However, as I walked to my car after leaving Dr. Ashford's office, I began thinking about what she said about the other men with whom Freddie was involved. I admitted to myself that she could be right, but I knew my fear wasn't enough to make me stop. An even greater fear was what Det. Kamon had alluded to—without more evidence, Freddie could get out of this. Someone out there who knew Freddie could have the answers we needed and I was going to keep looking.

Arriving home, I took out all the history I still had on Freddie, spreading the papers across the kitchen table. I scanned Freddie's mug shots and the pictures Robert had given me. Noticing differences in the facial features between the pictures, I got out a magnifying glass

David Allen and Donita Woodruff in happier times.

Sam and Jessica, Donita Woodruff''s children.

After being asked to bring a large sum of money into Romania, Donita's concerns regarding David started to escalate.

Donita Woodruff became suspicious after meeting Valerie Taylor for the first time.

David Allen denied to Donita Woodruff
any wrong doing.

Valerie Taylor (right) had an ongoing
relationship with David Allen.

POLICE DEPT.
GREENVILLE, S.C.

Freddie Lee Turner in a
mugshot from June 17, 1974.

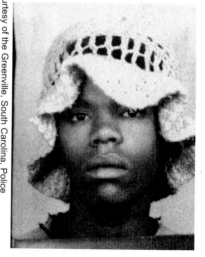

Freddie Lee Turner in a different
mugshot taken in Greenville,
South Carolina.

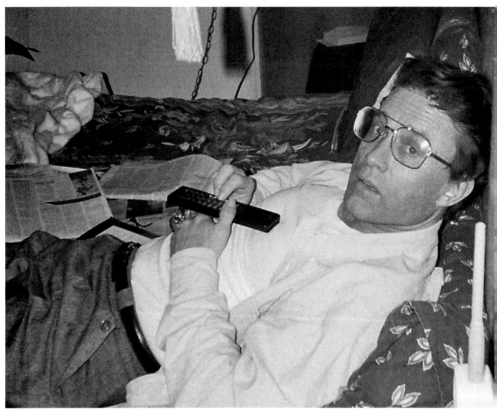

David Allen relaxing in his and Donita's home in Burbank, California.

David and Donita in Romania where he admitted to his relationship with Valerie Taylor to Donita.

Donita thought the past was behind her as she prepared for her wedding to David Allen.

David's missing wedding ring was discovered in Donita and David's backyard.

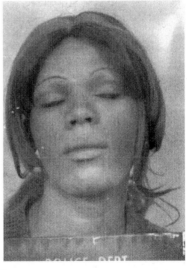

A mugshot of Valerie Taylor taken in Greenville, South Carolina in 1977.

Valerie Taylor was extradited to stand trial for murder in Greenville, South Carolina.

Photo courtesy of the Spartanburg Herald-Journal, Les Duggins Sr.

Valerie Taylor on the day of her sentencing in Greenville, South Carolina.

Although sentenced to fifteen years in prison, later the judge suspended Valerie's sentence to three years behind bars.

Donita Woodruff appeared on national television in disguise in order to avoid retribution from Valerie Taylor.

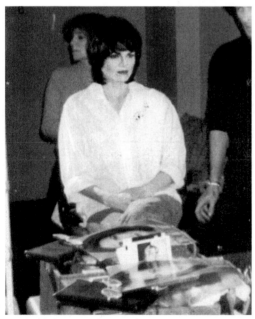

Donita Woodruff preparing for an appearance on national television.

Donita Woodruff as she appears today.

to get a closer look.

I studied the changes between the early and late pictures. Early on he was pictured with semi-open lips in one of the mug shots; there was a big gap between his front teeth. Then I glanced back at the newer pictures Robert gave me. The gap was closed; Freddie's teeth were perfect. I looked at Freddie's nose, first in the early then in the later pictures; it seemed Freddie had also had the bone at the end of his nose smoothed out. In addition, the knot on his chin, apparent in every mug shot, was also gone.

I remembered David telling me he had taken Freddie as his date for the Academy Awards, just before the sex change. I knew they had to have panned the camera at David when his name was called out as a nominee. David and Freddie must have been sitting in the audience somewhere up front. Thinking of all those celebrities who were unknowingly sitting next to a cold-blooded killer with a double identity gave me the chills.

I decided it was time to talk to Roger Mills; I got his phone number from information and wrote it down. I hesitated, feeling uneasy and not knowing if he knew about me or would be willing to talk to me. Nevertheless, I thought that if I approached him as I had Robert, he might be willing to meet with me.

Taking a deep breath, I picked up the phone and began dialing.

"Hello?" A man with a New England accent answered.

"Is this Roger Mills?" I asked.

"Yes, it is, who's this?" Roger calmly asked.

"Do you know a Valerie Taylor?" I asked.

"Who is this?" I noticed a slight edge had crept into his voice.

I took a deep breath and then went on.

"I don't want to say who I am right now. I just need to know if you know a Valerie Taylor," I replied.

"Yes, I do," Roger replied.

"Okay, I know I have the right person then," I said.

"Is there some news about Valerie?" Roger asked.

"Yes, I know a lot of things you might be interested in," I replied.

"Such as?" Roger asked.

I fingered the paperwork spread out before me.

"I have documents and pictures that would surprise you. But I first want to know if you'd be willing to share what you have or know about Freddie with me," I said.

"I might have something you'd be interested in. Did you want to meet somewhere?" Roger asked.

"I think that would be a good idea," I replied.

"When and where?" Roger asked.

"Do you know Baronies Restaurant on Riverside Drive?" I asked.

"Yes, I do," he replied. "I used to take Valerie there."

"Okay, can you meet me at the bar, tomorrow afternoon at one o'clock?" I asked.

"Yes, I can do that, but how will I know who you are?" Roger asked.

"Just sit at the bar and wait for me. Tell the bartender your name and I'll ask him to point you out," I said.

"Okay, that's fine with me," he replied.

"Please bring whatever you have on Freddie," I said.

"You too," Roger replied.

Getting off the phone, I remembered Dr. Ashford's warning and had an uneasy feeling about the meeting, so I called Det. Kamon, filling him in on my meeting with Robert and telling him I was going to meet Roger, another of Freddie's many acquaintances, the next day.

"What's Roger's last name?" Det. Kamon asked.

"Mills," I said.

"And where is it you two are going to meet, and when?" Det. Kamon asked.

"A restaurant on Riverside Drive called Baronies. We're meeting at the bar at one o'clock tomorrow afternoon," I said.

"I know where that is," he replied.

I told Det. Kamon that I wanted to handle this myself. I didn't want the police involved, as it might scare Roger off.

"Just be careful and make sure he doesn't follow you when you leave," Det. Kamon advised.

Promising to call Det. Kamon back after the meeting with Roger, I hung up and went into the desk drawer to look for a business-sized envelope to put Freddie's pictures and documents in. I also found a mini-cassette recorder and slipped it in my purse, figuring it might not be a bad idea to record the conversation. I spent another restless night tossing and turning with thought; the morning and my meeting couldn't come soon enough.

Arriving at the restaurant, I parked my truck in the lot and sat for a few moments mapping out my plain of action. Not wanting to tell Roger my real name, due to the uneasy feeling I had about him, I decided to introduce myself as Sandy.

I made my way to the bar. Italian music played in the background as the flicker of candlelight illuminated the cramped world of secrets I had just entered. Between the old-fashioned music and the creeping shadows, I felt as if I were in one of David's movies. Approaching the bar, I noticed a few men sitting alone. I walked up and leaned towards the bartender, asking in a low voice which one of them was Roger. Without saying a word, the bartender pointed out a tall, balding forty-ish man sitting at the end of the bar.

Walking towards Roger, I said hello. He glanced over at me, smiling. Nervous, I held out my hand to shake his.

"Well, you found me. I'm Roger Mills," he said.

"Donita Allen," I said. My shoulders collapsed as I realized that in my jumpy state I had just blown my cover, giving my real name.

"I kind of figured it was you I was going to be meeting," Roger said.

"Then I guess you know I'm David's wife. But he told me he'd never met you before, so how could you have known it was going to be me? How?" I asked, in confusion.

"I know a lot about you, Donita," Roger replied, chuckling, as he raised his eyebrow and took a sip from his drink. I stood still, staring at Roger, my uneasy feeling about him growing.

"I'm sorry, but I find this a little strange. We've never met before and it was only recently that I even heard your name," I remarked.

"I've known about you for a long time now," Roger replied.

"Huh, interesting. I'd like to know what it is you've heard about me and from whom. I need to go to the ladies' room first. Then we can sit down at a booth and talk," I said.

"Okay, meet me over at that booth," Roger replied, pointing at one.

As I walked away from Roger, I took a deep breath, questioning whether what David had told me about Roger was just another lie. In the bathroom, I went into a stall and locked the door. Opening my purse, I pulled out the mini-tape recorder and slipped it into the front compartment where it could pick up whatever Roger would tell me, then I zipped the purse closed.

Strolling back to the bar area where Roger was waiting, I reached in my purse unobtrusively and pushed record. Then I sat down close to him.

"So, Roger, tell me; what is it you know about me?" I asked, smiling.

"Enough that I hated your guts without ever meeting you," Roger replied, with a slight smile.

Shocked at Roger's comment, I reminded myself to keep my cool.

"Let me guess—Freddie? And I assume you met him from the personals?" I asked.

"As a matter of fact, yes," Roger admitted.

I realized I had to be careful with him. I knew I needed to get his trust and, in view of his bluntness, I felt the best way to do it was to fight fire with fire.

"Look, Roger, whatever you've heard about me, I can promise it isn't true. Do you want to tell me about it?" I asked.

"Well, first off, Valerie told me you've gotten her fired from several jobs—that you'd call her boss, spreading lies about her, making her life miserable. She also told me you've been harassing her for years, calling her apartment and hanging up, and when she'd volunteer her time to help the community, you'd find out, call there too and cause trouble for her.

"According to Valerie you were jealous of her friendship with David and made her life a living hell. Now she's saying, because of you, she's in jail for a murder she didn't commit. So, if that doesn't explain why I've hated you all this time, I don't know what will," Roger said.

Amazed, I listened to the lies Freddie had told Roger, realizing Freddie had manipulated him as well.

"And you believe all this?" I asked.

"Well, why would Valerie lie? I mean, what would she have to gain from it?" Roger asked.

"Because he was jealous of David and me being together," I said.

"Yeah, well, I guess that part may make sense," Roger replied.

"Maybe after I show you some of the things I've found out about Freddie, you'll believe my side of the story," I said.

"Well, let me see what you've got," Roger said.

I leaned over, picked up the yellow envelope off the seat, pulled out Freddie's mug shots and handed them over to Roger.

"Whoa!" Roger said, as he quickly sat back against the booth. His face grew more and more horrified, as I continued passing him more mug shots. "Yeah, well, hmmm, I have to admit; these are shockers," Roger said.

I nodded and then handed him Freddie's name change document.

"It's right there in black and white. Valerie Nicole Taylor, AKA Freddie Lee Turner," I said.

"Well, she told me that part was true when she called me from jail, but these mug shots are a further surprise," Roger said, a look of concern on his face.

I watched him closely as I filled in all I'd learned of Freddie's criminal past, proving what I could with the documents I still had and then explaining, "Freddie has a habit of manipulating people to get what he wants." I shook my head. "As for all those hang-up calls I supposedly made..."

"Yeah?" Roger bit his lip.

"Well, Freddie was making those hang-up calls to me, not the other way around. And all the other things he told you are nothing but lies. None of it ever happened. And by the way, if you didn't already know, David is the one who paid for Freddie's sex change operation and helped get his name changed. David did all that, knowing all along that Freddie was wanted for murder.

"Who had more to lose—Freddie or me? I'm just a housewife with two kids. Moreover, it was Freddie who was jealous over my, well, let's just say fake relationship with David—now the truth is out that my kids and I were used by David, while he carried on with Freddie," I said.

Roger looked at me; when he spoke again his voice was weary, strained and newly sympathetic. "Well, I don't have anything big like you do, but I do have an interesting copy of the phone bill from Valerie's apartment," Roger said. "She said she had to keep changing her phone number because of you, so she asked me to put it in my name, so you couldn't find her number. Anyway, she left a big phone bill behind and I got stuck with having to pay it. I was curious why it was so big and ordered a copy of it. There were a lot of 976 numbers she called. I called one of them and it turned out to be one of those telephone dating services. There were also a few calls made to South Carolina," Roger said.

"When did you have the phone put in your name?" I asked.

"Oh, I think it was the summer I met her," Roger replied.

I quickly realized that it was around the same time that the phone company had called David's studio saying they were going to disconnect a phone under David's name for nonpayment.

"Can I see it?" I asked.

"Yeah, I have it right here. It's from the last two months before she was arrested," Roger said, as he handed me a copy.

Looking the bill over, I saw rows of calls made to 976 numbers and a few to Greenville, South Carolina that had been made in the last days before Freddie's arrest.

"Roger, do you know how Billy was killed?" I asked.

"Only what I was told by Valerie, that it was out of self-defense," Roger replied.

"No, I mean do you know about Billy's wounds?" I asked.

"No," Roger replied.

"Freddie unloaded a .44 magnum into Billy's groin. Now does that sound like self-defense to you?" I asked adamantly.

"No, that sounds deliberate." A pained look crossed his face.

"Think about it: shooting a man to death, beating David on several occasions, not to mention the time Freddie punched David in the side of the head in front of me. Then he convinces you everything is my fault. Now, what does that tell you about Freddie?" I asked.

"Yeah, I'm wondering that myself, now that you've told me all this and shown me the documents," Roger said.

"There's something else you should know. David's not to be trusted any more than Freddie. He's just as much a manipulator and liar. In fact, David not only has been financially helping Freddie this whole time, even when he was with me, but he's also refusing to talk to the police about what he knows concerning what Freddie told him about Billy's murder," I said.

"You know, I was wondering who was paying all of Valerie's bills. I knew she wasn't working, because she'd sleep half the day away, and then she'd go out almost every night. I couldn't understand how she could afford the fancy clothes, furniture and jewelry either," Roger said.

"Well, I know now David paid a majority of Freddie's bills, like rent and other things, but there was also another man Freddie was seeing who he drove into bankruptcy," I said.

"That strikes a chord," he said slowly. "I do remember one time asking Valerie who was paying for her other bills. She got angry and said if I wasn't paying them, then it was none of my business, but I kind of figured David still was involved. Valerie talked about him all the time," Roger said.

"David told me Freddie told you to call him if you had any questions?" I asked.

"Yes, that was when Valerie called me from jail to tell me she was arrested for a murder she didn't commit, but then later she admitted to me she did it, but said it was in self-defense," Roger said.

"Did you see on the news that Freddie denied ever being a man?" I asked.

"Yeah, I saw that and it reminded me of an embarrassing situation Valerie told me about," Roger said.

"What was that?" I asked.

"Well, a maintenance man came over to fix the bathroom plumbing and Valerie hadn't shut the front door all the way. Anyway, the maintenance man showed up and found the door ajar, thinking it was left open for him. He entered the apartment and went to the bathroom to do the repairs, where he found Valerie in front of the bathroom mirror with shaving cream all over her body. They startled each other and the maintenance ran out of the apartment," Roger said, trying to hold back from laughing.

"Did the maintenance man ever come back?" I asked, as I laughed.

"I don't know; she never said," Roger replied. "But there was another situation that happened with Valerie that's bugged me for a long time."

"What's that?" I asked.

"Well, I bought her a kitten as a surprise, along with all the stuff she'd need for it and, not too long after I had gotten it for her, I came over and it was nowhere in sight. When I asked Valerie where the kitten was, she said she had the bathtub filled with water and the kitten fell in and drowned," Roger said.

"How big was the kitten?" I asked.

"Too small to jump up on anything; I know that. That's why I found the story she told me so strange. Anyway, I felt badly, went out and got her another kitten to replace the first one. I went over her apartment soon afterward and again no kitten. So I asked where it was, and she told me she gave it to her cousin, because it was clawing up her furniture," Roger said.

"Cousin? I've been doing some research and Freddie doesn't have any family out here; they're all in South Carolina," I said.

As our talk came to a close, I asked Roger if he would give me a call if he remembered anything else. He agreed, I wrote down my number and we parted.

As I walked to my car, I thought over my meeting with Roger. I was surprised to find how open he was, even more so after being told how much he had hated me.

On my way home I kept wondering if Robert had ever seen either of the kittens at Freddie's apartment when he went to visit. Later that night I called to see if he had.

"Hey, it's me, Donita," I said.

"Hi, how are you? Did you find out anything new about Valerie?" Robert asked.

"Yes, but nothing that would win the case against him. But I have a question for you," I said.

"What is it?" Robert asked.

"Do you remember ever seeing a kitten at Freddie's apartment?" I asked.

"No, only fish. Valerie didn't like animals," Robert replied.

I paused, thinking a moment of Valerie's cruel streak and what had probably happened. I winced.

"Why?" Robert asked.

"Well, I met with Roger Mills today and he told me he had given Freddie a kitten as a gift, but when he went back over there, it was gone. Freddie said it drowned in the bathtub. Then Roger went out and bought Freddie another kitten, which supposedly Freddie gave to his cousin. The thing is, Freddie doesn't have any family here, so what happened to the second kitten?"

"I don't know, but it does makes you wonder," Robert replied. "Do you think Valerie killed both of them?" he asked.

"Well, it does sound suspicious, especially now that you told me he doesn't like animals." After we got off the phone, I wondered if

Rev. Posey could add to my knowledge of Freddie's cruelty to animals, one of the signs of being a sociopath.

After getting off the phone with Robert, I called Rev. Posey.

"Rev. Posey, how are you?" I asked when I got him on the phone.

"Hi, Donita, I'm all right. And you?" he said.

"I'm doing okay. I just called to see if anything was happening out there and to tell you a little about a meeting I just had," I replied.

"Well, you know, I'm glad you called," Rev. Posey said. "I want to fill you in on something kind of strange and unbelievable, but true, that might help the case," Rev. Posey went on.

"What is it?" I asked.

"Now, as I said, it's going to be hard to believe, but I know it to be a fact," Rev. Posey said.

"Okay, what is it?" I asked again.

"Gaffney had a police officer by the name of Jack Jones. He was small but very muscular. Some jokingly called him Tom Thumb. Anyway, he was working the night Billy was killed. Now, this is the part that's going to be hard to believe, but I'm telling you, it's the truth," Rev. Posey insisted.

"What is it?" I asked.

"Well, Jack didn't know how to read or write. The thing is, he wanted to be a police officer so badly and bugged the Gaffney Police Department so much that they finally gave up and swore him in. Anyway, he was so proud of his job and so nice to everyone that he was well respected in the community," Rev. Posey explained.

"Wait a minute, I'm sorry to interrupt, but how could he make reports if he couldn't read or write?" I asked.

"I was just going to get to that part. Jack used a tape recorder; then someone at the police department would write the reports from the tapes he made," Rev. Posey explained.

"This is unbelievable, but I believe you," I said.

"Wait, there's more. The reason why I'm telling you this is because it was Jack who was called to the scene after a taxicab driver called about Freddie. He was the first one to arrive there," Rev. Posey said.

"Go on," I said, curious to hear more.

"Well, there was an article written in the newspaper years ago about Jack Jones. He solved every crime he ever came across except for Billy's, and that haunted him. He was even quoted in the newspaper saying he was going to solve Billy's murder and then he was going to heaven. He also said he was hot on Freddie's trail and hoped to get the criminal before he died," the reverend said.

"Can I meet this Jack Jones?" I asked.

"Unfortunately no. Let me explain the rest. One day, while I was at the dentist, I got a call on my pager—a number, followed with a 911. I got scared, thinking something bad had happened to someone in my family, like a car accident or something, so I called the number immediately.

"It was Jack who answered when I called. He was trying to stay real calm over the phone. He made it clear to me he couldn't tell me what it was that was going on, but that I should leave from where I was and drive straight over to his house right away. He told me not to talk to anyone from that point on, until I got to his house, not even the police.

"So I got in my car and did just what he said and drove straight over to his house. When I got there, he quickly shut the door behind me, locking it, then looked out the windows, like he was nervous about something. He told me to sit down, that he had something shocking to tell me. I started getting really nervous too, because he could always keep his cool, but that day he seemed really on edge. Anyway, when I sat down and asked what was going on, he told me Freddie had just been arrested in California for Billy's murder," Rev. Posey explained.

"So that's how you found out, huh?" I said.

"Wait, there's more," Rev. Posey said.

"Please, go on," I said, my interest piqued.

"Well, what happened next is that Det. Jones showed me a tape, telling me it was the one he made in the motel room the night of Billy's murder. He said he knew Freddie killed Billy, that it was no case of self-defense, but clear-cut murder. Now here is the bad part: Jack died of a heart attack shortly after Freddie was arrested. His poor wife is really going through a horrible time right now," Rev. Posey said.

"Oh no," I replied.

"He really wanted to catch Freddie and solve Billy's murder, even when he retired, but nobody really knows what proof Jack had. It's too bad you didn't get to meet him. He would have been really proud of all the work you did bringing Freddie to justice. My main concern now is that tape Jack made," he said.

"I would have been honored to meet Jack, and as far as the tape goes, couldn't it still be in the house with his wife?" I asked.

"I hope so, but his wife is in bad shape," Rev. Posey told me in a concerned tone.

"We need to get that tape!" I said.

"Yes, before someone else does, but I don't want to bother his wife right now; she's still shook up over her husband passing so suddenly. We need to wait a little longer," he said.

"I wish we could get to her right away," I said. "But I understand you should be the one to determine when. Just don't wait too long. Proving Freddie is a cold-blooded killer is very important to both of us and all the others he hurt or will hurt in the future if he gets off and goes free."

chapter thirteen

Diabolic
Plan

The next day, I called Det. Kamon, asking him to meet me for lunch. "I have a lot to tell you," I informed him.

With a heightened sense of anticipation, I walked into the diner, finding the detective already there.

"So, what happened with that Roger guy?" Det. Kamon was quick to ask.

"I know, I should have called you, but I needed a day to let it sink in and then I got into a conversation with Rev. Posey, which I also need to tell you about," I began to explain.

Just then the waitress came over and we both ordered sandwiches, which she quickly brought.

After explaining my apprehension about the meeting with Roger, I said, "And I blew my cover when I accidentally revealed my real name."

"I guess we'd better sign you up for Detective 101. So should I expect you next Monday when we're initiating the new recruits?" he joked.

"It's not a bad idea considering all the narrow escapes I've had trying to bring all this out in the open," I laughed.

Then I filled him in on my conversation with Rev. Posey. Pausing to take a bite of my sandwich, I caught Det. Kamon staring at me with a serious look upon his face.

"What?" I asked.

"Freddie is a psycho-sociopath who may get away with murder," Det. Kamon said.

"I hope not to let that happen," I told Det. Kamon. "I'm going to Gaffney to meet Rev. Posey"

"Just be very careful down there," he warned me. "We've heard some rumors that Freddie still has some friends."

After lunch I headed back to the house and found a message from Roger on the answering machine. I quickly dialed his number.

"Hello?" Roger answered.

"Hi, Roger, it's Donita; what's up?" I asked. "Did you find something out?"

"No, but something has been bugging me and I feel I should tell you," Roger replied.

The tone of his voice gave me the impression there was a problem and it involved Freddie and me. Immediately I grew concerned but tried not to show it.

"Please, start with me," I replied.

"Do you live near the Automobile Club, on Alameda?" Roger asked.

"Yes," I replied cautiously, wondering what his question meant.

"Are you across the street from a grocery store called Pavilions?"

"Yes," I replied, once again cautiously.

"And do you live closer to a bakery called Martino's, something close to that name?" he asked.

"Yes, I do, but why are you asking?" I said.

"Wow, this isn't good," Roger replied.

"Roger! What's the problem?" I demanded, my concern creeping into my voice.

I heard Roger take a deep breath. Then he began to explain.

"There are a couple reasons why," he said.

"I'm listening," I answered back.

"Well, when I was seeing Valerie, I'd go over to her apartment after work and she'd always want me to take her for a drive. But what was so strange about these drives we'd take was that they were always at night and always the same streets she'd have me drive. One street in particular, she'd ask me to slow down on, almost to a stop, and always in front of the same house. And she'd just stare at it, and then tell me to drive on. This was all around the same time Valerie talked about you, convincing me enough to hate you. I think it might have been your house Valerie had me drive by all those times. But she never said anything, so I never thought to ask," Roger explained in concern.

I sat in silence, trying to get a hold of myself. So I had been right: Freddie had been stalking the house. It scared me, but at the same time made me angry.

"How long did this go on, Roger?" I asked sharply.

"Almost as long as I was seeing her. About a year," Roger replied.

"Roger, if we were to meet over at Freddie's old apartment, would you be able to remember the route he had you drive? I need to know for sure if it was my house Freddie was stalking," I said.

"Yes, I'd remember the route we went," Roger replied.

"Could you retrace it?" I asked.

"Yes, I'm pretty certain I could."

"Good! Now what was the other thing you were going to tell me?" I asked.

"Well, you're not going to like hearing this, but after Valerie was arrested, I, along with Rick, the friend of Valerie's you know as well, went over to her apartment to get her stuff to put into storage. While we were packing her things, Rick showed me a picture taken at a Christmas party he said you all attended one night. Anyway, he pointed you out in the picture and told me Valerie told him that she wanted you dead and wanted to do it herself," Roger said, his voice trailing off.

Hearing what I had long suspected enraged and alarmed me at the same time.

"Can you meet me tomorrow in front of Freddie's old apartment at one o'clock?" I asked.

"Yes, I can do that. I'm very curious myself to know if it was your house," Roger said.

"Okay then, I'll see you at one tomorrow," I said.

"Okay, see you then," Roger agreed.

Hanging up the phone, I sat there thinking about Freddie plotting to kill me. Through my mind passed several scenarios. Had Freddie in fact been driving by my house, manipulating Roger all along to hate me enough so that he would do the dirty work, or had Freddie really been planning to do it himself? What if I hadn't informed the police about the murder? Would I have been his next victim? Quickly getting up, I called Roger back.

"Roger?" I said.

"Yes?" he replied.

"When was the last time you remember Freddie having you take him by that house?" I asked.

"I believe it was a few days before she was arrested. That's why I called you about it. I think maybe all those times we were driving by she was using me, or planning to," Roger replied.

"I was wondering about that as well," I said.

"I remember she'd always be talking about how much she hated you when we took those drives," Roger commented.

"Freddie might have been setting you up or planning to do it herself and blame you," I said, curious to hear his reaction.

"I'll see you tomorrow and at least we'll know for sure if it was your house," Roger replied.

Finding it difficult to sleep that night, I tossed and turned for a long time before I fell asleep. Visions filled my dreams of a violent death at the hands of Freddie. Awakening from the nightmare, I asked myself how much longer it would have been before something horrible happened to me if I hadn't found out about the murder Freddie had committed.

I began thinking back to when it was that I began discovering the truth about Freddie. If Roger had started seeing Freddie a year prior to the arrest, then it would have been around May of 1995 when they met. It wasn't until July of that year that David had admitted to me that Valerie had once been a man.

With both David and Rick knowing Freddie's dark past, and Rick telling Roger that Valerie wanted me dead and wanted to do it herself, it made sense to me that Freddie would try to manipulate Roger into hating me.

The next afternoon, as I drove away from the house, I reset the trip odometer, wanting to know exactly how far Freddie's old apartment was from my house. Arriving at Freddie's old apartment building, I found Roger wasn't there. I looked at the mileage. It was not quite two miles from my house to Freddie's apartment, too close for me. While waiting for Roger to show up, my thoughts turned to the knife I had decided at the last minute to bring with me. I carefully positioned it down the side of the truck door, where I could grab it easily if I needed to defend myself against a brainwashed Roger. Maybe I was overexaggerating, but my greatest fears had already come true, and I wasn't about to put anything off as impossible.

Just then, Roger pulled his car up behind mine. I got out of my truck, slipping the knife into my purse, and walked back to his car. Entering the passenger side, I looked over at Roger.

"Ready?" I asked.

"Yep," Roger replied.

"Okay, show me the route Freddie would have you drive," I said.

Silence filled the car as we drove down Verdugo Road in the exact direction of my house. The closer we got to my street, the more nervous I became. But I tried not to show it, as I didn't want to give away where my house was, in case Freddie had him driving somewhere else. Turning down my street Roger began to slow the car down. "Freddie asked me to do this many times before," he commented. My heart began to pound hard, as Roger pointed to my house. "Over there, with the blue shutters," he said.

My body shook with fear, as tears fell down my face.

"Drive on, Roger," I said.

"Was that house yours?" Roger asked.

"Yes," I replied, trying to keep my voice steady.

Roger shook his head but said nothing.

The minute I got home, I called Det. Kamon, telling him about the drive Roger and I had taken. I confirmed it was, in fact, my house Freddie had been stalking and that he indeed had wanted to kill me and had been manipulating Roger to hate me as much as he did.

"Listen, I think Roger may be harmless, but I'm not taking any chances. I'm sure Freddie knows I'm the one who turned him in. The thing is, I don't know if Roger's still talking to Freddie or not, but I want you to keep Roger's name written down, in case anything happens," I said.

"Is there anyone else you're concerned about?" Det. Kamon asked.

"Yeah, that Rick Cooper that Roger said pointed me out in the picture. David told me Rick knew the whole deal with Freddie also and I don't trust him at all," I said.

After getting off the phone with Det. Kamon, I broke down in tears from all that I had learned. Feeling I should talk to Dr. Ashford, I called, only getting her answering service. I left a message and then called Gayle.

"Hello," Gayle answered on the first ring.

"Gayle, you're not going to believe this," I said.

"It must not be good; you sound upset. What happened?" Gayle replied, concerned.

"Remember I told you someone was stalking my house? I found out that Freddie had one of his lovers drive him by my house for about a year. And this guy told me that Freddie convinced him to hate me. Gayle, I'd never even met this guy before David mentioned him to me. And worse yet, another one of Freddie's old lovers, Rick Cooper, pointed me out in a picture to Roger and told him Freddie wanted me dead and was going to do it himself!" I said, as my chest began to tighten.

"Wait, wait, back up. Who is it that told you this?" Gayle asked.

"Roger Mills—he was seeing Freddie for about a year before the arrest," I replied.

Before I could explain to Gayle all that had happened in the last few days, I heard a beep come over the phone. Telling Gayle it was most likely Dr. Ashford; I quickly ended my call and clicked over to the other line.

"Hello?" I answered.

"Donita, it's Dr. Ashford. You sounded really upset. What's going on?" she asked. "Donita?"

"I'm sorry; I have a choking feeling in my throat, my chest is tightening up and I'm finding it difficult to breathe. I don't know why."

"It sounds like you are having a panic attack. Donita, listen to me. Take in a deep breath slowly, and let it out. Do this a few times; let's see if it helps," Dr. Ashford said.

I followed her directions.

"I'm feeling a little better now," I told her.

"Donita, you're going through a lot of turmoil. I don't have a license to prescribe medication, but I seriously feel you need to see someone who can evaluate whether you need it," Dr. Ashford said.

"No!" I said. "I don't want anything that's going to fog my mind or take control of my senses. I just need to come in and see you, Dr. Ashford," I said. "Do you remember when I said I thought Freddie had been stalking me at the house for a long time?" I asked. "Well, I found out not only was I right about that, but he wanted me dead."

"What? What do you mean wanted you dead? When were you being stalked. How? How did you find this out?" Dr. Ashford asked.

I explained the story behind my learning about Roger and how he told me Freddie had him drive by my house time after time.

"Oh, God, are you sure about this?" she asked with a concerned tone.

"I had Roger show me the same route Freddie had him take and he pointed out my house. So yeah, I'm 100 percent sure," I replied.

"Do you trust this Roger person? Did you tell this to the police?" Dr. Ashford asked.

"Yes, I already told Det. Kamon. He knows everything," I assured her. "I've been working with him to get more evidence for the trial. Listen, Dr. Ashford? I think I'm well enough not to come in now," I said.

"Are you sure?" she asked.

"Yes, if I change my mind, I'll call you back," I said.

"Okay, but I'm here if you need me. Donita, please, be careful. I don't think you realize the danger you're putting yourself in," Dr. Ashford said.

"I think, if anything, I saved my own life. What if I hadn't contacted Roger? I wouldn't know for sure that Freddie wants to kill me. Now the police and I can take some measures for me and my family to be safer now and in the future. If not, who knows what would have happened to us if Freddie gets out of jail?" I said.

I got off the phone with Dr. Ashford, walked into the living room and stood in front of the window, staring out while deep in thought. Not only did I need to get more evidence against Freddie, but without David's support I needed to find work to pay the bills. I began looking in the newspaper and started applying for positions, soon landing a job as a substitute teacher's aide.

Since I didn't want to give up on helping the police, the job was to my advantage, because I could choose to work or not on certain days.

Next, I decided to call Det. McMurry in South Carolina, to see if there was anything new on Freddie's case.

"Det. McMurry? It's Donita," I said when I reached him.

"Hi, how are you?" he asked.

"I'm all right. How are you?" I asked.

"Keeping busy," he replied.

"Is there anything new on Freddie?" I asked.

"Only that she's been clogging up the jail sink shaving every morning. They're not allowing her to have hormone pills right now," Det. McMurry said, laughing.

"What jail is he in?" I asked.

"The women's jail. We had no choice but to put her there. She might have liked it in the men's jail too much," Det. McMurry replied, joking.

"It's hard for me to laugh when it comes to Freddie," I said soberly.

"I know what you mean, but a sense of humor helps," he said, hearing the anxiety in my voice. Then he became serious. "Donita, it would really help us if you could try and find out something more about Valerie. Your documents and summary helped us a lot, but we still need to know a lot more," Det. McMurry said. "Perhaps you could try to get something out of your husband again; he's really not cooperating."

"Well, I know David is aware of more than he's telling me, but how far do you want me to go to find out more?" I asked.

"Do whatever you can without breaking the law or putting yourself in danger. Any new evidence at this point might help our case against Valerie," Det. McMurry replied.

"I'll do what I can. By the way, who is the prosecutor going to be?" I asked.

"Bob Kane," he replied.

"Can I have his telephone number?" I asked.

He gave it to me. "I'll let him know you'll be telephoning," McMurry said.

When I called Bob Kane's office, Mr. Kane told me that he had planned on getting in touch with me. "We may want to put you on the stand during Freddie's trial."

My heart quickened, "If you need me, I'll be there," I said. "But until then, I'd like to keep my identity secret."

He agreed and then told me Freddie was refusing to talk or give anyone any information.

"I'm going to try and find out more," I said. "I'll get back to you and Det. McMurry when I have something."

Since I was being asked to help by the police in both California and South Carolina, I was worried about the case against Freddie.

Adding to my concern was that I knew David was doing everything he could to keep himself out of it, even withholding what he knew. I called Det. Kamon.

"Donita, how are you? I was just going to call you," Det. Kamon replied. "Are you holding up okay?"

"I'm doing the best I can under the circumstances," I said soberly.

"How are the kids doing with all of this?" he asked.

"They're fine, but I may have to tell them more than I have."

"Why's that?" he wanted to know.

"They pick up on things. Like me constantly talking on the phone in the bedroom with the door locked. I'm jumpy around them and not giving them the kind of attention they're used to getting from me," I replied. "Anyway, there is something I need to tell you. I talked to Det. McMurry and he asked me to try and find out from David anything else I could about Freddie. I'm trying to figure out how I can do it and get David to open up."

"Yeah, Det. McMurry and I have been talking about it. We're going to try and come up with a plan to help you get David to talk. I'll let you know our thoughts in the next few days," Det. Kamon replied. "Meanwhile, try to get a little rest and spend some extra time with Sam and Jessica. Very soon, things will be heating up."

chapter fourteen

Diverting
Justice

During the next couple of days, I tried to give Jessica and Sam, who seemed to have accepted our new circumstances better than I had, some extra attention. I resolved to keep their lives as normal as possible to give them some added stability in this traumatic time.

I also tried getting my thoughts off Freddie's case, but my mind always came back to it. I began to wonder if there could be anything at the Glendale courthouse on Freddie. I realized I was obsessing, but asked myself who wouldn't, with a person like Freddie out to get them? The following morning I drove over to the Glendale courthouse to see if there were legal documents or court records on Freddie.

Arriving home from my trip to the courthouse, I sat down at the kitchen table and added together all that I knew of Freddie's arrests. The total came to eight, with numerous different counts on several of those arrests. His arrests were splashed all over the United States. First he was arrested in Greenville, South Carolina, then Atlanta, moving up north to Columbus, Ohio, and eventually returning south to Florida. His last known arrests were in California starting in Glendale, moving to Burbank and ending up in Toluca Lake, where Freddie finally found out that whatever else he altered, he couldn't change his fingerprints. Aliases he'd been known to use across the country were Johnny Tribble, Freda Turner, Freda Keith, Keith Freda, and Valerie Nicole Taylor, as well as Nikki.

Next, I examined the hit-and-run and name-change documents. Gary Moore was the attorney on record. He had recently been on the news as Freddie's defense attorney for the murder case. I wondered if Det. Kamon knew about Moore representing Freddie in the earlier cases. Surely this could be important. Knowing I had to be careful because of possible later defamation claims, I wanted to discuss the matter in private.

"Homicide, Det. Kamon."

"Hey, it's Donita," I replied. "Can you come over to the house? I've got some new information I don't want to talk about on the phone," I replied.

"Huh, okay, I'll be right over," Det Kamon replied, a little confused about my secrecy.

I stood outside and waited for Det. Kamon to pull into the driveway.

"Hey," I said, "I'm really glad you were free."

Det. Kamon could tell I was eager to share some new information on the case. He smiled back with a curious look.

"Let's go inside the house where we can talk. I don't want the neighbors to see us. Some of them are friendly with David," I said.

"Sure," Det. Kamon replied.

I brought out a tray of cookies and coffee to the living room while he got comfortable on the couch.

"Well, my little detective, what have you found out this time?"

"Well, I decided to do a little digging at the Glendale courthouse and you're not going to believe what I found," I said.

"What did you dig up?" Det. Kamon asked.

"Get this. You know his attorney, Gary Moore? He's all over the news now since he's representing Freddie in the murder case. He's also all over the court documents for the hit-and-run and name-change a few years back," I said.

"Well, Freddie has been sent back to Gaffney," Det. Kamon said pensively, "so he will have to find a lawyer down there if he has the money."

"Well, Moore's been his lawyer for a long while. If it were only the hit and run document from 1991 that I had seen his name on, it wouldn't have grabbed my attention. But there seemed to be more to it."

"His name also appears on the name-change document from earlier that same year? It doesn't make sense to me why someone would use a criminal attorney to change names." Kamon nodded. "Go on."

"David already admitted to me that he helped Freddie change his name to Valerie. It made sense to me, since David had supported Freddie for so long, that he also was the one who paid Gary Moore's attorney fees, meaning David knew the attorney."

"Well, we'd better follow up on that," he said looking at the time.

"I intend to," I said, "right away."

He laughed, "I thought you would."

After Det. Kamon left, I quickly jumped into the truck and drove over to David's studio, hoping to get some answers. I bounded up the stairs to his office, my investigatory juices flowing. David, who must have heard my heavy footsteps running up the stairs, opened the door just as I was about to knock.

"What are you doing here?" David asked, surprised.

"I want to talk to you," I replied.

"Now what?" David groaned.

"I want to know who this Gary Moore attorney is," I replied.

David took a deep breath, looking frustrated at having to face more of my questions.

"Donita, what's the point of all this?" he asked.

Looking David in the eyes I said, "Well, you and Freddie seem to have known him a long time. Either you tell me or I'll find out myself—like always."

David sighed in defeat. "All right, I'm very reluctant to tell you anything, but I know how persistent you are," he replied.

"It's your choice, David, but if I find out from someone else, I'll go straight to the police with the information," I said.

David sighed again, looking troubled. From the way David was acting, I could tell there was something else he knew. I had learned to trust my gut instinct. I followed David into his office and sat down in a chair across from his desk. He just sat there, his face taking on several expressions, as he tried to decide where to start.

"Let me ask you this, David, and maybe it will help you get a start," I said.

"Okay," David replied.

"It's obvious you know and have met Gary Moore, because you helped Freddie get his name changed," I said.

"Yes, I've met Gary Moore on several occasions over the past years," David replied.

"When was the first time you met him?" I asked.

"I'm not sure. I'd have to think back a moment," David said.

"I have all day." I smiled.

"What happened to you? You use to be so sweet," he commented.

"You happened, David. Now let's just get back to the question," I replied.

"Well, I do remember it was within the first couple of years after I met Valerie," David said.

"And how did you come to meet him?" I asked.

"Well, Valerie was living with me at the time and she'd talked to me several times about this operation she wanted to have," David recalled.

"The sex-change operation?" I asked.

"Yes," David replied.

"Go on," I said.

"Well, I knew there was risk with this surgery being done, that it was very dangerous for me because I knew she was—or at least, what she told me was that she had killed a man. So this caused me to question how the surgery could be done without getting myself involved, although I agreed to pay for the operation," David said, continuing his story.

"Okay, but how does this explain your meeting with Gary Moore?" I asked.

"Well, I felt if I was going to be the one paying for the operation, which by the way was very expensive, I thought I should first get some legal advice as to how it could be done without me being connected to it. So I called an attorney and Gary Moore happened to be one I came across in the phone book," David replied.

I wondered if that was true. Gary Moore was a criminal attorney.

"Then what happened?" I asked.

"Well, then Valerie and I went to see him," David said nervously. "Valerie explained the dilemma she was in and that she had a criminal record and had run away from a crime scene. So the first thing Moore did was run a background check on Valerie, to see if the police were still looking for her," David explained.

"Okay, so what happened next?" I asked.

"Well, we had to come back for a second visit. Moore said it would take a few days to get back any information, so we had to wait. Valerie was very nervous those next few days, not knowing if the police might still be searching. There were some very dramatic crying scenes and she couldn't sleep much because of it," David said.

"Then?" I asked.

"Well, we finally got a phone call back from Moore, asking us to come to his office," David replied.

"And?" I prompted.

"Moore told us nothing was found in the background check," David said.

"Huh?" I was taken aback. "Go on," I urged, in total amazement about where this story was going.

"Well, I remember Moore saying at that point it would be safe to have the operation," David said.

Thinking aloud, I said, "I remember seeing in a newspaper article about the FBI dropping their search for Freddie in 1984 and that it was placed in the inactive files. It makes sense to me that Moore, when doing a background search in 1985, wouldn't find anything, but it sure didn't mean Freddie was in the clear." I shook my head vehemently. David quickly clammed up when I said this. Realizing I might blow it before David finished, I calmed myself. "Okay, so what happened next?" I asked.

"Well, I remember Moore telling Valerie, 'Wait a few years before putting in for a name change,'" David replied.

I nodded. Now I understood why there was such a time gap between Freddie getting the sex change and getting his name changed. This was especially true since the name change document showed that it only took two months for him to get that order through the courts. And Moore's name, I clearly recalled, was on the documents as the attorney.

"The question is, why did you help a confessed killer get away with changing his identity?"

"My purpose in helping Valerie was not to help her escape justice. I was just trying to help fulfill a dream of hers," David claimed. "I thought I was being compassionate."

I looked him in the eyes for a long moment.

"By the way, David," I said slowly, "did you know Moore was defending Freddie when he was first arrested? On the news I heard him say he had known Freddie for a few years and that he would never kill anyone. And then he went on to demand fingerprints to prove Valerie was Freddie Lee Turner."

David nodded. "Yes, I recall seeing that too."

"Like all the rest of it, this also is unbelievable," I said, shaking my head.

"I don't know what to say. You wanted to know and I told you." David sat quietly in his world of grief and confusion. At times I forgot that in some sick way David probably still loved Valerie, despite the lies and violence. The arrest was hurting him as well.

I drove home from the studio dismayed at David's revelations about his tortured love. A shudder passed over my body, knowing how twisted and dangerous the relationship between David and Freddie had become. It almost made me feel sorry for him.

As I walked into the house, an overwhelming feeling of frustration and anger came over me. Too many people had gotten away with not only having knowledge of Freddie's crime, but helping him financially to escape justice.

chapter fifteen

Buried
Evidence

———

Soon after my discouraging meeting with David, which I reported to Det. Kamon, I called my divorce attorney. I wanted to know how soon David's and my divorce would be final, only to be told it would be a while longer. I abruptly hung up the phone, angry it was taking so long to separate myself from a man who'd put my children and me in such danger.

But no matter how stressed out I felt, I knew I had to keep myself together for the kids' sake, hoping once David was out of my life, Sam, Jessica and I could start anew.

I wanted to walk out the door with the kids in tow and turn my back on everything that had happened, I wanted so badly to believe that this period of my life was over. But I had to finish what I had started and make sure Freddie stayed behind bars.

If I didn't follow this through to the end, I knew it was possible that David and Freddie could cover up their guilt with money and lies just as they had done for so long. However, knowing the truth as I did, I wasn't about to let that happen.

Several days after my talk with David, around the middle of the afternoon there was a knock at my front door. It was Det. Kamon stopping by. "I could tell on the phone you weren't doing well," he said, "and I wanted to come over and give you some added support. Listen, I've been a police officer for twenty years and I've seen a lot of things happen, but this one threw me for a loop. You didn't deserve this to happen to you and your kids, but you're a strong person and you've held up pretty well through all of this. Not too many people could handle finding out something like this about their spouse and then have the guts to help the police bring the killer he shielded to justice. It sounds outrageous just saying it, but it's true."

"I wish David would just drop off the face of the earth," I replied in anger, as tears welled up in my eyes.

"You're going to pull through this. Just hang in there. You're doing well so far. Now listen, the other reason I came over is we've got an added problem," Det. Kamon said. "The police in Gaffney buried their old documents in a hole in the ground on the property where their new building was going to be erected," he explained.

"Why would the police bury evidence to an unsolved murder?" I asked.

"It wasn't just evidence against Valerie. A lot of evidence that no longer seemed relevant was dumped in that hole," Det. Kamon replied.

"And they built the new police station over it?" I asked.

"Yep."

"So what you're telling me is, right at this moment, Freddie is sitting on top of all the evidence against him?" I asked, in shock.

"Yep, right on top of it. Now we have to build a new case against Valerie or she could go free," Det. Kamon replied.

"I can't believe this! This is crazy!"

"I know it sounds crazy. I was pretty surprised myself, but Det. McMurry told me that it's routine after a number of years to get rid of old evidence and documents and that was a safe way to do it so no one could get hold of it," he replied.

I stood dumbfounded, looking at Det. Kamon as he looked back at me and began to chuckle.

"What's so funny?" I demanded, staring at him with confusion.

"When you called me to report an unsolved murder and told me it was a man who committed the murder, but had a sex-change and is a transsexual now, and your husband paid for the sex-change and they're lovers... Well, after I got off the phone with you, I sat at my desk and started laughing. I thought someone in the office was pulling a trick on me. By law I had to check it out and when I did, I found information that matched up with Valerie's in a hit-and-run accident. I was amazed you hadn't been kidding. If I saw a movie with this plot, I'd label it fiction, and the strangest twists and turns keep on coming," Det. Kamon said, as he pursed his lips.

Shaking my head in disbelief, I told him, "Once I proved the murder really happened I thought the case would end up in a trial and the conviction of Freddie. Now it's spiraling out of control."

"Donita, we need to apply desperate measures. We were thinking of wiring you and having you meet David at a restaurant, but from what I was told by Det. McMurry, there are all kinds of legal problems about testifying against a spouse and we don't need any more of those. But you're our best hope," Det. Kamon said.

"Well, I'll try and talk to David again, but I think he's getting sick of me harassing him for information," I said.

"And you've done a great job so far; if you can just go a little further," Det. Kamon said.

"What can I do that I haven't already done?" I asked.

"Do you think you can get David to talk about the weapon used in the murder?" he asked. "He just might know what Valerie did with the gun."

"I don't know." I shook my head in doubt.

"See what you can find out and let me know. I've got to get back to the station now," he said.

I walked him to the front door and waved goodbye before sitting back down on the couch to think. How was I going to ask David if he knew anything about the gun Freddie used to kill Billy? It wasn't going to be easy, but I was willing to try anything. Plan after plan kept on popping up in my mind, but I discarded them all, knowing none of them would ever work.

I called Rev. Posey and told him what was going on with the case and the sudden discovery of the loss of evidence that had been buried under the foundation of the new police station. Rev. Posey was shocked.

When I told him Det. Kamon wanted me to find out about the gun used in the murder, I convinced Rev. Posey our chances would be better if we could get the tape the police detective had made the night of the murder. Rev. Posey and I both realized that Freddie could be set free without more evidence to convict him. I told the reverend I would fly out to South Carolina as soon as possible. After I hung up, I made a reservation to fly out there the following weekend.

As I sat there deep in thought, Det. Kamon called. "I'm going to slip my card into David's studio mailbox," he said. The plan was to scare David enough that he might talk to me instead of the police. "If David contacts you after finding the card, act scared. Tell him the police paid you a visit as well."

I wasn't sure it would work, but I said I'd try. Later that day Kamon called again. "The deed's done. Now let's see if it produces the effect we need."

An hour inched by. Then two. Suddenly the phone rang again. It was David asking if I knew anything about Det. Kamon trying to contact him. I acted dumb and scared, telling David I had gotten a personal visit from the police that day.

"David, I'm really worried," I said.

"What did the police want?" David asked.

"They were pressuring me for information about you and Freddie," I answered.

"Like what?" David asked in a concerned voice.

"Let me call you back. Someone's calling on the other line and I want to see who it is," I said. "Maybe it's Det. Kamon again."

"Okay," David replied.

Buying myself some time with the excuse that someone was calling on the other line, I hung up the phone and quickly ran into the kitchen. Pulling open a drawer, I grabbed the tape recorder I had used on David before, along with a wire that connected the recorder to the phone.

I quickly thought through how I was going to approach David so he might tell me something that would help the police. Then, taking a deep breath, I dialed David's studio and pushed the record button.

"Hello," David answered.

"Hey," I said.

"Who was that calling?" David asked nervously.

"Just the kid's doctor, reminding me of an appointment for their school checkups tomorrow," I lied.

"Oh," David replied.

"Look David, this is really getting serious," I said.

"What did the police want? What did they ask you?" David asked.

"They said we're looking more and more guilty by holding back and not helping them with the investigation," I replied.

"I don't care how they think it looks, I'm not talking to them," David growled.

"Maybe if we give them something, they'll back off," I said anxiously.

"Like what? What can I tell them that wouldn't directly involve me in some way?" David replied.

"There has to be something you can help with," I said, pleading.

"I don't want to meet or talk to the police," David replied sternly.

"David, listen to me. Freddie is going to get away with murder if you don't. By the way, did you ever stop to think that he knows it was you who told me and might come after you if he gets away with this?" I asked.

"Yes, that thought has crossed my mind a couple times," he replied.

"Then you also know if he comes after the kids or me you'll be guilty of letting it happen, because you didn't help the police with their investigation," I added.

"Donita, I'm very sorry you got involved in this. I can see it's tearing you apart, but you have to admit you were the one who brought this whole situation with Valerie to light," David replied.

"David, he was stalking me and you know this. Why do you continue protecting him? Freddie is a dangerous person," I said.

"I know; I know. You don't have to remind me," he replied.

"David, even a little information about Freddie's past might satisfy the police. I mean, Freddie is the one they're really after, not you. You might be able to cut a deal by cooperating," I said, forcing a sympathetic tone to my voice.

"They might not be able to involve me anyway. Howell said without proof that I paid for Valerie's operation, they really can't nail me as someone who aided and abetted her," David blurted out, obviously worried.

A few silent minutes passed while I thought about my next query. I wasn't about to tell him I had found the phone records he had put in the trash. But maybe if I alluded to those calls, it would shake him up and make him realize the police could tie him to Freddie. Deciding to play David's bluff, I thought I'd shake him up into reality without telling him about the phone records I had found in the trash.

"David, let me ask you something. Freddie was living with you when he had the surgery, right?" I asked.

"Yes, but what's that got to do with anything? There's no proof she was," David replied.

"Who made the calls to the doctor in Colorado to get information about the surgery?" I asked.

"Valerie did, of course. I didn't make any of those calls," David replied.

"And where did Freddie make the calls to Colorado from?" I asked.

Silence fell as David realized the calls were made from the studio house.

"Don't you think the police are smart enough to subpoena those phone records from the studio house? The phone was in your name, right? Don't you think Freddie could and would tell the police that? And the records would lead them right to you and connect you to helping Freddie while he was a fugitive," I pointed out, pretending to be concerned.

"Yes, I suppose that could happen," David replied. I could tell from his voice he was becoming agitated.

I was ready to spring the big question Det. Kamon wanted answered. I took a deep breath and began. "What about the gun he used to kill Billy with? Did he ever tell you what he did with it after?" I asked.

"Well, I recall her telling me something about it," David replied, cautiously.

"What did he tell you?" I asked, surprised at the admission.

"I remember Valerie saying something about keeping the gun with her as she made her way across the country," David replied.

"So he kept the gun with him after killing Billy?" I asked.

"That was the understanding I got," David replied.

"What did he do with it?" I asked.

"Donita, please," David said, trying to avoid my question.

"David, come on; please tell me," I said softly.

After a pause, he began again. "You know, I'm very reluctant to tell you anything, Donita. I mean, how do I know you're not going to go running to the police with what I tell you?" David asked, in a suspicious tone.

"I'm not stupid, David. I'm trying to keep them away from me," I claimed.

"What good would come from me telling you what I know? What would be the point?" David asked.

Now knowing that David knew more than what he had told me in the past, I took a different angle, hoping I could convince him to tell me more. My feelings were mixed, as I spoke to this man I had loved so much and for so long, knowing all along I was deceiving David in order to get information. Although I found it uncomfortable, I realized with each new admission, not only had David deceived me for years, but he had knowingly put me and the children in danger to selfishly conceal the double life he had been living.

Now I had to do whatever it took to make us safe. I prodded him.

"I don't want to get myself in deeper trouble, no way! I just want to know the truth so I don't fall apart as all this unfolds."

More silence spilled between us, as David debated whether or not he should share what he knew about the gun. Patiently I waited for David to speak.

"Someday I'm really going to regret that I ever told you about this, but I feel guilty about the trouble you're in. I do, Donita," he said slowly. He went on, "Okay, well, I remember in the days just before Valerie moved into the studio house, I received a call from her. I guess she wanted me to feel comfortable with the fact that she got rid of the gun before moving in with me."

I tried not to gasp, to sound sympathetic in order not to blow it. I knew David was about to tell me something; I could feel it.

"So you knew all along Freddie had the murder weapon with him?" I encouraged him, calming my own anxiety.

"Yes, well at least that was what I was told by her. Anyway, Valerie said she buried it somewhere on the property at the house at which she lived in San Bernardino," David replied.

"The one you showed me?" I asked quietly.

"Yes," David replied with a sigh.

"I'm curious, why would he be so willing to tell you this?" I asked.

"I don't know and I wished she hadn't!" David snapped in a frustrated tone.

"What exactly did he tell you?"

"I remember she made several prior calls to me, always in a panic, making tearful pleas for help. Apparently these thugs moved into the house and she told me they were running drugs in and out of there and harassing her. The understanding I got was these drug dealers eventually took over the house," David explained.

"How did Freddie end up there anyway?" I asked.

"Well, from what I remember, she said she felt the police would be looking for her, so she wanted to get as far away from South Carolina as fast as possible. Anyway, Valerie said she was running low on money but had to keep moving so as to avoid getting caught. And somehow, and I'm not sure exactly when, she ended up on a Greyhound bus. By the time the bus arrived in San Bernardino, she had no money at all," David explained.

"What did he do then?" I asked.

"Well, she had to get off the bus, of course, because she couldn't pay the additional fare. Apparently she hung out at the bus station deciding what to do next and was in a panic at that point," David replied.

"Where did he go before he ended up in San Bernardino?" I asked.

"She told me Las Vegas," David replied.

"And why did he leave there?"

"Well, that's another strange part of the story," said David.

"And what was that?" I asked.

"I'm not sure I can remember all the details, but as I recall she met a taxicab driver and ended up staying with him for a short while," David replied.

"Only a short while?" I echoed.

"She said something happened with the taxi driver and she had to leave town quickly."

"What do you mean, 'had to leave town quickly'?" I asked.

"She didn't give a detailed account of what caused her to leave so fast, but I do recall her saying there was some sort of fight between them, that it had to do with sex. I guess Valerie didn't want to keep her end of the deal, even though I remember her telling me that was the understanding they had in order for her to stay there," David explained.

"Do you think Freddie did something to the taxi driver?" I asked.

"You mean killed him?" David asked.

"Well, think about it. Freddie already killed a man; he was on the run, desperate, trying to get money any way he could," I speculated.

"Yes, it's possible something like that could have happened, but she never admitted anything like that to me. Anyway, this whole situation with Valerie has gotten me in enough hot water. The less I know the better!" David said, his voice rising.

Realizing he was becoming irritated and could close up on me, I felt it was best to back off the Las Vegas story for the time being.

"David, we need to talk about the gun. What do you remember Freddie telling you about it?" I asked.

"Well, I agreed to let her move into the studio house and, the weekend before I was to go pick her and her things up, I had gotten this call from her. And I don't know why she felt the need to tell me this, maybe to glorify her story, but I remembered her saying she buried the gun somewhere on the property. She didn't say exactly where, she just buried it. She told me it was buried somewhere on the property. I would assume somewhere in the backyard where no one would see her digging and become suspicious. She must have done it at night when everyone was sleeping, just before she moved in with me," David sighed.

"Wait, back up. What do you mean just before he moved in with you? Like, days?" I asked.

"Yes, that's what I recall her saying. Anyway, Valerie said that I wouldn't have to worry about her having the gun still with her when she moved in with me," he explained.

"Did you ever see the gun yourself?" I asked.

"No! Although Valerie did ask if I wanted to see it, I said 'no'! Even then I felt the less I knew, the better for me," David sounded stressed.

"David, you need to tell Howell where you think the gun is so he can tell the police," I said pensively.

"Or what?"

"You're going to be guilty of another crime. It's called withholding evidence. Think about it. If you don't tell him, then, yes, I will have to tell the police myself now that I know," I replied.

"I knew I shouldn't have told you! Damn." David murmured a few more curse words under his breath, which I could still hear.

"Which is it going to be, David? Me or you?" I pushed him.

"I guess you leave me no choice but to tell Howell myself," David replied, frustrated.

"When are you going to call?" I asked.

"Now is as good a time as any, I suppose," David replied, the irritation in his voice becoming pitched.

"Good. You may not realize it now, but you're doing the right thing for once," I said.

"Well, not out of free will, I can tell you that."

"Just call me after you tell Howell; I'll be waiting," I said.

"Fine," said David, in a defeated tone.

Curious to see if David would telephone Howell right away and tell what he knew, I waited before calling Det. Kamon to tell him what I learned. Suddenly, the phone started ringing.

"Hello?" I answered.

"Donita, it's Rev. Posey."

"I'm so glad you called, I have something big to tell you!" I said.

"I have something to tell you too," Rev. Posey replied. "Do you want to go first?"

"Mine's good news, if it's still there," I replied.

"If what's still there?" he asked.

"David told me Freddie buried the gun at a house he lived in before he moved in with David," I replied.

"That's great news! When did you find this out? Do the police know yet?" he asked. Quickly I explained the situation that had just taken place. "Now, tell me your news," I said.

"Mine isn't that good," he said dispiritedly. "I just wanted you to know after I talked to you on the phone, I went down to try and get a copy of Billy's autopsy report, but I couldn't get it."

"Why? Billy was your brother; you have a right to have it," I said.

"That's not why I couldn't get it. They said it's missing," Rev. Posey told me.

"What do you mean, it's missing?" I asked.

"They said they can't find the original. I find it really strange," Rev. Posey went on. "There are a lot of things that were buried or can't be found. It makes you wonder."

Suddenly my other phone rang. "Listen, I have another call. I'll try to call you as soon as I know anything," I said, rushing to pick up the phone, thinking it might be David.

"Okay, I'll be waiting," Posey replied.

Answering the other phone, I said, "Hello."

"It's me," David replied.

"Did you tell Howell?" I asked.

"Yes, and now I have to go down there and get the address so he can give it to the police," David replied, sounding nervous.

"I'm going with you then," I said.

"Why? You think I'd give them the wrong address?" David asked.

"Well, you've lied before," I observed.

"Fine, but if you're going with me, let's go. I want to get this over with," David replied.

"I'm leaving now," I assured him. "Give me a few minutes to get to your studio."

As soon as David and I hung up, I quickly called police headquarters.

"Homicide, Det. Kamon speaking."

"Hey, it's Donita. Did you get a call from Howell yet about the gun?" I asked.

"Yeah, Lt. Sims just got off the phone with him. You did well; I'm proud of you," Det. Kamon replied.

"I just wanted to make sure David called. I'm going down there with him to make sure he gives the right address," I said.

"You've been there before?" Det. Kamon asked.

"Yes, I once had David show me where Freddie lived before he moved into the studio house. Listen, I really have to go now; David's going to get suspicious about why I'm taking so long," I said.

"Okay, but be careful," Det, Kamon cautioned.

"I will," I promised and left the house. Getting into my truck I drove as quickly as I could to David's studio. He was waiting outside. "Get in," I said.

David and I were silent on the way down to San Bernardino. Both of us were emotionally drained. Driving up to Freddie's old house, I stopped the truck and got out two pieces of paper and a pen. I wrote down the address to make sure it was the right one, making a copy for myself and giving David one to give Howell. As David and I drove back home, I found it hard to hold back my pain. "I just want you to know, David, how betrayed I feel by you."

"You brought all of this on yourself, Donita," he said.

"How do you figure that, David?"

David looked distraught and broken. "You don't understand. I was in love with Valerie," David replied, almost mechanically, as if he was in a trance. At that point I knew David was going to stick by and protect Freddie at any cost, even his own future.

Looking at his pale face and his hand gripping the truck door handle, an uncomfortable feeling overcame me and I felt David might jump out of the truck as we were driving on the freeway.

Realizing how dangerous the situation had become and fearing David might make a desperate move, I immediately backed off. The rest of the ride became very quiet and surreal. We were both deep in thought. As I drove, I found myself torn between trying to get the information needed to help convict Freddie and not wanting to cause more harm than had already been done.

Dropping David off at the studio, I headed home and called Det. Kamon to let him know I'd made it back safely.

"Hey, it's Donita again," I said when he answered.

"Are you all right? Did you get the address where the gun's buried?" Det. Kamon asked.

"Yes to both. Howell should be calling with it soon," I replied. "But let me give it to you anyway."

"Good," Det. Kamon replied, taking it down. "Donita," he said excitedly, "you've done it this time. We can move forward. Freddie's not going to get away with what he did. Congratulations."

Hanging up I felt exhausted but deeply gratified, since Freddie's trial would now proceed. As I sat there going over the past in my mind, the phone rang. I picked it up to find David on the other end.

"Hello?"

"Hi," David said, in a defeated voice.

"Yes?" I waited.

"Well, I just got off the phone with Howell. I was worried about what you were going to do with the information I gave you, since you seem so bent on making sure Valerie is put away for good," David said. Caught off guard by David's accusations, I was silent.

"Why are you so bent, as you put it, on making sure Freddie doesn't?" I finally asked.

"You would have to know where I'm coming from to understand why," David said.

Fearing I'd completely lose it, I changed the subject. "What did you say to Howell?" I asked.

"Well, I gave him the address, of course; you left me no choice," David said disgustedly. "I also told him of the conversation we had over the phone today and he was very angry I was even talking to you about anything. Then we discussed the confrontation you had with him at his office. He feels at this point you can't be trusted," David explained.

"Well, tell him I'm not the only one," I said in a sarcastic voice.

"He also said he doesn't understand why I paid him money to defend me if I'm risking myself by confiding in you," David continued. "He also told me he had everything under control and I might have been able to get out of this mess. But now, with me telling you about the gun, he feels I blew that chance. He says the information now has to be given to the police or they'll for sure be able to connect me to helping Valerie, because I knew where the gun was, or at least was told where it was, if they're able to dig it up. Donita, have you been in contact with the police?" David asked, in a suspicious tone.

"Why would I talk to the police?" I tried not to convey my anger and frustration with him, but it came out in an evasive but deeply felt way.

"Are you sure about that?" David asked, again.

"I'm quite sure, David, that I never wanted to be involved in a murder. And I damn well don't want to be now."

"Okay, okay. Calm down. I believe you," he said.

Quickly I made an excuse to end the conversation. "The kids are coming home soon," I told him. "I have to get off the phone now."

After we hung up I sat there. I began thinking about my life before meeting David. Until now, I never realized how much I missed the quiet and slow pace of living in a small town. I recalled my reason for moving back to Los Angeles from Oklahoma had been because I missed all the excitement and lifestyle of living in a big city, having everything at my disposal. But those aspects of city life were of little worth compared to the fears and danger I found here.

Becoming teary-eyed, I recalled the peaceful, happy times the kids and I had in Oklahoma and how uncomplicated life had been while we were there. I yearned to be back in Oklahoma sitting on the front porch with the kids, being with loving family and making small talk about the simple things in life with a friend.

chapter sixteen

Searching
for the Gun

With Freddie extradited to South Carolina but the case against
him not as strong as it needed to be since so much time had
gone by, I racked my mind for another way to get more evidence
against him. Stuck on what to do, I finally decided I needed to meet
with Rev. Posey, Billy's brother, face to face. I felt badly for the Posey
family, knowing that my discovery forced them to relive the murder
of Billy. But at the same time I knew they needed closure even more
than I did. Calling Rev. Posey, I told him I was coming to South
Carolina that Saturday.

The evening before I was to leave, I packed my things, including
the envelope of information I had kept hidden under my mattress this
whole time.

Early Saturday morning, after dropping the kids off at a friend's
for the weekend, I drove to the airport.

During the long flight I had many hours to think about the murder. Knowing I only had a short time to spend with Rev. Posey, I

decided finding the police tape would be my first priority. I also
wanted to see for myself where Billy's murder occurred, the bar he
and Freddie were at that night and where Billy was buried.

As the plane approached the landing strip, fear seized me; I was
now in South Carolina and would soon be within miles of the murder site and the jail where Freddie was currently incarcerated.
Despite my fears I pressed on and grabbed a shuttle to the motel in
Spartanburg.

As I walked to the motel's reception desk, my fear mounted when
I saw several newspapers stacked on the counter top. Freddie's story,
Rev. Posey had told me, was continually being covered in the South
Carolina papers and as I glanced down at the headlines, I saw today
was no exception.

I reassured myself that the media didn't know about me, but I also
knew the police did. I didn't want to risk using my real name and
having someone find out why I was in Gaffney. Telling the hotel clerk
I had lost my I.D., I made up a fake name and paid cash for my room.

I put my suitcase down and rested on the room's bed for a short
while. Refreshed, I called Rev. Posey to let him know I had arrived
and where I was staying.

"I'll come over around eight thirty in the morning," he told me.

Exhausted, I slept through the night, but I rose almost at dawn,
dressed and waited for Rev. Posey to arrive. Exactly at eight-thirty
there was a knock at the door. Peering through the peephole, I cautiously asked, "Rev. Posey?"

"Yes, it's me," he replied.

Opening the door I stood face to face with Billy's brother. "Please
come in," I said. "I've been waiting to meet you." We solemnly shook
hands and sat down at a small round table in the corner of the room.

"I'm really happy to finally meet you, too," he said with a smile.
"Donita, I want to thank you from the bottom of my heart, as well as
from my family, for turning my brother's killer in. I'm just sorry you

had to go through such turmoil and pain in your own life in doing so. I know this must be horrible for you too, but I am very grateful to you. Now Billy can rest in peace," Rev. Posey said.

I tried to hold back tears from the reality of my own pain as Rev. Posey leaned over and gave me a hug. Putting my own distraught emotions aside, I knew what was more important was to share what I knew about Freddie with Rev. Posey.

I showed Rev. Posey what I had brought with me, from court documents to mug shots, and filled him in on how I forced David to give the police the location where Freddie buried the gun. In turn, Rev. Posey shared with me several articles he had photocopied for me regarding Billy and Freddie. As I skimmed them over I found that three were especially interesting. I put these three to the side and then went back to read them in more detail.

The first read, "FBI, SLED asked to help find slaying suspect... GAFFNEY – The FBI and State Law Enforcement Division have been asked to help find a man wanted in connection with the slaying of a Spartanburg man here. City Police Chief said Friday that the other police agencies are assisting his department in its search for a known suspect."

The rest of the piece told how Gaffney police found the body of a man in a room at the Sansing Motor Court and identified the dead man as Billy M. Posey, twenty-five, of Spartanburg. According to police he had been dead for a couple days.

Finishing that article I picked up the second that had caught my eye: "Female transsexual denies being male murder suspect – A woman identified as the man wanted for a 1979 slaying in South Carolina denied Thursday that she is the suspect as a judge ordered a new fingerprint comparison to settle the issue."

This piece gave the information that a Los Angeles municipal judge ordered tests after Valerie Nicole Taylor's lawyer asked for them. Gary Moore, his lawyer, admitted Taylor had been Freddie Lee

Turner—who was the suspect in a shooting death in the small town of Gaffney, South Carolina, seventeen years ago. But the lawyer said Taylor, now forty years old and an unemployed model, denied that she is the fugitive sought by police.

However, Burbank police proved him wrong. They said her fingerprints match those of Turner, who fled South Carolina after the killing and has evaded state and federal authorities since. Police arrested Taylor at her apartment on May 9. The lawyer also conveyed that he represented Taylor when she changed her name. He said Taylor's sex change had nothing to do with the case.

Moore went on to remark, "When I first represented her on the name change, she was already a woman. I don't know when or where she had the operation... I don't think she changed her sex because she was trying not to be found. I think her reasons go much, much deeper than that."

The article showed that Moore, like so many others including David, had been charmed by Valerie. "She doesn't strike me as the type of person who is capable of murder," he added. "That's out of character. She is a very quiet, shy and gentle person." Moore also said Taylor does not deny having once been a man named Freddie Lee Turner, only being the suspect sought in the case.

My heart quickened as I read that "Police had all but forgotten the case when, a few months ago, Burbank police got a tip from a citizen who said Taylor had admitted to killing someone long ago in Gaffney. According to Moore, Taylor denies making such an admission."

Shaking my head, I looked up at Rev. Posey and then picked up the third article and carefully went over it. "GAFFNEY – Transsexual Valerie Nicole Taylor said she might want the services of the local public defender during her arraignment Monday on murder charges. Taylor, 40, is charged with the 1979 shooting death of Billy Marshall Posey, 30, of Spartanburg, at Sansing Motor Court. At the time of Posey's death, Taylor was known as Freddie Lee Turner." It also told how she had been extradited from California the previous week. I read on about how she shielded her face Monday from a television cameraman who photographed her through the glass on the municipal courtroom door.

"Oh, my God, the cameras," she said when they brought her from the jail into the courtroom. A city detective directed Taylor to stand before the judge.

The judge repeated to Taylor the accusation of murder, then he went on to say that the hearing was to inform her of court procedures. As the municipal judge he could not set bond, since the charge of murder is punishable by the death penalty. Hearing this, Freddie began shaking.

"Will you repeat that?" he asked the judge.

The judge did and then Freddie asked when the bail hearing would be. Freddie was told a circuit court judge would have to schedule a bond hearing.

The judge then gave Taylor the opportunity to say something.

"I just got into town this weekend. My attorney from California is trying to find a local one. I thought maybe you could refer me to the public defender," Taylor said.

The judge referred her to the police, saying, "They will help you get a lawyer."

The article also brought out that an informant had tipped the California police that Turner lived in the state with a new identity and sex. Reading over that remark, I knew it was only a matter of time before reporters would identify and be looking for me. I had to be careful.

With Rev. Posey and me already questioning what was going on in Gaffney and the evidence on Freddie having been buried or having simply disappeared, we both felt I could easily place myself in danger or have my name revealed when I started poking around.

We agreed it was better for me to wear a disguise. Rev. Posey had brought a hat and sunglasses for me to put on.

As we sat in the car, Rev. Posey explained how cagey some people were in Gaffney about outsiders and reiterated that I should be very careful as we searched about town for clues and answers.

First, Rev. Posey took me to the bar where Freddie and Billy were last seen the night of the murder. It was a long and narrow stone building and was boarded up. Stealthily, we got out of the car and I peered inside the window while Rev. Posey pointed out where Billy had been standing.

We then took the same route Billy would have taken that night to the small, bungalow-style motel. At the motel I asked Rev. Posey where Room 10 was. We silently walked up to the building. Just as he pointed out the door to the room, a heavyset woman who had been in conference with two men in what looked like a drug deal started walking towards us, yelling obscenities.

We jumped back in the car and I cried out, "Let's get out of here!" as she got closer to the car and began banging on the hood.

"Wow! This place is still bad," Rev. Posey said, as he quickly put the car in reverse, pulling out onto the main road.

"I'd like to see where Billy is buried," I said.

Silently, Rev. Posey drove me to the cemetery. We both prayed for a few moments for Billy's soul and that he finally would be able to rest in peace.

Driving back into town, Rev. Posey turned down a side street, pointing out the jail where Freddie was being held. "He's in a cell on that side," Rev. Posey said, driving over there. I ducked down in the car to avoid being seen.

Our next plan was to get the tape Jack Jones had made. Rev. Posey pulled the car into an old gas station, asking me to stay inside while he went to call Jack's wife from a pay phone. I sat anxiously waiting, watching Rev. Posey from the car window. He was frowning as he walked back to the car and opened up the door to get in.

"May be more bad news," he said.

"What?" I asked in concern.

"Somebody's already been to the house and got the tape," he replied.

"What? Who?" I asked.

"I don't know. All Jack's wife said was someone came over and said they were investigating Billy's murder and needed the tape for evidence, so it must have been someone involved in the case," Rev. Posey replied.

"Well, if it was the police, then that's good," I said.

"Let's hope so, because that tape and the gun are the main evidence left against Freddie now," Rev. Posey replied. "Donita, have they told you the old police chief as well as the room clerk have passed away? The primary investigating officer who signed the original warrant is dead. Even the cabbie who took Freddie back to Spartanburg from the motel is dead."

Rev. Posey pulled up to the motel. Both of us sat there not speaking, frustrated that our efforts to get Freddie to pay for his crime were meeting dead ends.

Agreeing to continue to keep close contact, I got out of the car and said goodbye, waving as he pulled the car away. Entering my room, I fell on the bed, exhausted and wanting to get back to my kids.

By the time I got back to California Sunday night, I was wondering and worrying about what had happened to the tape. After a joyful reunion with the kids, I called Det. McMurry first thing Monday morning, only to be told he had no knowledge of a tape. Now I began to fear who else would have known about it and what reason they would have to retrieve it. I called Det. Kamon to find out what was going on with the search for Freddie's gun.

"How are you? I tried to call you over the weekend. Where were you?" Det. Kamon asked, sounding concerned.

"I went on a fruitless search." I said.

"Don't tell me you went out and tried to dig up the gun yourself," Det. Kamon said, with a chuckle.

"No, I didn't, but don't put it past me," I replied, only half joking.

"Oh, I believe you would. So where were you?" Det. Kamon asked.

"I flew out to South Carolina," I replied.

"What did you go out there for?" Det. Kamon asked.

"Among other things, to try to find a tape," I replied.

"What tape?" Det. Kamon asked.

"I can't get into the whole thing; it's too long a story, but in short, it's a tape Rev. Posey and I were trying to get that was made by the officer who was called to the murder scene the night Billy was killed. He couldn't write, so he recorded a tape at the crime scene. It told what he saw in the room that night, so the tape could prove it was murder," I replied.

"Huh. Did you get it?" Det. Kamon asked.

"No, unfortunately the detective is dead and when Rev. Posey called his wife, someone had already been to the house and taken it," I replied.

"Huh, I wonder who got it," he said.

"I don't know, but I do know Det. McMurry doesn't have it; I already called and asked," I sighed and then went on. "So, by the way, what's going on with your search?"

"We're waiting for a search warrant. There's a process we have to go through," Det. Kamon replied.

"Will you keep me informed?" I asked.

"As soon as I know anything," he promised.

After a week went by and I had heard nothing, I called Bob Kane, the prosecutor, to find out if a trial date had been set yet. He said it hadn't, but told me when David and I would be expected to testify.

"What do you think Freddie's defense is going to be?" I asked Mr. Kane. His reply nearly knocked me out of my chair.

"From my understanding, Freddie's going to plead battered woman's syndrome; can you believe that?" He laughed.

"I really can't even laugh," I said, grimacing.

Another week inched by. Still I heard nothing. I grew more and more anxious about what was going on with the missing gun; it seemed too quiet. I called Det. Kamon again.

"Hi, it's Donita," I said.

"There's no gun," Det. Kamon replied grimly.

"What do you mean there's no gun?" I asked.

"Just what I said—no gun. Det. McMurry took a plane out here with a couple of other people and we all went down to the house in San Bernardino, got together with the sheriff's department there, rented a bulldozer, dug in the yard and no gun," Det. Kamon replied.

"I can't believe this!" I groaned, frustrated.

"David must have lied to you," Det. Kamon said.

"But that's what Freddie told David," I replied, in a defeated tone.

"Then Freddie lied to David. That's not much of a surprise," Det. Kamon replied, jokingly.

"Did you dig up the whole yard?" I asked.

"Everything but the side of the yard where a slab of cement was. We didn't have a jackhammer," Det. Kamon replied.

"Well, did you ask how long that slab of cement has been there?" I asked, desperately.

"Yep," Det. Kamon said.

"Well?" I waited.

"The new people who own the house put it in there," Det. Kamon replied.

"Then the gun could be buried under that slab of cement, right?" I said.

"Might be," Det. Kamon replied.

"So why don't you go back down there and jackhammer it apart?" I asked.

"Too expensive," said Det. Kamon.

"How much would it cost?"

"About four thousand dollars," he replied.

"Well, I'll pay for it, if that's what it takes. You've got to get that gun!" I said.

"They won't let you pay for it, but let me talk to Det. McMurry and see what we can do. I don't have any control over what they okay or not," Det. Kamon explained.

"By the way, did you hear that Freddie's defense is going to be battered women's syndrome?" I asked.

"Yes, I heard," he laughed. "In my opinion, she'll definitely look like a fool in court with that plea."

After waiting another intense and agonizing week, I finally received a phone call from Det. McMurry in South Carolina, who astonished me with his report.

"I have some good news," he said. "We used your write-up to back up the murder."

"And what happened?" I asked.

"We interrogated Valerie, told her we'd been talking to David, making Valerie think the information came from David. Well, she confessed that the gun was buried in a backyard," Det. McMurry replied.

"So he doesn't know you've already been there and haven't found it?" I asked.

"No, we didn't want to give that away; we bluffed just to see if she would fall for our act and tell us where exactly the gun was buried in the yard," Det. McMurry replied.

"Where did he say it was buried?" I asked.

"Along the side of the house."

"So, it's got to be there! That's the only place you guys didn't dig up." I grinned in excitement.

"No, it's not," Det. McMurry replied.

"What?" I said, shocked.

"Unfortunately, we went back with Det. Kamon and broke up the cement, but we didn't find the gun," Det. McMurry replied.

"Then why did both David and Freddie say it was there?" I asked.

"I don't know. I guess they both lied about it," Det. McMurry said.

"But how can that be? It doesn't make sense," I said, feeling confused.

"I don't know. It doesn't make sense to us either," Det. McMurry replied.

"So, what else did Freddie lie about in his confession?" I asked.

"Just what we expected her to lie about, that she killed Billy in self-defense," replied Det. McMurry.

"Well, we all know that's a lie. Remember David told me Freddie admitted to him it was a relief killing Billy, that it was revenge for all the men who wouldn't accept him as a real female," I said.

"Look, Donita, we know you're not giving up and we're not either. Det. Kamon and I believe where Freddie shot Billy pretty much tells the story," Det. McMurry said.

"Now what? No gun, everyone but the old Chief of Police is dead; someone stole the tape—how are we going to prove in court it was murder?" I asked.

"Well, I have to admit it's not looking too good," Det. McMurry replied.

As soon as I got off the phone, I called Det. Kamon.

"Hey, what's up?" Det. Kamon asked.

"I just got off the phone with Det. McMurry. Why didn't you tell me you went back down to San Bernardino?" I asked.

"I knew it would upset you when we didn't find the gun," Det. Kamon explained.

"It has," I replied.

"I'm sorry, Donita; it is discouraging. We have to keep the pressure on or Valerie might actually get away with this," Det. Kamon said.

Tears streamed down my face. "I can't believe this. You know, Freddie could come after me if they release him," I said, concerned.

"Let's hope she's not that stupid with all the media attention she's gotten."

"I'm not so sure," I said, still upset.

Knowing I had to keep myself together for Sam and Jessica's sake, I once again fought to keep from falling apart. What was I to do now? Was Freddie going to get away with murder? Had I fought so hard only to meet defeat? I gritted my teeth. I wasn't going to go down without a fight.

chapter seventeen

The
Sting

Bringing all the evidence I'd accumulated into the living room, I read it over once again, trying to decide what to do next. Suddenly, I heard a knock on the door. I got up and, peering through the curtain, saw Det. Kamon with another officer standing at the front door. I opened the door.

"Hey," Det. Kamon said, looking concerned. "I wanted to give you some encouragement."

"What's going on?" I asked.

"This is Officer Cuso," Det. Kamon replied, introducing me to the other policeman.

"Hi, nice to meet you," Officer Cuso said, as he extended his hand to shake mine.

"Well, after we got off the phone, I called Det. McMurry. We put our heads together and we've come up with a plan that we need your help with," Det. Kamon began.

"What plan's that?" I asked.

"Let's sit down and I'll tell you," Det Kamon said.

"Okay," I replied. We all made ourselves comfortable in the living room.

"First off, we're going to try and talk to David one more time," Det. Kamon said, leaning towards me.

"There isn't much hope of that. He'll go out of his way to avoid you," I warned in a dejected tone.

"Well, we're still going to set up a sting, that's where you'll come in," Det. Kamon said.

"Okay, I'm listening," I said.

"If we can't get David in front of us to talk, if he keeps running to avoid us, then we need you to trap him to where we can," Det. Kamon replied.

"Go on," I said, curious as to what their plan was.

"We want you to set up a place to meet David, a place that's not suspicious—like a restaurant you two used to go to a lot. From there, we'll move in on David and you just go along with it and act surprised," Det. Kamon explained.

"It's a long shot, I think," I said.

"I agree, but it's worth a try, don't you think?" Det. Kamon asked.

"Yes, anything to make sure Freddie doesn't go free is," I replied.

"Can you try and set up having lunch with David tomorrow afternoon?" asked Det. Kamon.

"I can try," I replied.

"Okay, call him and try and set it up, then call me at this cell phone number and let me know where you'll be meeting him and when, but don't let him pick you up. We're going to follow you from the house when you leave," Det. Kamon explained.

"It won't work then," I said.

"Why is that?" Det. Kamon asked.

"As soon as David sees a patrol car and a uniformed officer, he's going to avoid you," I replied.

"Don't worry about that. We'll be in an unmarked car and plain clothes," Det. Kamon assured me.

"Okay, I'll call you as soon as I reach him," I said.

"Okay, good. I'll be waiting," Det. Kamon replied.

After Det. Kamon and Officer Cuso left the house, I began thinking of excuses to get David to meet me for lunch. Suddenly, the phone rang, startling me out of thought.

"Hello?" I answered.

"Hello, Mrs. Allen, it's Det. McMurry."

"Hi, funny you should call; Det. Kamon was just here," I said.

"Yeah, I heard he was going to get you to help set up a sting for your husband," he told me.

"I don't know if it'll work though," I replied.

"Well, it's a good idea and it may," Det. McMurry said, trying to encourage me.

"I'll do everything I can," I said. "By the way, have you found out who got the tape I told you about?"

"I have no idea. I wish I knew who took it," Det. McMurry replied. "Most of all I wish I had the case report, bullet shells, Bill Posey's autopsy report and the rest of the evidence the police here once had."

"And why in the hell did the police in South Carolina bury evidence from the old police station?" I asked in anger.

"They say it was part of a routine destruction of old evidence," Det. McMurry replied.

"Makes you wonder how many other unsolved crimes and murders won't get solved because of that," I said, frustrated.

"We'll never know," Det. McMurry sighed.

"This whole thing makes me sick," I couldn't help but say.

"I agree; it makes me sick too. This is the first big case I've ever had where all the evidence needed to convict someone is right below my own feet," Det. McMurry said in disgust. "And I can't get to it."

"Listen, I hate to cut you off, but I've got to find an excuse to get David to meet me for lunch tomorrow and then call Det. Kamon," I excused myself.

"Okay, good luck. I mean that," Det. McMurry said in a sincere voice.

After shuffling several ideas through my mind, I finally decided to use the divorce as an excuse. David had been calling and complaining that I was going to clean him out; maybe if I played on that, he'd be willing to meet for lunch and talk it over. With my plan ready, I picked up the phone and called David. His assistant said he was on the set and would call me back.

Frustration was the mood of the day. When he failed to call me back, I kept calling and pestering people until I got him on the line.

"David, hi, it's Donita," I began innocently.

"Yes?" he said coldly.

"We really need to talk," I pressed.

"About what?" he asked.

"The divorce. I'm willing to be fair about it, but we need to meet, because I want us to agree on the terms face to face before I finalize them with my attorney," I replied.

I could hear his sigh of relief.

"Okay, I can do that. Why don't you come over to the studio?" David said.

"Well, I have some things I have to take care of today for the kids. Why don't you meet me for lunch tomorrow at the Bay Club?" I asked.

"We can do that. I have to run over some things at the other studio in the morning. Why don't we meet there around one o'clock?" David suggested.

"Okay, I'll see you then," I replied.

David and I got off the phone and I quickly called Det. Kamon.

"Donita, did you get a meeting place set up?" he asked, recognizing my voice.

"Yes, the Bay Club near David's studio at one o'clock tomorrow," I replied.

"Good, just act casual and we'll take care of the rest, okay?" Det. Kamon said.

"Okay, see you later," I said and hung up the phone.

It was another restless night. I hardly ever seemed to get a good night's sleep anymore. The next morning dragged by. Minutes seemed like hours as I watched the clock slowly tick away. Carefully, I applied my makeup and put on a blue silk dress David liked. I paced the floor nervously while practicing the surprised look I'd have to fake so David wouldn't think I had something to do with the set-up.

Finally, it was time to go. I looked around the house but didn't see Det. Kamon anywhere. Pulling the truck slowly out of the driveway and onto the street, I stopped and looked out the rearview mirror hoping Det. Kamon wasn't running late. After waiting a few minutes, I still didn't see him. I slowly drove the truck down the street.

At the stop sign, I looked right and left one last time for Det. Kamon, but he wasn't there. I just figured something must have happened and that he couldn't make it, so I drove on to the restaurant as planned, hoping not to cause David any suspicion.

Arriving at the Bay Club, I parked the truck and got out. I walked slowly, still looking around, just in case Det. Kamon had decided to go to the restaurant instead of the house. If he was there he was well hidden. In the restaurant I began looking for David, but he too was nowhere in sight. Finding it strange, as David had never stood me up; I called the studio in LA to find out where he was.

"Hello, Production," an assistant answered.

"Tom?" I asked.

"Yes, this is Tom," he replied.

"Hi, it's Donita. Listen, do you know where David is? He was supposed to meet me at the Bay Club at one o'clock and he's not here," I said.

"He should be, he left thirty minutes ago," Tom replied.

"What? I was just at the Club in Burbank and he was nowhere," I replied, my voice rising with worry.

"No, he's at the other location," Tom said.

"Shoot! Okay, I'm on my way!" I said, as I quickly hung up the phone.

I swiftly walked out of the restaurant and jumped back in the truck. Driving out of the parking lot, I looked around again for Det. Kamon. I still didn't see any sign of him, so I headed up the street towards the freeway.

Wondering what had happened to him, I decided to pull the truck over to see if he might be behind my vehicle. I couldn't see him and now I couldn't tell him I had the right restaurant, but wrong location. After waiting there for ten minutes without anyone approaching me, I felt for sure that the set-up was not going to happen. I sped off to get on the freeway, worried David might think something was awry by my tardiness. I knew it would take at least fifteen minutes before I could get to the Club. I pushed my foot down, weaving in and out of lanes, as I frantically made my way towards Los Angeles.

Five minutes into the drive on the freeway, all I could see up ahead was bottleneck traffic. I swerved the truck over to exit and took side streets the rest of the way.

Once again, I found myself having to weave in and out of traffic, but I finally made my way to the Club where David was waiting. As my car came up to a stoplight, from nowhere, a black sedan zoomed just feet ahead and swerved, making a sharp left turn in front of me. For a moment I wondered if it was Det. Kamon, but couldn't see who was driving the car through its tinted windows.

When the light changed, I continued speeding down the street, then slowed down to turn into the parking lot. I quickly parked and jumped out of the truck. Turning around I saw David standing outside the front door of the restaurant, obviously disturbed because I was late.

"Where have you been?" David called, angrily.

"I'm sorry; I had the wrong location. I thought you meant the one in Burbank," I replied.

Suddenly, just as I got close to David, four undercover cars quickly closed in on us from both sides and slammed on their brakes. Police swiftly got out of their cars and stood behind their car doors, yelling at David.

I was in shock, now realizing Det. Kamon was on me the whole time, along with five other undercover officers; one of them, Officer Cuso, jumped in front of me. David looked dumbfounded.

Since their appearance was a shock, I didn't have to put on much of an act to feign surprise.

"Stop right there!" an undercover officer yelled.

"What the hell's going on?" David asked, looking at me in confusion.

"I have no idea!" I replied, my voice scared and confused.

"Don't move! Put your hands up in the air where we can see them! Now slowly, both of you turn around and put your hands on the car and spread your legs apart!" several officers yelled from behind their car doors.

All six undercover officers, including Det. Kamon, descended quickly on David and me, shouting questions. I shot Det. Kamon a knowing look without David seeing me.

"Do you have any weapons on you?" they asked, as they patted us down.

"No, why would I have any weapons on me?" David snapped.

"No, I have none," I told them.

"They're clean," an officer stated.

"You stay with her."

Det. Kamon and three other undercover officers then took David to one side of the parking lot, while the two other officers walked me over to the truck. Glancing over at David, I could see Det. Kamon intensely questioning him while the two officers with me made casual talk.

"This is a nice truck. Man, you were flying in it. We almost lost you a couple of times," one officer chuckled.

"Oh, that was you who flew in front of me down the street," I said shaking my head.

"Yep, that was us and I have to admit, you really know how to handle this truck," he replied.

"Let's not look too friendly," I said, glancing over at David and the other detectives. I reminded them that David was to think I was surprised by the sting too.

"Yeah, we have to make this look legit," one officer said.

"Pour everything out of your purse onto the hood of the truck. We'll make it look like we're searching your stuff," he said.

While one officer acted like he was searching the contents of my purse, the other one took out a pad of paper and acted as if he were taking down information.

After intensely questioning David, Det. Kamon began walking towards me from across the parking lot.

"Well, any luck?" I asked.

"No, he's not talking. Says he wants his lawyer, but I have threatened him with a subpoena and jail for withholding evidence. He's still trying to protect Valerie, but let's see what he does now that he knows what's in store for him."

I felt as frustrated as Det. Kamon, but I still felt David, just like anyone else, had a breaking point and decided to keep my cool. As soon as everyone cleared out, I walked over to David.

"I can't believe this happened, David!" I said, sounding shocked and angry.

"Yeah, well, I assume it was bound to happen at some point," David replied, as he took a deep breath. "They're threatening me with arrest."

"That's frightening," I said, studying him. "But Howell told you that could happen."

"Yes, that's right," David replied, hanging his head down.

"What did Det. Kamon question you about?" I asked.

"Oh, I'm sure you know," David muttered.

My heart began to beat fast, wondering if David figured out that I was in on the sting with Det. Kamon.

"What do you mean, I know?" I replied, angrily.

"I mean, I'm sure you were asked some of the same questions I was," he explained.

"I won't know until you tell me," I said.

"If I knew anything about the weapon Valerie used, was one of the questions I was asked," David replied.

"What did you tell them?" I asked.

"I told them I didn't know anything else about the weapon, other than what you left me no choice but to tell," David replied, in an aggravated tone.

"David, why are you so bent on helping Freddie? Don't you realize how dangerous he is?" I asked.

"Well, I don't know that there's much danger. Valerie told me she killed that guy out of self-defense and I believe that's what it was," David insisted.

"David, don't you remember how many times he was violent with you? And I'm sure there's a lot more you haven't told me," I said.

"Well," David began. He paused.

"Well, what?" I said.

"There were a few other times Valerie lost her temper, I guess," David admitted.

"Let me ask you this, David. When did Freddie start hitting you? When was the first time you remember?"

"Oh, I'd say within less than a year from when we met," David replied.

"So what happened?" I asked.

"Oh, it was so long ago. But, well, there was this one time I recall Valerie came at me with a closed fist and the next thing I knew I hit the ground. She had slugged me in the head, like the night you witnessed, but this incident was much worse," recalled David.

"What happened?" I asked.

"Well, I didn't sit back and take it, if that's what you think. I got up quickly; I slugged Valerie above the eye and busted it open. And I remember this shocked look I got, because she didn't think I'd fight back," David explained.

"That's surprising. You never seemed to me the type to fight back," I replied.

"Yeah, well, there're a lot of things you don't know about me," David replied.

"Obviously," I snorted.

"Well, stitches were needed, so I took her to the hospital," David said.

"David, you're going to have to tell the court about Freddie's violent past with you," I said.

"I'm not saying anything! The less involvement I have, the better for me," David replied.

"I don't think it will be so easy to lie under oath when they question you," I said vehemently. "If you do, they'll send you to jail."

"We'll see," David replied.

"David, you make me sick!" I said, disgusted.

chapter eighteen

A Shocking Verdict

—————

Freddie had been placed in his own cell to adjust to the lonely confinement of the city jail, which always housed between eight to twelve inmates. He decorated the walls with pictures. According to reports from his new attorney, "She says she's realizing now how strong she is."

After the sting David refused to talk to me anymore about Freddie. Now Freddie's fate would be squarely on the shoulders of the prosecuting attorney. At some point they would have to inform me of the trial date and when they wanted me to testify. But as the weeks passed there still was no call from Bob Kane. Instead I received a frantic call from South Carolina.

"Hello?" I answered.

"Donita!" Rev. Posey said in a panicked voice.

"Rev. Posey, what's wrong?" I replied, fearing whatever it was, was bad.

"You are not going to believe this!" Rev. Posey said, his voice shaking.

"What? What's going on? What happened?" I asked, as my eyes grew wide with concern.

"Freddie's plea bargained and I just got a call from the prosecutor's office to be at the courthouse in one hour for sentencing!" Rev. Posey exclaimed.

"WHAT!" I yelled.

"I can't believe it either! There was no warning!" Rev. Posey replied.

"How can they do this?" I yelled, in a panic.

"I don't know. No one contacted you?" Rev. Posey asked.

"NO, just you. I haven't heard anything from anyone," I replied angrily.

"I don't know, but something strange is going on. You were supposed to be a witness and your husband was supposed to be subpoenaed. This is crazy! I don't know what's going on. No one knew they were going to do this. I'm telling you, something's just not right with this," Rev. Posey declared in a darkly suspicious voice.

"I can't believe they're making a deal with Freddie!" I replied.

"Donita, I have to get off the phone and get down to the courthouse. I'll call you once I get there and fill you in on what's going on," Rev. Posey replied, rushing off the phone.

I stood frozen in total shock and disbelief that something like this could happen. Rev. Posey was right: something strange was going on and it was being kept from us. Pacing the kitchen floor, I waited for Rev. Posey to call back.

A million thoughts raced through my head as I sat by the phone waiting for news of the case. Stunned that the court had given the Posey family only an hour's notice and no one had contacted me, except Rev. Posey, I was haunted by one thought: *what if Freddie was freed?*

Finally, Rev. Posey called. "This is terrible. Just terrible!" I could hear his voice shaking over the phone line.

"Rev. Posey, please tell me what happened," I begged, as I began to cry.

"When I got to the courthouse, no one was there but Bob Kane, the prosecuting attorney, and Freddie's attorney, Kate Collins. I was told to go into the courtroom right away," Rev. Posey began to explain.

"What do you mean they were the only ones there?" I asked.

"There was no jury, no newspaper, no media, nobody," Rev. Posey said, his voice growing in anger.

"What do you mean there was no jury?" I replied, my voice starting to quiver as well.

"Just that—there was no jury. They explained that there won't be a trial since most of the witnesses are dead and most of the evidence was buried. The prosecution and defense must have plea bargained. It's like when they know a mob leader has committed a murder, but they can't get him for it, so they get him for tax evasion instead.

"Freddie appeared at the courthouse with his new attorney, Kate Collins. The lawyer said Valerie Nicole Taylor had waited eighteen years to tell her story but was 'too shaken to speak.' Collins read statements Taylor gave police that told about her relationship with my brother Billy, which she said had turned into a very abusive one, ending in violence and death. According to the lawyer Valerie was afraid, because she was black and poor. Taylor ran away and began seventeen years in hiding. Her lawyer portrayed her or him as an abused victim who feared the man she was with at the time. We both know Taylor was physically a man—Freddie Lee Turner, but she wore a wig and dressed like a woman. They talked about the truth, that her sex wasn't known even by our family; we just knew him as Freda.

"Her attorney said even though Valerie still was male, emotionally she was female and lived as a female. Their version was that on the night of his birthday, Billy had been drinking and came at her drunk and mean at the motel they went to; she was afraid she was going to be killed if she didn't shoot him first. According to Valerie/Freddie, my brother had pulled a gun and pointed it at her head. Somehow she'd gotten it away from him."

The reverend paused for a long while. I pressed him to go on and he did.

"The judge listened in silence to Collins telling Valerie's story. When he spoke he called it 'tragic.' He sentenced Taylor to fifteen years in prison but suspended it to three years after the prosecuting attorney recommended a ten-year cap on her imprisonment."

"I can't believe this!" I said, as I sat down in total shock, still gripping the telephone in my hand. "This is insane; I can't believe this happened." My tears continued pouring out.

"I'm sorry Donita. I know you worked really hard to help get justice for my brother Billy, and my family will never forget it. We'll forever be grateful to you. Look, I've got to tell my mother now. We'll talk again later."

After Rev. Posey hung up, I immediately called Det. Kamon. His answering machine picked up and I left a message. A short while later Det. Kamon called back.

"Why didn't you tell me?" I demanded, agitated. "Freddie just got away with murder and David helped him the whole time!" I was an emotional wreck. Tears came at the mere mention of the case.

"Donita, I've been trying to figure out how to break it to you," Det. Kamon said, obviously upset. "In fact, I've been trying to figure out how to explain it to myself. You know, with the police chief dead, the investigating officer dead, even the cabbie who shuttled Freddie from the motel to Spartanburg dead, the prosecution had to take what they could get. At least Freddie's in jail and his crime is out in the open. I'm so sorry, Donita," he went on, trying to comfort me.

"I'm in shock as to how this could happen," I said, angrily. "There wasn't even a trial. What about Det. McMurry?" I asked.

"I just got off the phone with him. Apparently he wasn't notified either. He's just as shocked as we are," Det. Kamon replied.

"Where are they sending Freddie?" I asked.

"To a state penitentiary for women in South Carolina," Det. Kamon said.

"That son-of-a-bitch!" I said. "Det Kamon, I am afraid not only for myself, but for my children and Reverend Posey. I'm afraid that he'll come after us when he gets out."

"As far as Valerie coming back here, don't worry. We'll deal with it when the time gets near," Det. Kamon assured me.

"Can you guys protect the kids and me? There's no telling what Freddie will do when he gets released," I said.

"Donita, we'll watch out for you, and remember, if anything happened to you, she knows we know you turned her in, so she'd be the first suspect," Det. Kamon replied.

During the next several days, I saw Dr. Ashford in hopes she could help me deal with what had happened. I wanted badly to call David and tell him off for not helping to put Freddie behind bars for good, but I knew it was hopeless. I was concerned about Rev. Posey's mother, who was in poor health, and called to see how the family was holding up.

"Hey, Donita, it's good to hear from you. I'm doing better, but my mom's still a mess. She just can't stop crying," Rev. Posey told me.

"I'm so sorry," I said.

"We're just in shock at the light sentence Freddie got. It's just unbelievable. I've lost all faith in our justice system now," Rev. Posey said.

"I know what you mean. It's hard to see evil triumph, but I truly believe, as I know you do, that though we can't see it now, there is a higher court which judges us all. We'll be shown the way. Rev. Posey," I said. "Don't despair and tell your mom for me, Freddie and David will get their due justice in time."

He chuckled, "Donita, I should be telling you that and here you are—not only were you the one who brought all this out, but now you're comforting me."

"No, I'm promising you," I said passionately. "Freddie may have beaten the system, but I'm not going to let Freddie get away with murder." I didn't know how I was going to make my words come true, but I vowed to myself somehow, someday, I would.

chapter nineteen

Respite and Confrontation

Though I tried to get on with my life, I was still on edge and anxious about Freddie getting revenge once he got out or sending a friend to do the dirty job for him. Being in the house where my children and I had been set up and stalked, I could not stop thinking of the injustice of it all and the unfairness done to Rev. Posey and his family.

Though I had promised him I would do something, never had I felt more helpless. Between the fear I was experiencing and the sleepless nights I spent, I was becoming paranoid. I knew it was time to make a new start. I made the decision to move the kids to my old hometown in Texas, feeling it would be a good place to begin a new life. The following weekend I flew down to there to house hunt, eventually buying a house I felt the kids would enjoy.

Our remaining days in California were spent packing up boxes, calling the phone company and utilities, asking them all to send the closing bills to the new house in Texas. I requested an unlisted phone number for the Texas house and left no forwarding address from the Burbank residence. Then I sat down and wrote Det. Kamon a letter, thanking him for everything, and dropped it off at the police station.

The following morning, the alarm clock went off at 5:00 AM and the kids and I drove off to Texas. Only a handful of people knew where we were going; everyone else was kept in the dark.

It took us two days to make the drive. Once we arrived at the driveway of our new home, the kids jumped out of the truck and grabbed the dogs. I slowly got out, stretched my arms and smiled. It was, I thought, a new beginning, far away from all that darkened our lives for so long, and I knew in my gut it would be better here.

I unlocked the front door of the house and Sam and Jessica quickly darted past me, excitedly running through the rooms, each wanting to pick out the best bedroom in the house.

Soon after, the moving van arrived with the furniture, keeping the kids and me busy as we unpacked boxes and put things away. Before too long I noticed a change come over me. I was more relaxed and emotionally calm. It was the first time I had felt truly happy in a long time, but my main concern was not so much for myself as for Sam and Jessica. Making up for lost time, I spent every waking moment I could with them. We took trips to the beach and around the city, settling into our new surroundings quite comfortably. As the days passed into weeks, I was sleeping more soundly and began gaining back the weight I had lost due to all the stress.

I took care of the last bills from the Burbank house. Before long I received a surprise call from Det. Kamon, wanting to know how the kids and I were doing. I was glad to tell him that for once everything was going well.

One Monday, after being in the new house for over two months, I realized I hadn't received the long distance phone bill from the

Burbank house and called the company to find out what had happened to it.

The customer service representative informed me the bill had been sent out already and that I should have received it within the first week after we got to Texas. Thinking it was lost in the mail, I asked that they send me a copy. Strangely enough, that same day I received a phone call from my dad's new wife.

"Hello?" I answered, in a happy tone.

"Hi, Donita, how are you and the kids doing?" she asked.

"The happiest we've ever been in a long time! How are you and Dad doing?" I asked.

"We're doing fine Donita, but... I don't know how else to tell you this," she paused and then blurted out, "David knows where you are."

"What! How did he find out where I am? How do you know this?" I asked frantically.

"Your phone bill. Somehow David got it. The only thing we can think of is the company sent it to him instead of your new address in Texas," she explained.

"I can't believe this! How did you find this out? Who told you?" I asked.

"David knows where you were by the last calls you made from the Burbank house. He narrowed it down to which city you're in from the real estate agent you called. I don't know why he made it a point to call and tell us," she said.

"Why is he doing this?" I yelled.

"Donita, I don't know. Your father and I are also confused as to David's motives, but we both feel you should let the police down there know what's going on. That way, they can protect you," she said.

I broke down crying, feeling all the hard work I had been doing to start a new life for my kids was once again at risk. After getting off the phone, I took my stepmother's advice and drove down to the local police department. I tried to explain my situation, but they knew nothing of the case and unless something happened in their territory there was little they could do. Returning home, I called Det. Kamon at the Burbank Police Department.

When I explained that despite my precautions David had found out where we were and I was sure had or would eventually tell Freddie, who was getting out of jail soon, Det. Kamon said he knew from the past that my gut feelings were usually right. He advised me to sell the house, change my name and move to another state or move back to Burbank where the police could keep a close watch on the kids and me.

After getting off the phone, I reviewed my options. Going on-line, I noticed I had received an e-mail from the realtor in California and began reading it. It stated they had my long distance phone bill, which David had given to them.

Since David was listed as joint partner on the house, the realtor also had to send him copies of the closing papers on the house. It made sense to me then. David had to have gotten the phone bill from the Burbank house. The only reason I could think of for him to give it to the realtors was to taunt me, letting me know that he knew where I was.

The e-mail also said that the phone bill had been taped shut, that it had obviously been opened. Angry, I got off-line and began making calls to find David. I called his studio, no answer. After calling both studios and getting no answer, I called his mother's house, taking a chance that David would be there, but there was no answer.

Both angry and upset, I felt I was becoming seriously depressed. I called Dr. Ashford.

As I began filling her in on what was going on, she too was concerned about Freddie's plans and David's intention.

Dr. Ashford agreed with the police, that the kids and I needed to be where we could be protected the most. After getting off the phone with Dr. Ashford, I quickly made my decision—we would return right away to California and this time I would not try to remain anonymous. That ploy had only earned us a postponement; it had not saved us. This time I would go public.

I felt if I got my story out, Freddie would know; the media would make the public aware of anything that happened to my children and me. Our story would also alert citizens that although the innocent are sometimes punished, the guilty sometimes go free. Returning to Burbank, I reenrolled the children in school. Then I gathered the information I had written up for the police and documents and began writing to national magazines, local newspapers and television programs.

The first to answer me was a reporter from the *Burbank Leader.* The day she interviewed me, we sat down in my living room and I began telling my story, covering a nineteen-year span.

In the days afterward I began to follow up on my other queries to the media, while I waited anxiously for the *Burbank Leader* article. Finally, everyone would know my name and that I was the one who tipped off the police to the murder Freddie committed. After several days the reporter called me. "Tomorrow," she said. The next morning, picking up the newspaper I saw the headline: "Skeletons in the closet," the headline read. "Burbank resident Donita Woodruff's search for the truth led to a 17-year-old tale of betrayal and murder... and the capture of a fugitive killer."

The article continued to tell the bizarre story.

"Eighteen months after she told police her husband's transsexual ex-lover was wanted for murder, Burbank resident Donita Woodruff's life is almost back to normal. She soon will discard the boxes of meticulously collected court documents, phone records, mug shots and audiotapes that have cluttered her quaint, three-bedroom home for more than a year.

"She hopes Valerie Nicole Taylor—soon to be paroled from state prison in South Carolina—will have no reason to visit, no excuse to call, no desire to return to Burbank. 'I feel Valerie is a disease who has been passed to many people, and it will take years to cure the ones she infected,' Woodruff said recently during the second of four interviews totaling more than 20 hours.

"Taylor was arrested by Burbank police May 1996 in her Toluca Lake apartment for the 1979 murder of Billy Marshall Posey, authorities said. Posey, 25, was found by his brother in a Gaffney, S.C. motel. Court records show he died from gunshot wounds to the groin and leg. Once a cross-dressing man who underwent a sex change while on the lam, Taylor pled guilty to voluntary manslaughter in May 1997. She will be released from the South Carolina State Board of Corrections in January 1998.

"And if it hadn't been for a 34-year-old Burbank mother and substitute teachers' aide, the 17-year-old murder in rural Cherokee County, a peach-growing community with about 44,500 people, may have remained unsolved.

"Sitting in her living room, which is decorated with Egyptian art, Woodruff recounted the story she plans to someday write as a book.

"It started in 1990, when her sister's boyfriend suggested she go out with David Allen, a Burbank film director and visual effects designer whom Woodruff would ultimately marry.

"After dating a couple of months Woodruff said Allen told her about a woman he knew who claimed to have killed someone a long time ago.

"Allen last week said he didn't believe the woman at the time because she lived in a 'kind of dream world' and her stories had many discrepancies.

"'I made some mistakes in judgment, but they only harmed myself. I have many regrets and am going to be paying for them for years,' said Allen, who owns David Allen Productions in Burbank.

"Unbeknownst to Woodruff, the woman who told Allen the story about shooting a man to death in a South Carolina motel was Allen's friend, Valerie Taylor, whom he met in 1985 through personal ads. Valerie met Woodruff and eventually grew jealous of the couple's relationship, Woodruff said.

"One night in 1993, Allen said Taylor struck him after 'a neurotic episode.' The incident frightened Woodruff, and she said Allen promised he would have nothing further to do with Taylor.

"That wasn't enough for Woodruff, who began to suspect Taylor may have been the murderer friend Allen mentioned.

"Taylor is serving her sentence at Leath Correctional Institute in South Carolina—a state penitentiary for women. Prison officials would not allow Taylor to be interviewed by phone, and she did not respond to a written request for comment.

"Shortly after marrying Allen in August 1995, Woodruff checked Burbank Municipal and Superior courts for any records on Valerie Taylor. She was worried about her safety and that of her children. She found an accident report citing Taylor for suspicion of misdemeanor hit and run in 1991, a charge on which she was convicted.

"Another showed Taylor's alias as Freddie Lee Turner.

"Allen's ex-girlfriend used to be a man.

"'This was a person I met, believing she was a woman, later discovering she was born a man,' Allen said, noting he had been intimate with Taylor while dating Woodruff.

"Woodruff filed for divorce the next day. It will be final on Friday.

"Flashback to December 1995, when Allen provided Woodruff with further information on his yet-unnamed female friend's tale of murder. According to Woodruff, Allen told her his friend had killed 'a man named Bill, who was black, in a motel at night.'

"Woodruff asked her husband if the killer was Taylor. Allen said it was.

"Now Woodruff had to prove it.

"Connecting the name Freddie Lee Turner with Greenville, S.C., the city listed in court documents as where Turner was from,

Woodruff called small towns in the area inquiring about unsolved murders. She found nothing.

"Despite being worried she or Allen could be considered an accomplice in a murder she still wasn't sure occurred, Woodruff told the story to a Burbank police detective in February 1996.

"'I figured someone in the office was pulling a trick on me,' the detective said last week, until he called Gaffney police and discovered a murder warrant had been issued for Turner in 1979. After 17 years with no leads, the warrant had become inactive.

"Gaffney police buried the case report, bullet shells, Billy Posey's autopsy report and other evidence in a hole, over which was built their new police station, the detective said. Authorities in Gaffney said the burial was part of a routine destruction of old evidence.

"The former Gaffney police chief who signed the original warrant was dead. The primary investigating officer was dead. And the cabbie who shuttled Freddie Lee Turner from the motel to Spartanburg was dead.

"It took Gaffney police about two months to get another warrant and reactivate the case, the detective said.

"'If it hadn't been for Donita, there wouldn't be any justice done,' the Rev. Perry Posey, Billy's brother, said last week by phone from his South Carolina home.

"'She gathered more information than the police force itself,' he added.

"Like an attorney preparing the case of the century, Woodruff continued collecting data she hoped would help convict Valerie Taylor. She gave police Taylor's address, told them restaurants she frequented and people with whom she consorted.

"'This person committed murder and got away with it for 17 years. I'm not going to keep quiet about it,' Woodruff said, noting she may have to look over her shoulder for the rest of her life, but that it was the right thing to do.

"When Burbank police arrested Taylor on May 9, 1996, she was drinking wine in her Camarillo Street apartment with a married Glendale attorney, the detective said.

"Taylor was extradited to South Carolina, where she pled guilty to involuntary manslaughter in 1997. Having already served a year in county jail, Taylor will be released Jan. 21, 1998, said an officer at the South Carolina board of Corrections.

"Shaking her head at the brevity of Taylor's sentence, Woodruff said she has no regrets about what she did.

"Caller-ID and sensor alarms throughout her house are constant reminders of a chapter in her life she won't soon forget.

"'I helped get a murderer out of the community. For that I will never be sorry,' she said."

Within twenty-four hours, my telephone began ringing. The national media were asking me to appear and tell my story. Sitting down on the living room couch, I realized my anonymity was gone, but so was Freddie's. I'd kept my promise to Rev. Posey and, as I revealed to the first reporter to whom I disclosed my name, I had dis-covered within myself during these traumatic years of fear and terror the seeds of strength and courage impelling me to unearth the truth. And when I found it, I wasn't going to keep quiet, not now, not ever.

chapter twenty

Moments of Terror, Moments of Strength

Having to meet each other at a notary public to have some papers signed by both of us, I kept my distance from David. I just wanted to get the formalities over without any words spoken between us.

After I signed my name in the notary book, I turned and began to walk away, having to pass David as I headed for the door.

"You're going to regret divorcing me one day. You're never going to make it without me." David called out to me, with a confident look on his face.

Taken back by David's comment, I was speechless for a few seconds. Then I realized he was fearful of losing control of me as he had Freddie.

Stopping, I turned around and looked David straight in the eyes, then smiled.

"Watch me!" I said, returning the same confident look.

As I drove home that day I was feeling a sense of renewal. I had told my story to the public and was now free from David, but that night, as

I lay awake in bed, the fear that came from knowing that Freddie would soon be released from prison was a cruel reminder of all that I had hoped to put behind me.

Nevertheless, in the months that followed I focused all my attention on the kids and tried to live a peaceful, normal life. I was pretty much able to do so until 1998 rolled in. The news of Freddie's release date came in the form of a letter from the Leath Correctional Institution, stating his release from prison would be on January 21.

Worried about what retaliation could come from Freddie, I took every precaution I could to protect the kids and myself.

I got a restraining order against Freddie while he was still in prison and had a state-of-the-art home security system installed in the house. Wanting extra protection, I purchased a .38 Smith and Wesson and took lessons on how to fire it.

Soon Freddie was served the restraining order, which ordered him to keep at least 200 yards away from me and the kids, our home and the Burbank schools that the kids attended, as well as the place I worked.

I made a list of the key people affiliated with Freddie who I felt could be a danger to me and my children. I wrote down their full names and motives if anything should happen to us, along with taped conversations. I discussed this on an appearance in the national media and gave the list to Det. Kamon to keep in a safe place at the police department.

As the day on which Freddie was to be released drew near and passed, Det. Kamon kept in close contact with me. The Burbank Police were briefed and shown a recent picture and description of Freddie, as well as given instructions to frequently patrol near our home. It was hard to explain to the kids why the police were there so often, but I managed to make them think we had friends in high places. It seemed to work and the kids went on about their normal daily routines without added stress. I still had moments of fear, but I was growing stronger every day.

I began to relax more. Everything seemed peaceful and quiet. Unfortunately, it didn't last. Late one night the phone began to ring. Wakened from a dead sleep, I turned to look at the clock in the light of the night moon that glares through the drapes. Half asleep, I answered.

"Hello," I said, waiting for a response.

"Hello?" I said again.

"Hello?" I said a third time in an angry voice.

I knew it had to be Freddie. I quickly looked at the caller ID box, but it read unknown caller.

"You son-of-a-bitch, Freddie! I know it's you!" I said angrily. "You'd better not come near us or this time they'll put you away for good. And if they don't I will!"

No other calls came that night, but I was too fearful to fall asleep again. First thing in the morning, I called the police and an officer was sent over to my house. After I explained the call I'd received, the officer telephoned an operator, asking to have a tracer put on my phone in hopes of catching Freddie if he continued calling. After the officer left the house, between being tired and feeling the hell I tried to put behind me was once again being relived, I became enraged. I did everything I could to contain my anger, but it got the best of me. I grabbed the phone to call David at his studio.

I knew he must have been in some sort of contact with Freddie since he got out of prison, and wanted him to give Freddie a message for me.

"Hello?" he answered.

"David, its Donita!" I said angrily.

"Yes?" he replied, drawing the word out in frustration.

"I have a message for Freddie. The police are waiting for him and so am I, as he'll soon find out."

The police brought Freddie into the police station for a meeting, making it clear to him that under no circumstances would he be allowed in Burbank and that if he ever came there they'd find him, arrest him and send him back to prison. Freddie, angry that he was told to stay out of Burbank, in turn wanted me arrested for threatening him through David.

The police laughed it off and told Freddie to go home and that he'd better stay clear of Burbank city limits.

I began to see Dr. Ashford to work out all the feelings and traumatizing events that I'd been through and soon I went back to work for the school district.

Avoiding the side of town where David's studio was and places he frequented, I hoped to reduce the risk of running into him.

Then in the spring of 1999, I saw David in the parking lot of the grocery store.

"Hi, Donita," he said. He seemed desperate to tell me something but didn't seem to know how to get it out. "I'm dying of lymphatic cancer," David finally said, in a soft voice. Stunned, I stood in silence, staring at David as he spoke. "I only have about a year or less. At least that's what the doctors tell me," David continued.

"I'm sorry to hear that," I replied, feeling tears spring to my eyes as I recalled how much I'd once loved him, but I couldn't forgive what he'd done to me and my children. "David, what you did was pure selfishness and evil. I was in love with you and you took advantage of that," I said.

He sighed deeply. "I realize that now. And maybe my getting cancer is payback in some sort of way."

"David I feel sorry for you. Not that it would wipe out what you've done, but is it so hard for you to say you're sorry for the pain you caused me?" I asked.

David just stood still with a blank look on his face.

"Donita, you don't understand the relationship Valerie and I had. I don't think it's possible you could," he replied.

I was shocked by David's response. He had almost seemed to have gained some grasp on reality before he made that last comment to me. I smiled in disbelief while shaking my head.

"Well, David, good luck," I said, walking off, as tears fell down my face.

Getting in, I started the truck, took one last look at David, backed the truck up and drove off. As I drove I began to have flashbacks of the good memories I had with David, but those memories soon became distorted as I remembered the dark secret I discovered David was living and the horrific emotional pain it caused. At that moment I felt both sorrow and a total sense of freedom come over me. And somehow I knew it would be the last time I would ever see David.

Epilogue

In mid-August of 1999, David Allen passed away of cancer. It was later rumored he had left Valerie a lot of money in his will.

In February of 2002, Rev. Perry Posey was gunned down in the early morning hours outside Gaffney, South Carolina. To this day no suspects have been arrested for his murder.

On November 4, 2002, Valerie Taylor was arrested for committing a violent act. Count 01: Inflicting Corporeal Injury on spouse, resulting in a traumatic condition. Count 02: Battery against former spouse/fiancé. I never discovered the names of the victims, as they were crossed out with a large black permanent marker on the copies that I saw of the records. Ruling on count 01: Convicted. Ruling on count 02: Dismissed due to plea negotiation. Imposition of sentence suspended. Defendant placed on summary probation for a period of three years under the following terms and conditions.

Serve two days in Los Angeles County Jail less credit for two days, plus $200.00 Domestic Violence Fund, no alcohol, perform 30 days of

Cal Trans. Defendant shall pay restitution in the amount of $100.00 to the State Restitution Fund by 02/10/03 total due $300.00. In addition enroll and complete twelve-month batterer's counseling program and return with proof on 01/10/03. Obey all laws and order of the court. Defendant in open court is handed a copy of the above conditions of probation.

And, with this book, I have fulfilled the promise I made to Reverend Posey and his family, and fulfilled my words to reporters and the media that I'm not going to keep quiet about my efforts to get a murderer out of our community. I've never been sorry and I am sure if you see or know evil has been committed and you speak out, you won't be sorry either. That is both a gift and a lesson for our children and a way to better the world in which they dwell.